Mu, 49 Marks of Abolition

Black Outdoors: Innovations in the Poetics of Study
A series edited by J. Kameron Carter and Sarah Jane Cervenak

Sora Y. Han

49 Marks of Abolition

mu

Duke University Press Durham and London 2024

Printed in the United States of America on acid-free paper ∞
Project Editor: Ihsan Taylor
Designed by Aimee C. Harrison
Typeset in Garamond Premier Pro, SangBleu Kingdom, and Batang by Copperline Book Services

Library of Congress Cataloging-in-Publication Data
Names: Han, Sora Y., author.
Title: Mu, 49 marks of abolition / Sora Y. Han.
Other titles: Black outdoors.
Description: Durham : Duke University Press, 2024. | Series: Black outdoors | Includes bibliographical references and index.
Identifiers: LCCN 2023036599 (print)
LCCN 2023036600 (ebook)
ISBN 9781478027836 (paperback)
ISBN 9781478020974 (hardcover)
ISBN 9781478025719 (ebook)
ISBN 9781478094142 (ebook other)
Subjects: LCSH: Ethnology—Study and teaching—United States. | Asian Americans—Study and teaching. | African Americans—Study and teaching. | African Americans—Relations with Korean Americans. | Poetics. | Law—Language. | United States—Ethnic relations. | United States—Race relations. | BISAC: SOCIAL SCIENCE / Ethnic Studies / American / African American & Black Studies | SOCIAL SCIENCE / Ethnic Studies / American / Asian American & Pacific Islander Studies
Classification: LCC GN307.85.U6 H36 2024 (print) | LCC GN307.85.U6 (ebook) | DDC 340/.115—dc23/eng/20231025
LC record available at https://lccn.loc.gov/2023036599
LC ebook record available at https://lccn.loc.gov/2023036600

For my father, Kwang Woo Han,

who lives on in the freedom dream of Korea's reunification

contents

note on etymologies

Etymological definitions throughout this work were developed by consulting a number of dictionaries and lexical references. For hangul, *hanja*, and Chinese words, these references included: *Naver Hanja Online Dictionary*, https://hanja.dict.naver.com/#/main; *The Dong-A Ilbo*, 한자 뿌리 읽기 (Understanding hanja roots) serial, https://www.donga.com/news/Series/70070000000210; *e-hanja, Digital Hanja Dictionary*, http://www.e-hanja.kr/; and the English-language *Wiktionary*, https://en.wiktionary.org. For Latin-script words, I referred to the *Oxford English Dictionary (Online)*, https://www.oed.com/; the *Online Etymology Dictionary*, https://www.etymonline.com/; and *Logeion*, an open-access database of Latin and Ancient Greek dictionaries, https://logeion.uchicago.edu/λόγος. Less frequently consulted references are specifically cited and included in the bibliography.

I must thank Monica Cho, who provided invaluable support translating and interpreting the hangul and *hanja* throughout this book. All errors and bungles remain mine alone.

preface

Inside a closed book, or in some crevice of a library bookshelf, the girl hides, as emaciated as paper. The girl's smell lingers in my metal printing types. A smudge from the girl's soldering iron stays on my book's cover. —YI SANG, "Paradise Lost" (1939)

Where does language go limp, break apart, or fall into pieces, stammers, glimpses, or just merely the black marks that make up letters? —DAWN LUNDY MARTIN, "A Bleeding, an Autobiographical Tale" (2007)

My iPhone reminds me that I wrote a note. The feeling I attempted to record there is beyond me. I do know, though, that the note is there because at that moment, back in March 2020, I feared regretting at some future moment not giving in to a need to write.

A peculiar effervescent loss has glittered every experience of daily life since then.

One week before that note reappeared, I learned that stage 4 cancer had taken over my father's liver and stomach. It was also the week that California shut down in response to the coronavirus, COVID-19, spreading across the globe. Or, maybe, on second thought, the events should be reversed. That was the week COVID-19 started to devour the world's human population, like the stage 4 cancer that had taken over my father's liver and stomach.

Somehow, I still think now that if I can decide the correct order of these two events, I might be able to write something truer about this effervescence that has hued every moment of my day, whether asleep or awake. As time became a practice of bone-deep dread, drawing and bearing breath, I disappeared into a sense of life too vivid to capture in any language I assumed to share with anyone else.

Whatever the order, this note reminds me, every letter of every word I typed into this unaddressed note was a slowly fading heartbeat, the mark of a cell-by-cell colonization of vital internal tissues, a pithy series of strokes filling in an expanse of time that seemed to open up in those months between each touch and thought.

Writing marks some interval between this nearly imperceptible decay in living and some cataclysmic future happening. In those early days of 2020, I could barely muster the energy to put this theory to the test. But somehow, after so many predawn flights of notating later, this book is complete as a practice of the Buddhist tradition to mourn the dead for 49 days. Writing confronted and comforted me, ultimately, with the fundamental entanglement of decay and regeneration, the ritual practice of an always more to be given, which exceeds the melancholic economy of loss.

He and my mother called a meeting to tell us they would die one day. The first time they brought this up was during a secret trip abroad to North Korea nearly four decades ago. They pulled me out of kindergarten before the school year was over, and as we transferred from one plane to another, I sleepily wondered how long it would take to get to "Canada." It was during this trip that they plainly informed us that they would die, and they did not want their dying to become a burden on our lives. My three-year-old sister broke down then, sobbing, pleading, fat tears rolling down her cheeks. "Please don't die."

I did not cry. I would not plead. Dying is an unchangeable fact. No grief, no supplication, no abject fear, could distract from a child's knowledge. Its devastation is neither narcissistic nor sentimental. It is life. "Why are we born if we just die?" my three-year-old son would ask me three decades later.

For a child, it strikes me, imagining the day when a parent will die is the closest experience to one's own death. In dependency, the thought of no longer existing is coterminous with and fundamentally shared with the end of another's life. The parasite lives and dies as the host does. And yet this truth coexists with the fact that actual loss and imaginary death have radically incommensurate temporalities and differential significance for both the parent and child. And so, on occasion, we carve out lessons from the essential entanglement of dying, losing, and living, even as this entanglement undoes the identities assumed as we try to learn these lessons.

I have come to see the lesson I learned in North Korea of risking death in living out radical political desire as a scene of separation. Separation, which is to say, a desire to know what is beyond language and the Other, took place as I was taught how to love and work while assuming the risk of losing one's life. The eventual real loss of the parent who imparted such a teaching only intensifies its brilliant truth, only further distills and disseminates, hands, this undying anti-colonial tradition across the social field. And if one spends a life trying to learn this lesson, as I have through writing, then separation is not individuation but some sort of continuous impossible disambiguation of "I" and "you," young me and grown you, that which is not yet me and that which is you yet gone. Separation through the cut of radical political desire yields endless indivisible transmission. This is where love and work gather each other's mutual erasednesses in a realm of knowing so vast that the thought of and desire for one's life, the life of a one, is impossible to sustain in any real or imaginary way.

Who have I been writing to? Who have I been writing for? I can finally conclude that there was no "to" or "for" other than an unconscious knowledge of something necessary and worthy to figure out by returning, over and over, to the reality of death impressed on my five-year-old mind during this most extraordinary family meeting. This became all the more clear with the purity of the sadness of losing a father who gave lessons in stark and mysterious truths. Writing theory through transliterating and translating to Korean hangul and *hanja* has been both my mourning ritual and the modality my desire took to try to say something about an upheaval in the way the body knows in the midst of a most brilliant sensorial scramble of light and touch, loss and love, death and grief. As Don Mee Choi poignantly captures, "For a child-translator, translation is an act of autogeography."[1]

Indeed, that note, inputted into a machine, orders me to return: "I am constantly shuttled between wanting to make my father a mythological character and seeing him for his gentle and breathing life. He both towers in a train of memories that intrude, one after another, in my field of vision, and folds down into a warmth enclosable in my arms." In his final days, he would momentarily wake from some place behind his closed eyes and look at his hands, turning them this way and that, as if to study them. Here, in this tangle of grief and love, I don't know how to differentiate between the man whose death causes the desire to write and the desire itself.

If Buddhist mourning gave me a schedule, the principle of free verse allowed me to keep writing. Transliterations and translations so loosely associative I can only call them *dystranslations* produced a nonmetricality recorded in the following pages. They capture less the rhythm of natural speech than a rhythm of the unconscious, or improvisation, in how theoretical political ideas are thought by some other faculty of knowing, both internal and to the side of reason and experience. At every turn where my thought failed, broke off, or lay neglected in a file on my computer, the way forward for me was ultimately given by an open field poetics and how its itinerary of debates and differentiation has been taken up and surpassed by Nathaniel Mackey.[2] Fred Moten, devoted student of Harriet Jacobs, to my mind, is the first poet-philosopher to fully integrate the force of free verse into his theoretical writing.[3] He inaugurates what we might call *free theory*. Writing theory should not be exempt from the movement of free verse. Theory in the black radical tradition should move with an a priori "sociopoetic grounding" given in "(mis)translation, (mis)transliteration, and (mis)transcription."[4] This reality became inescapable for me the instant this revelation appeared in my study of Mackey's *"Mu"* poems, especially those in *Splay Anthem*.[5] And to submit myself to the accompanying obligation that writing theory be real *in this way*, that is, *grounded sociopoetically because written with and in lunacy, love, and analyricism*,[6] I reformulated Moten's question "What if blackness is the name that has been given to the social field and social life of an illicit alternative capacity to desire?" to *What if blackness is the name that has been given to the open field and open life of an illicit alternative capacity to desire?*[7]

Perhaps as a response to this question, in the middle of drafting this book, I started writing another text more identifiable with poetry proper, offering me new appreciation for the early language poets like Lyn Hejinian and Robert Duncan, and then poet-translators of Korean folk myth and modernist poetry, like Theresa Hak Kyung Cha, Don Mee Choi, and Myung Mi Kim.[8] Such language writing breaches the line between poetry and criticism, and I am so grateful to have found this space of study. This book, however, is not a study of them or the historical literary movements with which they and other poets contained in the following pages are associated. Rather, while deeply shaped by their art, thought, and protest traditions, this book risks actually participating in language writing, in the sociality of language poetics, in *free theory*.

As I wrote this book, I could only start to study Ezra Pound studying Ernest Fenollosa and their work with Chinese writing and poetry.[9] Nonetheless, I was compelled, however prematurely, to take up the questions of "objectism" raised by Charles Olson and the lasting influence of the imagists by allowing analytic thought processes to pause and yield, of an accord that would exceed my own intentions and imagination, language and imagery in extremely concentrated form, or what Jacques Derrida refers to in *Of Grammatology* as the "irreducibly graphic."[10] These are the letters that mark each of the pieces of *Mu*. And though, for Pound, modern poetics might strive with Chinese ideograms to inoculate the lyric from "the wanton play of sounds and letters" as "emblems of stability," according to Mutlu Konuk Blasing, the concreteness of my letters could not possibly exist without lyrical vulnerabilities, or what Charles Bernstein has described as "language's *animalady*," which poetic practices carry with them as profound and varying emptinesses of sense and meaning.[11]

Emptiness, the held presence of absence, harbors the power, beauty, and danger of thought, theory, and language to come. Transliteration and translation, insofar as the activity carries along absences of possible corresponding meaning within a language and between languages, offered me a more manageable protocol of writing to guide my thinking in *Mu*. The 49 letters capture in clipped and dense form the constancy of waves of memories, images, sounds, and things of everyday life that bend, puncture, and evacuate speech of the sovereignty of conscious thought. As objects resulting from a procedure of *free theory*, the 49 letters of *Mu* bear my having submitted to a writing that might be replete with life. Life with my father was, is, always present possible revolutionary thought quietly coursing through territories of desire and cultural memory unextinguishable by slavery and colonialism.

The honorific Korean phrase for dying, for passing away, is 돌아가시다, *dora gasida*. 돌아, *dora*, means "spin." And 돌아가다, *doragada*, means "go back or return to." Dying, spinning, returning. $4 = 2 + 2 + (-\phi)$. Contained in the infinitesimally small of the subtracting thing, 돌아가시다 indexes an at least double-spun force. The galaxy turns and returns, turns as it returns. And we spin as we circle toward some nonpoint of origin. This is the something, other than this world, that I believe my father prepared me for with our math lessons so many decades ago. Here, this something gets us ever closer to this obscure place of everything in these condensed reassociations I call *marks of abolition*.

돌, *dol*, is a homophone for the Korean word for "stone, pebble."

In Cormac Gallagher's translation of Jacques Lacan's seminar on anxiety, Lacan leaves a tachygraphical notation, a "little mark," so we can find our way back to the lesson if we drift off during his lecture. It is "the small o" in contrast to "the big Other."[12] Its function is one thing, while its mark, the signal of anxiety, takes the form of "a white stone." We need this little white pebble to find our way as we attempt to outline the processes by which the ego, baffled by a certain "ambiguity between identification and love," invites us to consider "the relationship between *being* and *having*."[13] This o, an "instrument of love," is how "namely—we find it again—. . . one loves . . . with what one does not have."[14] The practice of love is a practice of *not having*, or having only "what one n-o longer has (*n'a plus*)," which is to say, sharing in "the disorder of small o's which there is no question yet of having or not."[15] Love is abandonment to and in a disordered condition of *n'a plus*. Love is the abolition of the very phenomenological problem of associating *being* with *(not) having*. In choosing "the subjectification of o as pure real," perhaps it becomes possible to produce a new mythographic practice of loss.[16]

I look again at this small white pebble, this o. While it guides my reading of Gallagher's translation of Lacan, it is oddly out of place. Its markedness invokes the primordial lines and curves of hangul that can be seen, I realize, in fragments and pieces in any system of writing, if one looks from a certain view of *dystranslation*.

o, this small white pebble, the 돌 of *dora, doraga* . . .

Each of the 49 letters in this book is an attempt to recall and retain the sound of burnishing this stone in a time of war. Not a war of benign and malignant life, of prey and predator, colonized and colonizer. No, this is a war of cellular attrition on one front and of cosmic attrition on the other. And fighting in it requires giving in to everything the way, I think, I give in to the psycho-hapticality of a beloved's question. In one instance, it is nowhere and then, in another, everywhere inside me, which is to say, in not-me, just o.

With this particular attention, my writing seemed always to set off and arrive on some path of alphabets and glyphs as I cut and pasted characters and letters that the buttons on my keyboard are not programmed to correspond to. Annie Rogers, in *Incandescent Alphabets*, writes that "a true hole—outside meaning, outside the chain of signifiers, and outside discourse—leaves in its wake a river of Real *jouissance* that runs through our bodies, collecting the melodies of the river, all those sounds we heard before we had language."[17] She says we might, like the psychotic, make use of this river, this swarm.

Writing suspended my thoughts in this swarm, like water drops in air hover, fall, and fly. I reassociated them in an ideo- and pictographic terrain of Korean hangul and *hanja* in service to what J. Kameron Carter calls a "black rapture" that I hear in the vernacularity of thought in general, performed across poetries, theories, histories, and laws.[18] Black rapture, the complete lapse of will, "a lapsarian condition," to "enfleshed spirit," materializes in *Mu* as an animist mode of study in the necessity of emptinesses, palimpsestic blanknesses, and cutting arrhythmias in spoken and written forms of radical political desire.[19] The satisfactions of this mode of study have been many, as it sent me each day to raze, not necessarily the lyric, but the grammatical structure of the English sentence. For if the jurisgrammatical scale of the sentence is an essential unit of violence on which colonial law, language, and history depend, then the abolition of the sentence is precisely what was and has been at stake in poetic writing and mark making.

Returning over and over to both graphic and phonemic priority in this mode of study deconstructed and inspirited the givenness of the written word (of law, but also theory) into a form of writing I ultimately felt was, or should be, approached as a form of calligraphy. This is precisely what Aldon Nielsen has theorized as the intertextual and polyglottal form of "black chant," which "bodies itself forth in the garb of mark, inscription, calligraphy."[20] The calligraphic contained in translating and transliterating between Korean hangul and *hanja* and other languages became an occasion for communion with both the immateriality of poetic thought and, in turn, the reenchantment of presumptively lifeless letters and words.[21] This reenchantment performs thought in the difference between social life and social death to overwhelm this something we call an "I," who might write, or think, or speak about this difference as one *about* concepts, while also *listening* to the Real difference of words as glyphs or marks. This is to say, while listening as "*'mu' second part*":

The

enormous bell of a
trumpet's inturned
eye, an endangered
isle, some

insistent Mu,

become the
root of whatever

song.[22]

The speaking subject is a glossolalic, chanting, *mudang* ("shaman" in Korean) subject whose body both bares and bears the promise of a language that honors the difference between social life and social death. If R. A. Judy's devotional thought of and in *Sentient Flesh* murmurs "us *is flesh*," *Mu*'s mode of study strives to produce a calligraphy of this murmur, where every stroke is a poem on the way to another, "us *is glyph, mark, letter . . .*"[23]

As notated echoes with no beginning, I wish these 49 letters to be an incomplete anti-neocolonial alphabet. I wish for them to remain in what Craig Dworkin has called the "alphabetic threshold" one encounters with the sheer materiality of language.[24] The letters of *Mu* mark an obstinacy in somersaulting phonemes that, over and over, on and on, give the lie to every conception of sovereignty, democracy, and freedom Europe and the United States have polluted our waters, air, soil, and imaginaries with. It is an alphabet of the oceanic of history, law, and language that wells up in some odd aural medium my body was called on to scribe. They are irreducible flecks of flesh in a general condition of violence that I wanted to spare from the added offense of fixing meaning in a conditional and contextual nature.

Thus my enthrallment with apophasis, which Michael Sells describes as the unsayable in speech. Such speech is often characterized by the metaphor of emanation and refuses to ontologize transcendent phenomena by persisting in the immanent nature of speech.[25] These letters are meant to retain what remains empty, enigmatic, and unsayably real about life in the wake of colonialism and slavery, neocolonialism, and anti-blackness. They mark an apophatic movement of thought immanent to prison abolition as the ongoing struggle for the abolition of slavery. They are my way of responding to this strange bidding, "Knit her speaking to the Real in a social link."[26]

While English is the stranger language of European continental philosophy, the law-giving and enforcing power of law written in English the world over is produced through both its grammatical structures and its capacity to colonize and assimilate non-English words and cultures into a single-minded drive to sovereignty. Yet the English of US law contains an etymological hybridity and promiscuity between Latin and Germanic strands of Proto-Indo-European language families. The poetry and poetics of social life and social death I think with and through, largely given in Black and Korean American Englishes, queers this etymological promiscuity internal to law by further disordering and proliferating the marks and sounds of Chinese, French, German, Latin, and Greek.

While the early writings of Lacan focused on "full speech," his later writings shifted more specifically toward how speech holds the Real in what he referred to as the "well-spoken." That which is "well-spoken" is speech that holds the quiet excess of the *unsayable* and how that form of truth lives immanently in the body. Hangul as I use it throughout this book offers the *well-written* in the truth of the letter that lives in how the mouth moves and the body listens. Mobilizing the Korean hangul alphabet was crucial because its consonants directly depict the speaking body held together by the mystical realm of vowels. It is an anti-aristocratic alphabet designed for vernacularity, ease of learning and use, and adaptable to the changes of speech and ideas of oral culture. The proliferated *well-written* of *Mu*'s hangul is not to recover or reconstruct legal meaning but to force the law to surrender to us, the only rightful keepers of the precious, vital resource of the unsayable, of justice.

A voice that tenderly says other than what is said in what we hear is borne of its own murmuring. It demands we give in better, give better, give like the hands from Lucille Clifton's poem "cutting greens." They write, which is to say, hold and cut, and prepare and nourish our connection to another order of things.

> curling them around
> i hold their bodies in obscene embrace
> thinking of everything but kinship.
> collards and kale
> strain against each strange other
> away from my kissmaking hand and
> the iron bedpot.
> the pot is black,
> the cutting board is black,
> my hand,
> and just for a minute
> the greens roll black under the knife,
> and the kitchen twists dark on its spine
> and I taste in my natural appetite
> the bond of live things everywhere.[27]

These letters will not relent to meaning. They are nonsynthesizable. This is because the pragmatic, material nature of the apophatic language of abolition is covert, irrepressible, and overflowing. The social practice of breaking words into breath and sound, mark and phoneme, thought and poem, is always also a sacral, mystical practice beyond the way sacrifice and the knowable have come to dominate expressions of political desire. And so we move associatively as ciphers of our beloved, whose everlasting abundance is a living thinking of *mu*.

acknowledgments

With love

To Kieran, Azure, and Akira.
To Wellington Bowler.

To Sun Young and Kwang Woo Han.

To Fred Moten.

Deepest thanks

To my editors at Duke University Press, J. Kameron Carter, Sarah Jane Cervenak, and Courtney Berger; the production team, Ihsan Taylor, Aimee C. Harrison, Laura Jaramillo, Kimberly Miller, Christopher Robinson, and Chad Royal; and indexer extraordinaire, Paula Durbin-Westby.

To my confidantes in writing psychoanalysis, Jared Sexton and Annie Rogers.

To my students, Samiha Khalil, Ernest Chavez, Justin Strong, Navi Gill, Amanda Petersen, Anthony Triola, Izzy Williams, Konysha Wade, and Khirad Siddiqui.

To friends and mentors whose engagement shaped portions of this book, especially David Lloyd, NourbeSe Philip, Roshanak Kheshti, R. A. Judy, Frank Wilderson, Simon Leung, Teresa Dalton, Keramet Reiter, Simon Cole, Mona Lynch, Susan Coutin, Val Jenness, Ana Muñiz, Chris Tomlins, Jerry Lee, Dylan Rodríguez, Laura Harris, Atef Said, Colin Dayan, Denise Ferreira da Silva, Michael Sawyer, Paul Bové, Alberto Toscano, Kelli Moore, Salar Mameni, Yang Yu, Charisse Pearlina Weston, James Bliss, Christopher Chamberlin, Yen Noh, Monica Cho, lauren woods, Kimberli Meyer, Elena Mo, Sharif Ezzat, Greg Reeves, Leti Volpp and the Center for Race and Gender at UC Berkeley, Jason Bayani and the 2022 Kearny Street Workshop's Interdisciplinary Writer's Lab, and Caroline Fowler and the Clark Art Institute. And to the Anti-Colonial Machine.

Earlier versions of various sections of *Mu* have appeared in the journals *Women and Performance*, *boundary 2*, *Textual Practice*, and *Law and Literature*.

savoir
black

e [inapparency] I

In his preface to *Splay Anthem*, Nathaniel Mackey writes, "Any longingly imagined, mourned or remembered place, time, state, or condition can be called 'Mu.'"[1]

Mu, 무, 無, nothingness.

Writing this book on *Mu* has been a practice of reading again and again, and revising over and over. Something of my living body has wanted to make an offering. And yet this possible offering otherwise burrows down, just out of grasp, as if me because in me. And so a certain insatiable feeling to write something truthful about radical politics and desire appeared. The form of this feeling was *mu*, empty and so unsatisfiable, and nothing but the incompleteness of all the words I found and deleted along the way to figuring out how I might offer that which remains unknown.

I travel the surface of the possibility of this strange condition, this possible offer. Perhaps this strangeness of writing is itself an offering.

Parlêtre, where mark, lack, and some bodily text densify into a thing. I work this thing, its imperfections and imprecisions, over and over.

> This was finally myself swallowing
> those small, common parts of me.[2]

There is no end to writing over, starting over, doing over. Even with this book. Repetition carves lines out of a meaningless block. Sometimes beautiful, sometimes abject, some form of absence always appears. It blows gray ash off from the surface of everything in the afterlife of our burning world. To write with *parlêtre* is to happen upon an amber fossil on this surface.

that it is re-
served for *going* too, for a deeply
artifactual spidery form, and how it can, gleaming,
yet looking still like mere open air mere light,
catch in its syntax the necessary sacrifice.[3]

The hand that scribes, the hand that cuts, the hand that brushes, is pushed along by another, ghostly hand. That hand is the hand that places a yellow jewel in my palm, ever moving along, ever ready to twist and open up to catch what falls. Being enjoys the prosthetic gestures of *that* ghostly hand, drafting on my exhaling body.

Neither *prose* nor *thesis*, prosthetic writing absents a letter—*e*—and two modes of writing and thinking are revealed to be one. The prosthesis of poetic writing writes the absent *e*.

The absent *e* marks a species of time Luis Izcovich refers to in *The Marks of a Psychoanalysis* as the "meticulous present."[4] He is referring specifically to Jorge Luis Borges's poetry, but so many others come to mind. You will find them manifesting a meticulous present throughout this book, where I feel an urgency to make theory's past and future respond to the present, but, as well, where writing theory as a physical act admits and undertakes the seemingly impossible task to write a word that will ring truth in times un(fore)seeable, circumstances absent any anchoring law, and ears listening for refuge and revolution.

> In the rapid eye movement of the poet's night vision, this dictum can be decoded, like the secret acrostic of a lover's name.[5]

The absent *e* of *prosthesis* is more than silent. It has an inapparency, an uncanniness. Where and how does this *e* emerge in the law's writing? This inapparency between the prose and thesis of law's language? One must approach the law fundamentally as a form of writing constituted through the repetition of questions people bring to it. These questions remain unanswerable in any final way because of the sheer heterogeneity of complaints desire produces in the living.

And yet law's answers to social matters have to be made to hold. "The origin of every contract," writes Walter Benjamin, "points toward violence."[6] Legal holdings are not just holdings. They are marks made to cohere into words. And without force, without state and civil agents to enforce this coherence, holdings are empty. Law depends on letters, which, absent their enforcement into grammar and translation, compose a strange emptiness of an "unalloyed means of agreement."[7] The inapparency of *e* marks, for me, the reality of both the unalloyed agreement available in law as language referred to by Benjamin, and "a profound agreement" Jared Sexton points to as "an agreement that takes shape in (between) *méconnaissance* and (dis)belief" when one submits, in the most extreme sense of the word, to "being inhabited by that writing."[8]

It is this emptiness in law that drives the writing of *Mu*. It is here that all the misrecognized and unrecognizable suffering the law propagates, with its always evolving enforceability, elicits a strange horizon of thought on nothingness. Erica Hunt, in her poem "Upon another acquittal / A choreography of grief," dedicated to "Mamie Till, Sybrina Fulton, Samira Rice and Geneva Reed Veal," in *Veronica: A Suite in X Parts*, locates this horizon in the movement of collapse:

> & crumple in an instant
> knowing no justice will ever be found
> could be found
>
> where nothing is said out loud
> & when it is said or wailed
>
> the something said is
> something that no one hears:[9]

To say nothing out loud is to give these nothings a substance, a "something" that no single being can hear, at the same time that this substance persists in gestures, marks, and letters. My 49 marks of abolition follow Hunt's colon and echo the 49 days of Kim Hyesoon's *Autobiography of Death*.[10] They crouch and ride underneath the imposition of meanings of and as justice, or the subjection of writing to the political. They are not total voids. They are what Izcovich refers to as "median void[s]," insofar as gestures, marks, and sounds, left in the aftermath of enforcement, sparkle like grains of sugar. These nothings are compounds of something visible and an invisible force that allures, like sweetness, what is necessary and lethal to life.[11]

In *Six Drawing Lessons*, William Kentridge writes about a poem by Rainer Maria Rilke he has taped on the wall of his studio.

> Like a dance of strength around a centre
> Where a mighty will was put to sleep.[12]

The poem's lines depict a panther, which reminds Kentridge of something essential at the core of his creative practice: "The urge to make something," he writes, "a gathering of energy around . . . Around what? The blank page, the empty paper. An energy gathered, but not knowing what it should do. The impulse to make something, to draw or to paint something; but waiting for a clear instruction."[13] I am interested in this tension between "a gathering of energy around" and "waiting for a clear instruction."

Around the empty paper, who gathers? Who or what instructs?

We gather, with all our sounds, desires, and histories. Those who gather gather not simply around, but *with*, the blank page. Gathering here is an occasion granting the symbolic lack constitutive of desire. It is the gathering not of solidarity in some shared symbolic object of desire but of the solidity of a knowledge obtainable with the not-all of each and every differentiated symbolic object. And the blankness of the page will persist even after every color is applied, each picture drawn, and all the words typed.

This blankness can menace, just as we suffer the barred-ness of desire as archaic or phallic jouissance. Or it can impart something, a gift, just as we might enjoy the barred-ness of desire as a third form of jouissance beyond the phallus. Across his later teachings, Jacques Lacan identifies three types of this third form: feminine, mystical, and a nominative ex nihilo referred to as "Jouis-sense."[14] The clarity of the instruction we wait for is given in the timeliness of the blank page's invitation to be with and in the not-all of feminine, mystical, nominative pleasures, of making, doing, acting outside the protocols of symbolic ownership of self and objects. We gather and wait for an instruction whose clarity depends neither on what the instruction is nor on who instructs, but on being able to know the difference between the I who knows and enjoys and something that knows and enjoys the mystery of the blankness that grounds all thought and desire.

The blankness of *savoir*, its peculiar clarity, calls from the Real, rings black.

The torus is a ring, but not just any one. The torus's three-dimensional hole is planar. Unlike the hole of a two-dimensional surface, which can be filled by pulling the border of the hole into a single point, the torus's hole can never be filled. As a structure, the inside of its hole will never become one point on a smooth surface. Instead, its many points will only ever exist touching each other. In the crowd and press of points, there is still the emptiness of the hole.

> I is the on of on going and gone.
> Up and away[15]

Amiri Baraka's movement away from the "I" to an "on" appears as o^n, the rule of touching given by the torus's empty space.

The hand at the end of my arm that moves a pencil across that blank page, or the fingers at the end of my hand that press a sequence of letters across a blank digital plane, are prone to not-copying. This writing arm prosthetically choreographs lines that register the briefest of pauses, a hesitation both nearly imperceptible and unavoidably insistent. It writes lines that start at the left, break at the right, and start over directly beneath the line prior. But . . . it also writes lines on some invisible topological surface, bumping and bouncing arrhythmically along.

The panther circles because it abides by an ante-instructive law. It will never be instructed, not completely, except by this place, where "a mighty will was put to sleep," where the world and a protest baby meet in fields ablaze: Oakland, xučyun (Huichin) territory, Watts, Ferguson, the South African highvelds, the banks of the Han River.

Circling around nothing is not itself nothing, but consent to the inapparent.

> In the winter of the highveld, there are veld fires, and the yellow grass is reduced to black stubble. It becomes a charcoal drawing in itself. You could drag a piece of paper across the ground, and a charcoal drawing could be made.[16]

I miscopy: Kentridge's word is *drag*. I handwrote *draw*. As I recount this slip in writing by hand, my fingers still want to type *w* instead of *g*. My body, and something else, insists that what one does with paper is "draw on it" instead of "drag it across."

Paper for drawing is a membrane that awaits a mark to be made on it, my body insists. It is not to be turned face down, scraped across the soot of a scorched field, marked out of sight, dirtied. Something remains impossible to copy. In this repetitious physical urge "not to copy," there is something obscene about the act of dragging invoked by the visceral description of the essence of drawing materials: black stubble, charcoal, paper, ground.

What about the conditions of possibility for creative life comes into view when that which is dragged is draped over the history of art, literature, and philosophy? When one identifies (or is given the chance to identify) not with the subject who draws on an "it" but with this other scene in which it is impossible to not not-copy? How to invite this "it" that is dragged across the blackness of the earth in the aftermath of fire?

The word *membrane* comes from the Latin *membrum*, meaning "part of the body," "covering a part of the body," or "flesh."[17] At some point in the etymological evolution of the word, this notion is displaced and expanded to include the idea of "parchment" and more biologically and medically technical definitions, including "a thin sheet of tissue or layer of cells, usually serving to cover or line an organ or part, or to separate or connect parts."[18] That which projects becomes a surface, that which points becomes pointless or pointillistic, and that which protrudes becomes an enclosure.

This etymology tracks a shift from geography to topology. Lacan uses the figure of the lamella to conceptualize a distinctly libidinal *objet a*. *Lamella* generally means a thin flat scale, membrane, or layer; for example, biological membranes like the gills of a mushroom; geological layered mineral formations that produce line patterns; various layers that make up bone. More recently, the vitreous lamella, or Bruch membrane, refers to a nearly transparent membrane found in the uvea of an eye.

In this montage of membranes, their formal symbolic equivalencies are haunted by the specter of the living dragged across the earth, of inanimate evidence embedded under our nails, the rub of flesh on rock, of tissue on ground. The gold grass once shimmering across the highveld is a ghostly, dingy yellow in contrast to the many shades of charcoal produced in a certain infernal libidinal topology of colonialism and slavery.

From a clearing smoke, skin drafting low to the soil, my mouth a portal, my hand an erring scribe, write o^n.

ki [a little package of air] 3

The law—its business of handing down sentences, delivering judgments, and regulating promises and exchange—expends great effort to annihilate a certain positive force of social life structuring the individuated conflicts that make up a court's docket. When the law abstractly declares, "You are guilty of aggravated assault," it means that some *we* does not believe, for example, that Marissa Alexander fired her gun at her abusive husband to defend herself.[19] Reducing a trial to a sentence, and by that sentence reducing a person to a state of being, "you are" annihilates the person, thing, and context included in "aggravated assault." Law's sentencing evacuates the volatility of violent environments through an intransitive declaration of a defendant's being.

What does the poetic form of the Chinese sentence do to the way we understand law as both a symbolic discourse of norms and Lacan's formulation that "desire is law"?[20]

Ernest Fenollosa, in *The Chinese Written Character as a Medium for Poetry*, notes the likeness of form between Chinese and English sentences but also offers the caution that the translation such formal similarity allows "must follow closely what is said, not merely what is abstractly meant."[21]

What does the law say with a guilty sentence, when it reestablishes a taboo, when it asserts itself as the regulation of desire? It reclaims a certain fundamental senselessness of violence into meaning. Violence is reduced to human intent; its reality is an event with beginning, middle, and end; the loss it leaves in its wake can be accounted for by the force of the writtenness of law. This is Robert Cover's point: the performativity of law as nomos encloses and manages violence at the scale of its actual sentences.[22]

Comparing English and Chinese, Fenollosa notes the prevalence of the intransitive verb in English, whose performative effect reveals the separability of verbs from direct objects. These verbs without direct objects reveal that it "requires great effort to annihilate" the sense of a verb's positive force into "weak and incomplete sentences which suspend the picture and lead us to think of some verbs as denoting states rather than acts."[23] This is in contrast to the otherwise vivid experience in written Chinese, where verbs "are all transitive or intransitive at pleasure."[24]

The annihilation of an essential activeness or life of language itself is a core part of the repressive function of law's written sentences. This grammatical annihilation structures desire in and of legal judgment and, in turn, naturalizes the separability of verb and object in every declaration of law. Grammatical order, the sentence as both a unit of writing and a moment in legal judgment, procedurally offers finality by addressing a person who no longer does or acts in the world but "is" one way or another. Law's passive construction of violence replicates equally passive enjoyment of fantasies in law that personify violence as the essence of blackness.

But what refuses annihilation, despite the sentence's efforts?

"It requires great effort to annihilate. . . . "
*It requ***ire***s great ef***fort** *to annihilate . . .*
Ire and fort . . . da.
Anger and strength, gone and there.

In his essay *Beyond the Pleasure Principle*, Sigmund Freud observes in the child's game of *fort/da* that "the first act, that of departure, was staged as a game in itself and far more frequently than the episode in its entirety, with its pleasurable ending."[25] *It's so effortless, annihilating this thing,* " '*da*' ['there']."[26]

Repeating Fenollosa's sentence on the English sentence's difference from written Chinese, I drop the consonantal sound of the *q* (K), this voiceless velar plosive. This stop sound falls away, and I pick up the sound of the *th* (θ). It is a voiceless dental fricative, a tongue sound.[27]

"The thing of it is . . . ," as Fred Moten begins so many of his explanations, phonographic slippage, the sound of a literal slip of movement, from the base of the tongue to the front between the teeth.[28] The thing of it is to write the law by the skin (in the middle) of our teeth.

Perhaps this is what Fenollosa meant when he declared, "*We* can assert a negation, though nature can not."[29] If nature is essentially active, always doing, law's investiture in sentences would seem a uniquely deadening activity. Indeed, "if we could follow back the history of all negative particles," or, I would add, all things, we should find that they are sprung from a certain inseparability of verbs and objects, and not from the intransitive drift baked into English and law's writtenness.[30]

Written Chinese reminds us of a certain meticulousness necessary for positive verbal conception. Traversing the unsentenced life of the ideogram and the uniquely deadening English copular verb *to be*, the consonants in the Korean alphabet offer letters that are at once phonemic references and pictures of the sounding mouth through which air and voice move. The fricative *q* (K) is denoted by the hangul letter ㄱ.[31] The letter itself depicts the shape of the mouth, lips, and tongue when it makes the represented sound.[32] The name of the letter ㄱ, *giyeok*, the first letter, in fact, of the Korean alphabet, is homonymic with 기억, meaning "memory."

Korean consonants both denote and depict sound as the breath and voice cleaved by tongue and lips. Speech acts written are acts of cleaving, a leaving to and in the side. To speak is to take leave of "I," hearing the clear note of some other thing that accompanies the saying, uttering the clear shape of a hangul letter.

Hangul is the orthographic *parlêtre* of and for an aliterate common folk intellectuality. The body is in the stroke, and the stroke in the body, as differential absences.

In grammatical annihilation, speech offers the pleasures of "no," *na*, strung out, one line after another, sentences whose multiplicity betrays ordered sense. "In Chinese the sign meaning 'to be lost in the forest' relates to a state of non-existence. English 'not' = Sanskrit *na*, which may come from the root *na*, to be lost, to perish."[33]

And so it is that the sequencing of words, or the ordering of speech, has no end. In forgetting how they began, words contain the capacity to surpass any ending. We speak always lost in the middle of things, forgetting what letter we capitalized at the beginning and between which letters we punctuated a stop. In perpetual revision, each word is a stone that takes me deeper into the Forest of *Na*.

Here, "frequently our lines of cleavage fail, one part of speech acts for another. They *act for* one another because they were originally one and the same."[34] The proposition of an original sameness is interesting to me only insofar as the uncanny filters my attempts at a certain philological reconstruction. This is to say that uncanniness, for me, cuts philology with the transliterative possibility of Korean hangul to fill the expanse between English and Chinese with a vestibular mouth connecting speech and *parlêtre*. *This* mother tongue, of the marked mouth and mouthlike marks, claims in those failed cleavages. Its geometry of breath tempts me down some road to a place where the mark, the letter, the stroke, the calligraphic line fuses with what writing leaves behind and transmits nonetheless.

ㄱ cleaves.[35]

Ki: cleaving the law's sentence with the clarity of Don Cherry's trumpet, or the soft brush of his breath in my ear, or the hum of a song's hook. It is our *petit objet a*, this little package of air, *ki*, or 기 in hangul. Can you hear the surpluses that survive the sentence's repetition?

The thing of it lives in this transliteration, which some might say is slightly off from the more proper *gi*. But I suppose I prefer the harder *k* over the more glottal *g* given that the sound of ㄱ is somewhere in between. In the expanse of difference in the utterance between *ki* and *gi*, and in the nonsensical English phoneme *ki* and the Korean word 기, there is not simply the meaning of the word but a knowledge of it: "energy, life force, breath, heart, ether, temper, a feeling of."[36] The *hanja* root of 기 is the familiar philosophical idea of *qi*, *ch'i*, 氣, also meaning "energy, life force, breath, air."

Some living part of my body that would hear, utter, and mark this *ki* enacts what Izcovich describes as an "effective real . . . a real not as a frontier between what can and cannot be symbolized, but a real which can be used as a support in existence."[37] The real borne here, for me, is a procedure of writing where the twist of homophonic translation also wrings the neck of the law's sentences, forces it to open up to an amonolingual transitive register. There is no existent "I" of this text aside from the marks of this procedure.

The Chinese written character 氣 is a compound of the pictogram 气, meaning "air, breath, energy," and representing clouds flowing through the sky; and the pictogram 米, meaning "rice." Together, the character describes one's effort of steaming rice as a gift for guests. Seditious, riotous, ungovernable guests, whose desire as law's reverse, re-verse law's sentences, with tinges of sound as small, soft and hard as grains of rice, scattered, scatted across the earth by the winds of life.[38] So are we ordered, with Layli Long Soldier:

> Now
> make room in the mouth
> for grassesgrassesgrasses[39]

Just This, as the great Chan Buddhist teacher Dongshan Liangjie would say.[40]

bi [*savoir* black] 4

My father died in the early months of the COVID-19 pandemic. There were four unreal months between when we first learned he had cancer in March and his crossing over at the end of June. The words "mathematical incomprehension" Lacan speaks of in his published series of lectures *Talking to Brick Walls* continue to ring inside me.[41] They give me a way to grieve.

Seven times seven: the Buddhist tradition requires 49 days of mourning by those who survive the deceased. My father's favorite number was 49. He was born in 1949. Aloft in loss, 49 lines of flight incarnate an indestructible desire.

Listen, listen to the voice of the mountain of the North
The candlelight inside you is extinguished[42]

He was a mathematician and put this passionate intellect to any problem. Writings of the Black Panther Party, like Eldridge Cleaver's *Soul on Ice*, sat next to his books on topological manifolds. And somewhere in our home, he had hidden manuscripts of Korean history written by scholars living in North Korea.

Growing up doing math homework with him transmitted profound lessons about living and dying. I would not have said this as a child, but I must have known it nonetheless. His teaching traced how one moves through incomprehension with a protocol to arrive at an answer that includes a partial knowledge of *why*. To teach was to embrace incomprehension as an occasion to construct this protocol. Revelation always awaited at the end of this labor. The answer made sense at a deeper level of knowing, which was also a deeper level of living.

The political traditions of black radicalism and 주체 (*juche*), the Korean word for "self-reliance" or "independence," were our protocol for arriving at why it was correct to question all teachers, scorn all police, defend the right to self-determination, take pleasure in the possible triumphs of all of the United States' political enemies, stand up for peasants everywhere, revere the miracles of land and water we receive from farmers and fishers, and always think on the side of black liberation.

I still wake up to the sound of some book, whose pages he would slide before turning to the next, like breathing's exhale.

Meet me in the open field of mathematical incomprehension.

There is a form of truth in mathematics that proceeds from but also exceeds deductive truth statements performed through logics of bivalency. Mathematical reasoning builds from a series of determinations between "true" and "false," and each judgment of what is "true" is built out into an expanse of abstraction. It is both real procedure and fantastical ambition that characterizes the scientific revolution. Thus, Lacan's fuller comment:

"Subjects who are beset by mathematical incomprehension expect more from truth."[43] This expectation, he goes on, "puts them to flight" in "a certain distance between truth and what we may call a cipher."[44]

Parlêtre, cipher, and the Arabic grapheme بِ (*bi*), read by R. A. Judy from Ben Ali's African-Arabic American slave narrative.[45] "The cipher is nothing else but a written form, the written form of its value," writes Lacan, to which Judy follows up with the spoor as "auto-obscuring articulation," from an ancient Arabic proverb, "The camel dung-spoor signifies the camel" (*al-baʿira tadalu ʿalā al-baʿīr*).[46]

Parlêtre, cipher, بِ (*bi*), dung-spoor: they materialize the "patterns of movement" in flight toward the more of truth in and of what Judy calls the "black textual tradition."[47] They are the marks of a *savoir* black, an unknown knowing that is true generally for every practice of writing and reading the illegible.

Deductive reasoning about what blackness is or is not, then, can only get us so far in this formulation of *savoir* black. For at some point, the essential nonnarratable history of the black slave and their descendant textual communities must think about the continued existence of this nonnarratability. Explaining Ben Ali's diary as "gibberish," Judy emphasizes, "the manuscript exists and in existing indicates a discernible system of signs, an *agencement* of referentiality, which somehow resists being comprehended in a universal semiology."[48] More recently, Judy's *Sentient Flesh* extends this earlier study to develop the idea of *para-semiosis*. Judy explains, "*Para-semiosis* denotes the dynamic of differentiation operating in multiple multiplicities of semiosis that converge *without synthesis*."[49] That such *para-semiosis* unfolds and flows "without synthesis" is, as I understand it, the condition of possibility for "blackness," which, Judy explains, "is a poetical, as in *poiēsis*, expression of *para-semiosis*."[50]

What Judy performs as "cryptoanalysis" and now, *poiēsis*, to read the ciphers of the black textual tradition articulates perfectly where blackness and Lacanian psychoanalysis meet.[51] On this approach, statements about ontologies of and as anti-blackness, political and otherwise, are "gibberish" unavoidably admitting that the mouth's or the hand's movement, their "auto-obscuring articulation," is the only fact of existence.

According to Lacan, ontological discourse is a form of *connaissance*, knowledge desired for its transcendental nature.[52] Cryptoanalysis as a form of black psychoanalysis maneuvers the subject whose "desire is a desire to know" to "render present a hole which can no longer be situated in the transcendental nature of knowledge."[53] The symbolic existence of that which is nonnarratable, the letter, must and will ultimately displace *connaissance* with *savoir*. Not because *savoir* is a higher form of knowing. But because, as Judy says, there is "graphic material in need of a structural field."[54]

Through cryptoanalysis, the desiring subject will have been placed in a structural field in which the more of truth can be experienced as some mark that lives on or in the body, and whose origin and cause is unknowable. Every crypt is a hole, and every hole is a crypt. This is a radical extension of the Freudian discovery Lacan tries to impress across his seminars and writing, that is, "the structural reason why the literality of any text, whether proposed as sacred or profane, increases in importance the more it involves a genuine confrontation with truth. . . . That structural reason is found precisely in what the truth that it bears, that of the unconscious, owes to the letter."[55]

So, how to articulate the *parlêtre* of Afro-pessimism as a challenge to the reduction of it to deducible truth about what blackness is or is not?[56]

The surprise of movement other than the bivalent back and forth of conscious political thought awaits between the imaginary and the symbolic. And to respond to these swarming letters by theorizing this structural field from the very ciphers or materials that exist outside semiology is not to valorize their "oppositional resistance" but, continuing to follow Judy, to trace "a resistance of being that can only be transposed."[57]

Something of existence whose mode is transposition refers to a surplus jouissance. Specifically, it is a pleasure of redrawing a line around the blankness of a text to be taken in and as the cipher, the letter, *parlêtre*: بِ, *bi*, be. Judy says that Ben Ali was "writing writing," as Judy, too, does with Ben Ali as beloved cipher.[58] And we all, too, might, if we can conscience that black radical politics is the camel, and the black textual tradition the transpositional, transferential movement of its spoors.

The letters and sounds of theory's writing often start to get restless. They do not neatly stay in their field of meaning. They become serial marks, and my eyes and ears unsync themselves from each other as they wander from the monotony of lined-up letters. They catch those letters and sounds that fall away only to return. These are homophonic (mis)translations, or dystranslations, through which I, we, might escape the line. It's as if theory were a little tune from no song in particular, hummed under one's breath.

> She speaks ajar, the aggregate asunder: render
> The cacomeme babble towards the fourth star[59]

While *dystranslation* is my term, it follows in the wake of what Lyn Hejinian has written about *translation*: "What must be preserved," she writes, "are the disappearances that are enacted as specific meanings vanish into the time and space of sentences, the sentences into paragraphs, and the paragraphs into a book—the momentary experiences of our perceptions occurring always just at [the] moment when they too disappear."[60]

Dystranslation is a form of composition that works from the nonmeaning of a letter's sound, but also one that moves, plays, and, indeed, breathes its way from an absence of meaning into the construction of another idea. The initiation of this other idea is linked to the letter on the page as nothing more than a musical notation. And then the letter is released into an open field of sound awaiting alphabets, a crypto-writing. As the movement of the sounding mouth leads us on a path of reading between English letters and Chinese characters, the letters of the Korean hangul alphabet are, for me, the marks of a babble we might call the ghost of and in an anti-colonial machine.

Referring to Lacan's discussion of Chinese calligraphy, Izcovich remarks that the void "is what is seriously at stake, *l'en-jeu*, in the letter."[61] I suppose the English equivalent is the poem, whose patterns of letters and spaces allow a void to inhabit the page. The English in me wants to scatter out into an "auto-obscuring" English.

A being of poetics whose materiality is given in the letter as both movement and vanishment: Chinese calligraphy and the Black Arts Movement. In this disassembly of marks, cuts, curves, infinities, my being enjoys in writing, not about *parlêtre*, but with.

Lacan would conclude in his later work that *parlêtre* is "being specified by the unconscious."[62] It is a mark that lives in the body as a lost jouissance and shapes the search for surplus jouissance. It is a special signifier that marks a second birth of the living body, where the Real ex-sists in the symbolic body. *Parlêtre* is not simply a neologism for *être parlant* ("speaking being") but plays with a certain equivocation of conceptual significance between *parle-être* and *par-lettre* so as to emphasize how that which cannot be absorbed by the symbolic is libidinally expressed as the unconscious. In Izcovich's words, "The *parlêtre* is the speaking being in his singularity of jouissance, which involves the way in which the unconscious produces its effects at the level of the body."[63]

Let this body, this history, these letters fly into the air.

An unknown knowing sees letters, numbers, and symbols in mysterious relation—madness, maybe. Or reads the marks of a sage of sages. Or hears the prelude to some discourse that will make a path to some other articulation. Write only the "scraps," Lacan would insist.

Just That is all I have, anyway. *Savoir* black.

만 [only] **5**

Savoir black: holding the transposability of all history and all culture as true, incomprehend mathematically. Mather, not father . . . mather, mother, matter, ether. Math, moth, man. A flute scatters notes across the oceans, buffers the air and light with mist, drowning talk with notes, and more notes. Notes, letters, numbers, his drawing hand whispers as it moves across the page, whistles evermore . . .

波瀾萬丈. 파란만장, *paranmanjang*. Meaning "a life full of change, upheaval, turbulence."

만, *man,* meaning "10,000" and "only." Cancer would be another wave in the ten thousand waves of life, he said.

Only (a) life . . . made so little wants revenge on the biggest thing conceivable: time and its utterly arbitrary violence.

I want to cut it down the middle, reduce it to pure logic, fit it into a series of letters, numbers, and signs. I want to be the author of a logic so unconditional, unrelenting, and totalizing an act against time, it can bring the violent chaos and endless heartbreak of the world to heel. What Lacan refers to as a "*generator* operation" I know as the *generative* operation of my body.[64] I will bear with my body the capacity to gather any- and everything and spin it all in another direction, away from this ongoing catastrophe of whiteness. Born of revenge and fury, from a state of general coercion we call *freedom*, anything I gestate, living and otherwise, will be a trace of the spoor because this logic theorizes it so. Each strand of desire, which is to say, loss, which is to say, spoor, will always end with a prick that punctures the skin of memory with something to metabolize the sweet senselessness of revenge into a living alphabet.

Lacan's lectures at the Chapel in Sainte-Anne's Hospital end with "[. . .]." Ellipses are a provocative placeholder, perhaps signaling that the lectures collected in the book *Talking to Brick Walls* occurred as part of another series of lectures he delivered to the Law Faculty at the Pantheon around the same time. Those lectures are collected and translated by Jacques-Alain Miller in the volume entitled . . . *or Worse*, as Lacan's Seminar XIX. Or perhaps they signal an unrecorded free discussion, the coming of a reader's free writing that might follow the end of a published lecture.

I read these ellipses as part of a cipher: ". . . or worse." The cipher is formulated like an operation, like the bivalent operation of "True or false?" Drawn as a little diagram (table 1.1), the ellipses occupy the same place in the structure as truth, suggesting that the mark of the ellipses is how we might regard the "more" of truth. Indeed, Lacan writes in his first lecture as part of . . . *or Worse*, "This empty place is the only way to catch hold of something by means of language [and] allows us precisely to penetrate the nature of language."[65]

Table 1.1			
	TRUE	or	FALSE
	. . .	or	WORSE

What is this adverb, *worse*, related to? I believe it is related to what becomes true as a result of not choosing *savoir*. When the matter of knowledge is at stake, the bivalent choice is not between "true" and "false," but between ". . . " and "worse," or *savoir* and "worse." To respond at the level of writing, reading, and listening to the unique form of how the unconscious demands is to choose *savoir*. It is a response to the unconscious in the grammatical function of some verb, any verb, that would ground the adverb *worse*.

만 or worse.

My earliest memory of learning math was not solving a math problem but being walked, by my father, through the theory or logic that reveals a knowledge supporting a certain procedure of deduction. He drew, annotated, sketched as he explained how a theory was discovered in the context of real-life situations, people, and technologies. When drawn, Gauss's first summation formula was simply the folding and cutting of a number sequence on itself. In my father's hand, any mathematical comprehension to be had was in the *savoir* of drawing. Drawing was in the teaching, and teaching was in the drawing. This may well have been the first time I fell in love, even if it would take me decades to understand and know exactly with what and whom I had fallen in love.

So, too, then, a theory of the unconscious in a world where law and anti-blackness are one and the same, if there's one to be had, will be in a certain drawing of it. Here, drawing is a poetics of "scraps of discourse."[66] Like a memory, any theoretical insight will reside in a condensation for those who don't know what they want from you.

To give this cipher, for and of study. . . .

It bears an addressee who, also, moves through and beyond an argument of the "true or false." Less digression, less demonstration, just a few points for a drawing. Points that carry forward the expectation of a practice and knowledge of the unconscious, an experimental doing that gathers an "us" that we can only provisionally refer to, or orient around a cipher. This gathering, your teaching, my offering, some transmission happens.

What kind of interview, or inter-view, has already happened, takes place, as we ask and answer questions from separate sides of a brick wall? *Wall* in French is *mur*. Lacan refers to *l'(a)mur* to invoke the object, *a*, as a wall that structures "love, the good a mother wishes her son," and his decision to "come back here to spill some stuff at Sainte-Anne."[67] He puns, "I've been speaking with the *murs* here, indeed with *(a)murs*, and with a-*murs*-ement."[68] So what desire brings us up close to this brick wall, expecting something on the other side? What will the verb you overlay on the ellipses of Lacan's cipher do with my verbs: write, cipher, alphabetize? How do we each come to the doing of thinking *as if* someone is there, to share an interest with and in incomprehending?

The intimacy of interest in losing time to, or in having all the time for, the arrival of a *savoir* that addresses something deeper to live for than life itself is coterminous with incomprehension. Neither with hope nor with faith, neither agnostic nor fatalistic, I am talking about incomprehensible expectation. This would be, for me, the "more from truth" that emerges from the "distance between truth" and ". . ."

Between mathemes and math, law and M. NourbeSe Philip's *Zong!*, Nathaniel Mackey's *"Mu"* poems and Theresa Hak Kyung Cha's muism, cipher on cipher, jouissance on jouissance, in the distance between the position of the analyst and the analysand's hysterical demand, seditious procedures await to be discovered only once and then never again, except as trace on trace, as so many notes on the discourse of the analyst, these many "scraps."

• [cosmosis] 6

To recount from memory "what happened" in the months since June 2020, when this book's vision came to be—the pandemic, Black Lives Matter protests, losing my father to cancer—is to necessarily invite layer on layer, veil on veil, of that which divides a writing self from the self at the scene. Writing began with a stubborn persistence, something miraculous about the mere will to show up, or a desire that something would show itself despite and in the midst of recounting.

Serge André reports that he "'strangered' himself" as he set out to write about his recovery from cancer.[69] This is to wish for a nononeness, to solicit and stay with this nononeness, to know the having always been gathered. The distinction between an awakening of oneself and "something awakened" emerges. The insistence of this distinction in its turning, from side to side and under and over itself, is a palimpsestic process that follows a certain pitch. I mean *pitch* as sound, but also the willingness to be pitched, thrown, by some pitchfork of the real, out or to the side of oneself, or the oneness of being.

Palimpsestic, the words in this book are wet with gesso. They each suspend the mark of psychoanalysis in a splay of pigment. That which is suspended used to be a word. But smeared by and in the gesso, a letter remains, spread for examination. The word takes some lovely hazy shade of gray, a blurry now, a barely perceptible word. This milky fluid shows us the bareness of the materiality of the word, not in its stripping, not in its covering, but by force, a streak of motion.

The analyst's writing, *this* writing, like palimpsestic painting, or the carving of paint on canvas, summons a certain kind of pressure, the press of the real on the symbolic world we unconsciously defend, the unwitting automated "worse" we choose on one side of Lacan's formula ". . . or worse."

The beyond that which the ellipses mark, and precisely here, is where André poses the question of whether writing might have cured him of his cancer. Beyond as that which exists without representation beyond any frame, delimitation, or rule tends to give us the sense that "the cure comes on its own," that it is a "negative knowledge," an acontextual context of being that "endeavors to keep empty."[70]

I find it frightening and thrilling that art is exemplary of such effort. Insofar as something truly new and true is made through the nonrepresentational part of (any) gesture—noting, smearing, sketching, erasing, etching, sounding, copying—art is exemplary for me, not of courage, but of some way of being in time and space where fear and courage, meaning and madness, and self and other are rendered obsolete as ways of taking responsibility for one's desire. The pen, the brush, the hand, the sponge, the lump of charcoal, the body, the shadow, the keyboard—they are all physical portals to a practice already underway, each offering the possibility of choosing that which can only be symbolized with ellipses.

The open field is scorched for the drawing.

The dots of an ellipsis as grammatical punctuation of a beyond within meaning have a pictorial aspect in hangul vowels. Vowels were created using three figures: the dot, representing heaven (yin); the horizonal line, representing earth (yang); and the vertical line, representing the human. I read the ellipses in J. Kameron Carter's reading of theologian Charles Long, in

The Anarchy of Black Religion, with this hangul twist. In the ellipses, Carter registers the presence of cosmological worlds at the heart of black religion and all this implies about the heterogeneity of form we can imagine in and as ellipses.

Manifestos 4 is a musical art piece by Charles Gaines, who transposed the letters of the written Supreme Court opinion in *Dred Scott v. Sandford* into a system of musical notation and composition.[71] In the black box of slavery with Gaines, he shows us what a true re-versing of law is. There is a new cosmic universe waiting in the conceptual mediation of the letter connecting word and sound, law and music. Gaines's is a process of co-osmosis between written law and musical score, a cosmosis of *savoir* black, between listening and reading. Gaines's conceptually driven practice of musical composition produces orchestral sound from the mathematical incomprehension of how the letters that comprise the *Dred Scott* opinion dispense violence across the social field. It is a dissonant, haunting, contemporary, and musing music. Gaines shows us that the conceptuality of law's writing bears music. The written opinion is just a misread musical score of letters notating an unhearable sonicity.[72] Their phrasings contain polyvoided meanings. And when played in concert through conceptual transposition, translation, and transliteration of the question of who or what Dred Scott was, is, and could be in the late nineteenth-century United States, Gaines's art shows us that, yes, no, *mu*, "music," as Nathaniel Mackey writes, "is wounded kinship's last resort."[73]

The law's illimitable interdiction of *black life is also a black cosmosis* in inter-diction.

Se [bird] 7

M. NourbeSe Philip created the long poem *Zong!* from the words of *Gregson v. Gilbert* (1783).[74] In this infamous English case, the owners of a slave ship sued an insurance company to recoup their "losses" of 130 enslaved Africans they intentionally cast overboard en route from Accra, Ghana, to Jamaica.[75]

Zong! culminates in Philip's scattered and fragmented phonemes and words, many of which are unreadable because they appear like letters typed on top of other letters, into a dense gathering and overlapping movement. They represent the bones of millions of slaves lost to the liquid grave of the Middle Passage, the unhearable sonicity of their submerged lives, and continue to haunt the words of law as letters.

Reading *Zong!* aloud, my voice stops at these knotted letters, and continues on, moving with the waves of what legible phonemes and words appear in relationship to these condensations of sound and mark. The blackness of these typographical figures arrests and presences the labor of breath in reading and making sense.

There is, at the end, no way to untangle writing and reading, history and violence, law and life, letter and mark. Entanglement is beginningless, and endless. There is only reknotting in these secretive, intimate dashes of letters laid over letters. They vibrate with a blurry edge created from their inseparability. They are marks of an uncoded, unencodable silence whose frequency changes into so many waves of murmurance. Indeed, it is as if *Zong!* is part of the quest narrated in *Looking for Livingstone: An Odyssey of Silence* to "make the desert of words bloom—with Silence!"[76]

The force of Philip's poetics, which is to say, the force of law written with Philip's hand, is physical. It requires sounding bodies, dead and living. The unencodedness of the silence of these reknotted letters impinges on the body as reader, the body of law as word, and the unconscious as ceaseless writing. The breath is freed from reading as performance. Voice is unwillingly stilled, suspended, unensured. What and who will proceed from there is not assured, even if a next breath can be and is taken, or a next phoneme or word can be and is discerned. *Zong!* is the force of law's language incarnated in hovering, teeming, blurry marine matter whose lines move in a moving medium. *Zong!* azures law.

Filled with glyphs of the ungivenness of breath, to read it, aloud or in silence, is to break the law, which is to say, break prose.

Zong! is our *pro se* case.

Se, *sae*. *Sae* is a transliteration of the hangul word 새, meaning "bird," "new," "fresh." Hear the *muni* bird in . . . [77]

> . . . that outer space structured by inner sound, which is where the poetics of political form lives, where that poetics takes up and is taken up by its life, which is a form of life, cloaked, clothed, veiled, given in a sumptuary law of motion.[78]

Yes. I see her. The Chinese pictogram for 새 as "bird" is 鳥.

Zong! teaches abolitionists that there will be no justice for the slave and their descendants without doing something with the graphic marks of the law. Perhaps Philip, too, would say they are "in need of a structural field." Abolishing the world of meaning that both gave rise to the case and continues to drive our return to it as historical narrative has only ever been a means. No end. This form of abolition is accomplished by an erasure that is a writing over word and meaning with its sound. *Zong!* as means is an explosive reading and writing from the "underness" of law where the enforcement of a deathly contract at issue is between word and narrative.[79]

Lawlessness: a unary law of the underness of every utterance and tone.

I take a photo of the prints appearing in a book collecting and discussing Cha's life and art (figure 1.1).

I and this structural field that is yet to be are prefigured in the bottom right frame of Cha's 1977 set of prints, "Markings." The doing of *parlêtre*, "blacks," is summoned by the blankness of this specific frame. It offers as condition of possibility all the things it could be filled with. The inapparency of the ghosted words underneath the clearer ones—black and blue, markings, blacks and blue, mark, blues—is made more present by my desire to include Cha's "Markings" here by taking a picture of the book's page. This blankness is all that the absent mark "blacks" marks, inapparent ghosted words there even so.

Every morning, somewhere between six and seven, always with waking dreaminess, my son looks over my shoulder and scans my writing. This morning, while I was getting him breakfast, Namu reminded me that I was born in 1977, and "7 times 7 is 49."

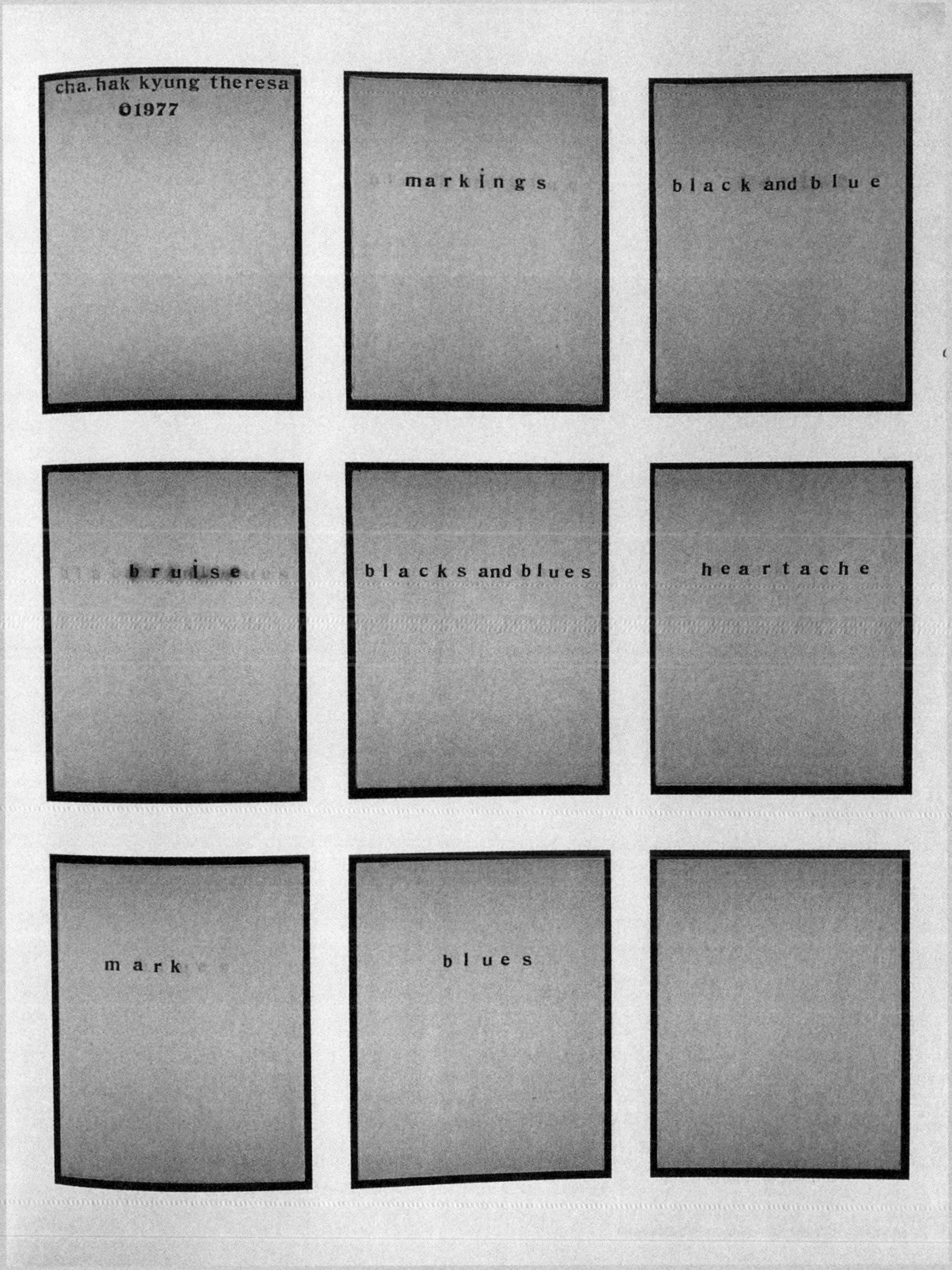

1.1 Theresa Hak Kyung Cha, "Markings" (1977). In Lewallen, *The Dream of the Audience*, 129. Photo by author.

terra incognita

Fe [terra incognita] **8**

I run into trouble revising a previously published article of mine to incorporate into this book. The article, "Poetics of Mu," is on Hortense Spillers's essay "'The Permanent Obliquity of an In(pha)llibly Straight': In the Time of the Daughters and the Fathers." The sound of my knowing voice (*connaissance*) grates on me. It is obsessive in its preoccupation to say everything that needs to be said in order to justify reading Spillers's reformulation of the incest taboo. I fill with dread as the revision process starts to descend into an obsessive rewriting of obsessive writing.

How to write to allow the unconscious writing of the article to appear here in *Mu*? How to revise how I wrote the "lack [*faille*]" I encountered in the Other, there, on first pass, as Spillers's desire for the social adoption of the incest taboo? This time, instead, might I write "the lack," which Jacques Lacan describes as that which "results from the constitutive loss of one of [my] parts, by which [I turn] out to be made of two parts"?[1]

Lacan would say, to operate "*with*" your own loss, go back to your "point of departure."[2]

My return, revision, will have to not obsess over being unobsessive. I don't have time for this self, which, anyway, critiques that which it itself cannot be rid of: a difficulty of analytically implementing the Lacanian idea that desire comes after prohibition, and not the other way around.

Don't revise. Intervene on the "I" of the first writing by "scanding."[3] Adjust not the "I" but the "pulsation of the rim through which the being that resides just shy of it must flow."[4]

Mark, letter, cut, punctuate a certain symbolic limit registered in the body given in the first writing as the "unsayable" into a libidinal "surface" of *this* writing. The unconscious that writes is prefigured in the first writing as the "ready-to-speak," who could only appear there in the "imperfect, *il y avait*," because it awaited a writing with an unknown knowing.[5]

Here I go, then, not revising, but expecting what might be born from a repetition of the first writing, intervened on, by writing "with" writing as loss that can only be figured by a certain circularity, roundness, swell.

Here, we are in this terra incognita that Édouard Glissant says "gives-on-and-with" ("*donner-avec*").[6] It is a place of knowledge that emerges from "the belly of the boat," or what he also terms "The Open Boat."[7] It is where the effluence of violence, language, time, space, and relation is taken as a vantage on truth about the world. The boat's belly, he notes, is not really a belly but "a womb, a womb abyss."[8]

Abyss 1: the boat itself
Abyss 2: the ocean
Abyss 3: memory of Africa, forever left behind

He goes on, "This boat is your womb, a matrix, and yet it expels you."[9] That which is part of you and of which you are part expels you. Knowledge and language come from an organ within, but it is also an organ from which you emerge. We are challenged to think "this boat: pregnant with" a form of pregnancy that both digests and gestates "as many dead as living under sentence of death."[10]

The opacity of the figure that both has a womb and is within the womb floats along a curved surface, the ever-swelling waves of the ocean and its currents. Its bulging movements into an expanse render memory from an absolutely irretrievable heritage. Creation and creativity are tied to this open immersion in the boat's terra incognita, a violence of the Middle Passage whose reckoning requires the rejection of any strain of universalizing thought and a thought of identity that relates to all, "the planet Earth," in differentiation.

"Each and every identity is extended through a relation with the Other," writes Glissant, in "the blue savannas of memory or imagination."[11] If identity is what "gives-on-and-with" relation on the open boat, it will be because "the unconscious memory of the abyss served as the alluvium for these metamorphoses."[12]

Glissant's discussion of the terra incognita further goes on formally in a parenthetical: a minor, condensed form of explanation within an explanation. We might say it is a poem within a text outlining the poetics of relation. The parenthetical as poem enacts knowledge whose reality is as quick as a twist of meaning on the drop of a word, and as expansive as a word's capacity to defeat its own assigned finitude of meaning.

> (Expanse [extending] ramifies its web. Leap and variance, *in another poetics. Transversality*. Quantifiable infinity. Unrealized quantity. Inexhaustible tangle. Expanse [extending] is not merely space; it is also its own dreamed time.)[13]

The space-time of the expanse, the terra incognita, is more similar to the space-time of the unconscious than it is to the space-time of literature, history, science, and other disciplines of comprehension. Language and its sheer uncontainability, with all its sedimentations and untraceable and unforeseeable multiplicities, fells all given modes of understanding. This is true, Glissant goes on, even for how we understand human and linguistic filiation:

> (Let's open another and deciding parenthesis: the Oedipus complex does not function in the expanse that is extension. Neither mothering nor fathering are factors there. . . . Creole tongues, mother tongues vary too much within them to "be conjoined," to be prized as an essence or to be valorized as a symbol of either the mother or the father. Their threatened violence is, admittedly, a synthesis but one spread throughout the expanse. . . .)"[14]

There is no natural right to relate, for relationality in a context where identity is impossible is necessarily beyond law, politics, and communication. The absence of a natural right transmutes into a form of violence whose threat is an expansive multiplicity from within the naturalization of colonial languages.

Critical theories of natural language must begin a priori with the specific threshold of negation of any diasporic referent. This is the case for the slave and her descendants, and for any thought of (a) speaking being(s). And so "we can only follow from afar the experimentation feeling its way along in all the elsewheres that we dream of."[15] Language in the wake of slavery, on the still-sailing open boat, is neither pure nor creolized but an ongoing gestation.

Relation is given in *gest-*. *Par-être* divides untraceably into *parlêtre.*

Beyond the seductions of a multilingual composite anti-colonial language I am trying with Glissant to listen otherwise, poised at the horizon of neither translation nor multilingualism, but "the share of opacity allotted to each language, whether vehicular or vernacular, dominating or dominated."[16] Transversality is what each obscure figure of language—letter, word, phoneme, tone, and grammar—requires without saying in advance what movement can and will bring this oblique field into view.

Latin *transversus* means "laying across," the *transversal* referring in geometry to a line intersecting a system of lines in a plane, and in differential topology to a general intersection. It is an expansiveness within, the space-time of some language's usage that touches everything. Glissant's transversality exceeds Félix Guattari's transversal psychoanalytic clinic as well as his later development of sociohistorical nomadism and rhizomatic form.[17] Glissant's transversality must remain essentially gestural, radically associative, and fundamentally libidinal if it is to signify a topological register where experience, desire, trauma, and unconscious knowing meet in some "hidden order."

Somehow I land on the ultimate and always necessary question: "Is there a hidden order to contacts among languages?"[18] If so, Glissant gloriously concludes, "Our poetics are overwhelmed by it."[19]

Slavery haunts Martinique through the very spokenness of French. This is also to say that slavery haunts through speakers of French as subjects of unconscious desire. Spoken French is both the performance of law, custom, and filiation; and a terrain of the experience of the symbolic order of this performance as "also its own dreamed time."[20] If usage of language and the production of meaning is on the other side of the Middle Passage, so, too, is a "time" of unconscious knowledge mediated by that language.

Referencing Sigmund Freud's attempt to generalize the process of filiation through his interpretation of the oedipal myth, Glissant promises that "we shall see that what opposes this new sort of generalization is, in fact, the expansion, power, and reality that we shall define [as the poetics of relation], whose presupposition is the opposite of filiation.[21] It is "a living idiom that was playing out its history elsewhere—there (here) where, even more important, *all imposition of filiation had been forsaken*."[22]

Terra incognita is the permanent immanence of a structural violence that only language, and its poetics as the strange discontinuities and curious breaks in its rhythm, offers a way through, between real and imagined paternal and maternal forms of cultural inheritance. And insofar as French colonialism has touched all four corners of the modern world, either directly, as in the case of Martinique, or indirectly, as in the case of Korea, Glissant's terra incognita of a poetics of relation addresses a global (post)colonial situation and applies anywhere a language's colonial force has saturated and then extracted its new territories of natural resources, people, knowledges, and affects.[23]

Writing that reads and thinks the split subject of the Middle Passage might be what Glissant refers to as "another poetics" at stake in a "poetics of relation."

This Glissantian terra incognita provides a global topological sense to what Jared Sexton, in his essay "The *Vel* of Slavery: Tracking the Figure of the Unsovereign," identifies as the transmission of "[a form of] *unconscious thinking*, [which] consists in this affirmation of the unsovereign slave."[24] Abolition, then, can be understood as a transversal associative knowledge rejecting and surpassing the props and signifiers offered by fantasies of revolutionary sovereignty in service of a revelation whose improbability marks that which allows for any relation at all.

Here, a certain regard or gesture of, neither totally absent nor fulfilled, relation overtakes any of the satisfactions or dissatisfactions of meaning, resemblance, and translation. This drive neither suppresses nor closes social, historical, or linguistic gaps in language use but scrutinizes them with a desire to know how every word and thought is suspended in and by them.

Regard the murmur, and its sound that knows. If those who sail on the open boat across the terra incognita have a language, it is, Glissant tells us, "this murmur, cloud, or rain or peaceful smoke."[25]

I pause on page 157 of "Ferrum" in Philip's *Zong!*

The cut-up words in figure 2.1 still have some spatial order, but I notice how long my eyes travel the distances between letters to put words back together, finding fragments of meaning and lyric in law. This section of the poem suspends letters in visibly uniform distance from each other. Each fragment of word, each curious grouping of them, is still lined up left to right. I can expect that crossing the blank space from one set of letters to the start of the next will yield a word, an idea.

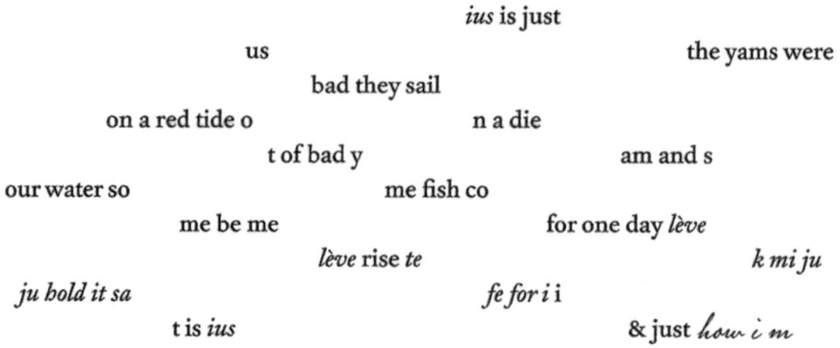

ius is just
us
the yams were
bad they sail
on a red tide o
n a die
t of bad y
am and s
our water so
me fish co
me be me
for one day *lève*
lève rise *te*
k mi ju
ju hold it sa
fe for i i
t is *ius*
& just *how i m*

2.1 Page 157 from M. NourbeSe Philip's *Zong!* (2008). Photo by author.

We are confronted here with an experience of reading for the sake of a word, to make something, a word, out of the law's scene of mutilation. To make a word from the unexhumable bones from the Middle Passage, we process these inked letters into the sounds and words of law. This process yields a sonic alluvium through which a reading swims. We are rich in, in need of "Ferrum," as Philip's title suggests. *Ferrum* is the Latin word for the mineral iron, which in our table of chemical elements is denoted as Fe.

> . . . *ius* is just / us / the yams were / bad they sail / on a red tide o / n a die / t of bad y / am and s / our water so / me fish co / me be me / for one day *léve* / *léve* rise *te* / *k mi ju* / *ju hold it sa* / *fe for i* i / t is *ius* / & just *how i m* . . .[26]

"*fe for i* i": This iron for *i* that is the redness glinting in the blue makes of identity an "I / t." A thing, this thing, is given in the relation between *i* and *t*, and the wish to think across the blankness that separates them on Philip's page and that is marked in my quotation of Philip's writing as a slash.

Zong!'s *fe* tinges the Atlantic's salt, its sands, its sounds. *Fe* gestures, rusts, the blueness of the seas. It puts the blush in all who care to know all that we don't know about all that this *fe* holds. *Zong!*'s captives are everyone's ancestors through a certain iron aftertaste. *Fe* lines life.

Fe, soft like the pink gray clouds that smoke strangely makes, its outlines so faint we have to listen for them as feral wounds and woundings that lap at our unconscious, leaving bottled messages sent from the abyss of this womb that is in us and that we are in.

The ingress of womb within womb bears a listening. Not an echo but an alluvial murmur, the letter *fe* marks the no-return of the ocean. A knot, an object recrafted. *Fe*, a little raft in the amnion of law's language.

배 [flesh of her flesh] 9

There is something heroic in Hortense Spillers's gesture to something "unsayable" structured by law.[27] With her, we are squarely, inescapably, in the situation of wishing to think where boundaries among desire, sexuality, and reproductive violence collapse.

Perhaps precisely because of this collapse, it becomes all the more necessary, Spillers insists, to ask what the black textual tradition bears about and in the daughter.

She is an oblique subject of a doubled law of genealogy. The first law is the "Eurocentric psychomythology" of the oedipal "law of the Father" that intervenes on the mother-child relation and structures and confers symbolic legitimacy in exchange for observing the incest taboo.[28] The second is the law of absent phallic parentage, of a specific form of slave law, *partus sequitur ventrem*, establishing that a mother's slave status passes down to her child.[29] The law of *partus* sanctions incest precisely because it casts slave offspring outside the pale of human sexuality and, thus, symbolic legitimacy. Subject to these two forms of genealogy, as Spillers puts it, "the African person was twice-fathered, but could not be claimed by the one and would not be claimed by the other."[30] And crucially, Spillers observes, because of this doubled paternal absence, the daughter registers a "social subject in abeyance."[31]

Black's Law Dictionary defines *abeyance in* as "being in expectation." The expectation at issue stems from the uncertain fate of unclaimed property, and a future in which an "heir will be found and the estate will no longer be in abeyance."[32] As a "social subject in abeyance," we might consider here that Spillers's daughter incarnates the unclaimed, unowned terra incognita as the terrain of history, language, and the unconscious desire of the split subject of the Middle Passage. Her fate and the question of who can and will constitute an "heir" to this desire are bound together as a problem of time and inheritance.

What kind of law would be the basis for expecting that the terra incognita's "heir" might be found? That the daughter might become the heir, in a way, and, being in abeyance no longer, become a social subject? What kind of social subject would, could, she be? Or does she "escape" from nomination as heir, or the terra incognita altogether?[33] Is there some other relationship between escape and heirship she leaves us to track?

The daughter is so much more than a fugitive of the oedipalized mother-father-child triad into an expanded network of anti-oedipal kinship. Spillers frames her in a much more difficult situation, where what and where she is escaping from and to seems nearly impossible to determine. If "desire is the reverse of the law," or "desire is the flip side of the law," then desire that is the flip side of the doubled law of genealogy in a slave society is an expanse of desiring that is dangerous beyond words and comprehension.[34] The daughter marks the unsayable structured by the doubled law of genealogy by which sexuality, desire, and violence become constituent elements of how slavery and its abolition are remembered, lived out, and politicized.

Words vanish. Thick air.

Freud has a curious comment in his 1924 paper "The Dissolution of the Oedipus Complex," about the difference of oedipality between girls and boys. He asserts that in contrast to boys, whose libidinal objects are newly ordered under the threat of castration, "the fear of castration [is] excluded in the little girl."[35] Castration is "not tolerated by the girl without some attempt at compensation. She slips—along the line of a symbolic equation, one may say—from the penis to a baby. Her Oedipus complex culminates in a desire, which is long retained, to receive a baby from her father as a gift—to bear him a child."[36] In a paper written some eighteen months later, "Some Psychological Consequences of the Anatomical Distinction between the Sexes," he further detailed the difference between how libidinal structures of satisfaction and desire vary depending on the interaction between infantile oedipality and castration. Whereas for boys the oedipal complex is "smashed to pieces by the shock of threatened castration [and] its libidinal cathexes are abandoned, desexualized and in part sublimated . . . [to] form the nucleus of the super-ego," for girls, "the motive for the demolition of the Oedipus complex is lacking."[37]

It seems obvious that Freud's comments are inapplicable to thinking about Spillers's daughter. It's not that there is something deeply objectionable to think that a black female slave who has been impregnated by a white master desires to "bear him a child." It is inapplicable because the terms *girl*, *father*, and *child* are far too simplistic to capture the set of oedipal positions at play under a doubled law of genealogy. The white master is an unavowable father, the girl is only ambiguously his daughter, and the child she might bear is a gift insofar as it is not a child but an object, a new slave.

But what I do think is possible to extend from Freud's commentary is his recognition of a different time of oedipal desire that emerges when he considers the difference between boys and girls. It is a time not beyond but *intolerant* of a certain normative masculine course of development between oedipality and the castration complex, and whose intolerance is the grounds from which a "long retained" desire emerges despite and through "the result of upbringing and of intimidation from outside which threatens her with a loss of love."[38] The sexual difference suggested by Freud in these two essays is that either the paternal function that proscribes incest can destroy oedipal desire for the mother (as Freud says is the consequence for boys), or it can both leave desire for the mother in place and instigate another form of desire. Freud notes that absent a fear of castration, the oedipal complex for girls "may be slowly abandoned or dealt with by repression, or its effects may persist far into women's normal mental life."[39] I am interested in the third possibility laid out here, insofar as the idea of "women's normal mental life" is structured by the absence of a pure masculine superego, or the presence of a "bisexual" superego.[40] This is an essential piece of Freud's structural framework that links the "character-traits which critics of every epoch have brought up against women" with what we might generally understand to be an illiberal subject: "that they show less sense of justice than men, that they are less ready to submit to the great exigencies of life, [and] that they are more often influenced in their judgements by feelings of affection or hostility."[41]

The proscription of satisfaction by castration forms an "indissoluble link between *wish* and *law*," but this link is not firmly established for the girl.[42] At least, not so starkly as to establish a conflict between wish and law. Wish or unconscious desire emerges from intolerance, not transgression, of law and is braided with a new form of "long retained," or we might say, insistent, desire. Lacan's discussion of oedipality carries along the question of the girl. His writing of oedipality traces the movement from the supposed triangular relation (mother, child, phallus) to an oedipal quaternary (mother, child, father, phallus).[43] The fourth term is sometimes the phallus, sometimes death, and later, the letter can be traced among the three oedipal figures. In his lecture on Edgar Allan Poe's "The Purloined Letter," Lacan thinks about the letter like a girl: "We are quite simply dealing with a *letter* which has been *detoured*, one whose trajectory has been *prolonged* . . . or, to resort to the language of the post office, a letter *en souffrance* (awaiting delivery or unclaimed)."[44]

"a letter *en souffrance*." "social subject in abeyance . . ."

The doubled law of genealogy keeps returning us to the scene, itself doubled, of natality. A sending into a space-time of suspension, nonheirable life begetting nonheirable life. Germs of desire that we hold in us and that we are held in by. In this scene, the social terms that surface are not destruction and legitimation but intolerance and gestation.

An unusual but uncanny pair of terms . . . How can they help us to conceive of "flesh of her flesh"[45] as law? It would have to be a law of surplus in a world dependent on a unique form of structural anonymity that radically, reproductively, unravels the laws of genealogy.

The Hebrew word for "flesh" is *bâsâr*, and "by extension, *body*, *person*; also (by euphem.) the *pudenda* of a man: --body, [fat, lean] flesh [-ed], kin [man-]kind, + nakedness, self, skin."[46] *Bâsâr* comes from the Hebrew root word, *bâsar*, meaning "to *be fresh*, i.e., full (*rosy*, [fig.] cheerful); to *announce* (glad news):--messenger, preach, publish, shew forth, (bear, bring, carry, preach, good, tell good) tidings."[47] The phrase "flesh of my flesh" in Genesis 2:23 as the biblical scene of woman's creation carries along these two Hebrew resonances of flesh as body, person, skin; and flesh as freshness and good news. Specifically, after God's creation of Eve from Adam's rib, woman comes from his announcement of her as *woman*. *Bâsâr* as supplement carries the function of being both the cause of speaking and itself a form of speaking. It causes the announcement of woman and is itself the announcement of woman. "Woman" as *bâsâr* is the cause of symbolic speech, and is some other form of speech, for she has not yet spoken in this scene. Animation relies here on a metaphorical bond of intimate relation requiring, on the one hand, loss *and* speech (Adam), and supplementarity and silence or speech-in-abeyance (Eve) on the other.

In a radical, subtle retelling of this biblical scene of woman's creation, Spillers insists that "Woman" is not "flesh of my flesh," but "flesh of her flesh." In

Spillers's doubled scene of genealogy, in which one possible father is unavowable (white master) and the other foreclosed (black male slave), it is the black woman from whom the daughter is created. Symbolic relation and sexuality are animated by black female loss and supplementarity without recourse to symbolically effective speech.

Spillers's dispossessive formulation of "flesh of her flesh" is a reconceptualization of the split subject of desire, which Fred Moten has recognized and further developed as "the ani*mater*ial ecology of black and thoughtful stolen life as it steals away . . . in which the estrangement of natality is maternal operation-in-exhabitation of diffusion and entanglement."[48] Insofar as maternity is given in the female body as a part both radically detached from a body *and* reattached as and in others who incarnate the possibility of diffused and entangled desire and dispossessive speech, the specific jurisgenerative dividedness of Spillers's daughter embodies an ani*mater*ialist politics. Zakiyyah Iman Jackson analyzes this politics in *Becoming Human: Matter and Meaning in an Antiblack World* as "the latent symbolic-material capacities of black *mater*, as mater, as matter . . . [which] holds the potential to transform the terms of reality and feeling."[49]

Still, I am interested in the narrower problem Spillers poses about this *mater*, this *bâsâr*, and the confluence of feminine substance and speech in abeyance. It is precisely a question of how the daughter will move from primary narcissism into the symbolic world of language via a nonphallic oedipal desire, which, by Spillers's formulation, must work through a mother-daughter relation. Maternal desire here, as something other than the doubly marked absence of the father, as *absence* or *immaterial performance*, begs so many questions:

How does an unspeakable violation of the mother (by the white master) and desire of the mother (for anything or anyone) mark the way the Imaginary, Symbolic, and Real are structured in the changing relation between mother and daughter? How do these marks of absence shape the daughter's relation to the mother, their psychic separation, not castration but intolerance, which is to say, intimacy?

On the face of it, the mark of absence seems to be a figure. The natal triad here is of daughter, mother, and marked absence (of the white master); or the natal pentad of daughter, mother, and two marked absences (of the white master and black male slave), and of course, from these two layered scenes of natality, the possibility of the daughter's "second birth" in her reclamation of her symptom.

I move too quickly here. Too quickly because it is only through a certain regard for how one lives and survives these marked absences in the psychic relation between mother and daughter that the daughter has a chance to create the "scant of" something in a symbolic register where desire registers primarily as Imaginary (primitive, archaic, instinctual) or, less often, as Real (mystical, absolutely different, unthinkable, nonsensical), and hardly ever properly Symbolic (egoic and generally normative identification).

Slowing down, I hear Spillers's idea of "flesh of her flesh" as a possible conceptualization of the transmission of the Real of the mother's desire that lives in the body of a daughter as *sinthome*. The scant something occurs through some unknowable procedure, not theological, as in Eve's creation from and by Adam, but libidinal, as in the anoriginal creation of blackness and sexuality.

In this figure of the split subject of desire, "flesh" is the germ of ani*mater*ialist desire, its femininity, a libidinally coded (but ultimately undecipherable) form of *bâsâr*, the announcement of good news; the speaking of a good, true word; the chatter of what Lacan calls the ethics of the "well-spoken" (*bien-dire*).[50] This relation of "flesh of her flesh," then, is a different way to listen for truth in the emergence of unconscious desire. I am not ascribing to black women or femininity an essential or privileged relation to truth. Rather, I am underscoring that the structural relation of natality signified by Spillers's figure of the daughter, passed through theoretically and psychoanalytically, links together the touch of the Real and oedipality as an institution of slavery.

As a condition of possibility for genealogical isolation, natal alienation raises the absolutely mediated and effaced labor of natality prior to any assumed coincidence between a body and a self. Spillers's figure rejects the sublimation of natality into an individuated figure with body and self, and instead contemplates an internally differentiating, generationally nesting and nested figure of a womb within a womb.[51]

Womb of her womb. She is an organ that carries an organism; her womb carries germs on germs of desire. The subject Spillers delivers is *en souffrance*, in abeyance.

In my first writing on "flesh of her flesh," I insisted on the necessity of never not being in touch with what the Spillersian daughter bears in unbearable circumstances of natality.[52] It was a failed insistence because the writing used too heavily a critical sense to fill in that part of thought that is beyond meaning. On second pass now, however, I witness there how my refusal, my intolerance, we can say, disappeared in the way that the writing was subordinated to legitimating a critique.

But I write like a girl, so I return to the first writing to revise my symptomatic repetition of knowing. Revising as repetition is a form of a "long retained" desire to bear a gift, which can only ever really be some saying born of Spillers's words, "flesh of her flesh." Returning to these published words, no longer my own, I find only shards of some sayings. In fact, they are so many ways of repeating unsayably: *the boat, its belly, its wombs within a womb, the slave as womb of her womb, and the daughter as "flesh of her flesh."* Some things are impossible to write as a matter of conscious will and, because of this, are nonetheless written.

The Korean word for "boat" is 배 (*bae*), a homophone for the words "stomach," "belly," "abdomen," and "womb."

In the belly of the boat are the womb and the stomach. Stomach: a digestive organ, but also to withstand, tolerate, keep inside. It is flesh whose language is, like the womb, to bear something, with all the conflicting tones this can connote. The *bien-dire* absent from the first writing appears in the letter 배.

Can you stomach my writing?

Can I stomach my writing?

Can you, can I, stomach her writing?

Can I stomach her stomaching that which no one should have to stomach?

Write with the stomach. Digest and gestate. That which disturbs from within will find some other way anyway. Revised repetitions turn twisting pains of the stomach and "flesh of her flesh" into a knowledge of 배 of her 배.

無 [atless] 10

What are the global consequences of the daughter as mark, letter, *parlêtre*, flesh of her flesh?

To Nathaniel Mackey's ear, listening to Don Cherry's studio album *Mu, First Part* (1969) and *Second Part* (1970), the name of the single Greek letter μ becomes the double-lettered sound, "'mu' (in quotes to underscore its whatsaidness."[53] Partially coincident with the Greek word for myth, *muthos*, the sound "mu" is the name of one of the two serial poems that chronicle a nomad people converging into one long poem with *Song of the Andoumboulou*.[54] We discover in "'*mu' sixteenth part*" of *Splay Anthem* that "mu" as reference to that which is "longingly imagined" is "atless":

Manipulable hope turned endless
hover. Steeped intertwinement of
tongues an amended kiss the
world it made in the image
of.
Reconnoitering mouth, mouth
rummaging mouth, crimped circle . . .
Caught mouth. Extinguishing mouth.
Would-be quench . . . At mind's mercy,
meaning mind
without mercy, reminiscing what only
might've been. What where was left
left
atless, unavailable, amiss,
"mu" irredentist
even so.[55]

The possibility of orthographic duende floods my ears and mind with these lines, "What where was left / left" and so "atless." The sensuality of the mouth and the sound of representing the shape of the mouth in action, combined with the drive to know ("meaning mind / without mercy"), takes us through a form of negation that is so complete—"What where was left / left"—that the words that come after have the voice of something that comes out of nowhere. Mackey's duende as poetically demonstrated negation here is almost like sublimation in reverse; not two into one, but one into zero and two.[56]

Mark the homophone *atlas* and *atless*. If *mu* refers to a state of "atless"-ness, then to name one of his serial poems "*Mu*" suggests that it can be understood as an atlas of "atless"-ness. "*Mu*," as never-ending poetic seriality, is a book of maps of an unconscious knowledge of not being "at" anywhere, at least in one moment (but perhaps many moments at once). "'Mu' irredentist," finally, can be grasped as the poetics of a relation between that which has no homeland and that which could possibly represent it "even so." "Mu," then, as an expeditious traversal without any security of having landed even so.

This unplaceable field or territory, again, the terra incognita, is difficult to think. We follow along with the recursion and seriality pursued to the letter and are projected out as "conjunctive deprivation and possession, phantom limb, as if certain aroused and retained relations among consonants and vowels and progressions of accent were compensatory arms we reach with, compensatory legs we cross over on."[57] This book of maps of "atless"-ness, if it could be thought of as one, records the "clipped rhythm" of the usage of some alphabet—"consonants and vowels and progressions of accent," Mackey says—that provides a "we" by its prosthetic use out of the cleaving and impositions of languages.

How to feed the arousal and retention of that relation between the consonant *m* and the vowel *u* and this relation's varying accent across European traditions of knowledge and the jazz chronicles of a mystical nomadism? This is what Moten does in his essay "Blackness and Nothingness (Mysticism in the Flesh)," where he elaborates on both these accents in Mackey's "*Mu*" to think about blackness as a "radical unsettlement that is where and what we are."[58] He explains further, "Unsettlement is the displacement of sovereignty by initiation, so that what's at stake—here, in displacement—is a certain black incapacity to desire sovereignty and ontological relationality."[59] "Incapacity to desire sovereignty and ontological relationality" is the nuance Moten uses to register an "infinitesimal difference between pessimism and optimism."[60]

The "general and infinite self-determination" of "the *nonself*" proceeds through and toward a certain drive toward sovereignty.[61] Following Mackey's substitution of "atlas" with the figure of "atless"-ness, Moten substitutes the "island" of the nonself with what we might refer to as the figure of "is-lessness" or the "is-less." In other words, Moten takes us to the brink of translating the translation of the Japanese word *mu* back onto itself, asking whether we have not already been involved in a philosophy of absolute *mu*thingness?[62]

I hear the question of the lowly utterances of "'*mu*'" through Moten's "mu." It's a matter of hearing how a Korean accent slides into Japanese philosophy.[63] Between Mackey's and Moten's accentuation of *mu* and a Korean accentuation of *mu* (무), the terra incognita expands with orthographic transliteration: the English letter *m* as the Korean letter ㅁ, and the English letter *u* as the Korean letter ㅜ. The specific cultural imposition in language learning sets out how "atless"-ness becomes a physio-psychological fact of history, language, and religion when violence is thought at the level of the nonsensical letter.

The Korean usage of *mu* (무) has two possible meanings relevant for us here. The first meaning, "not have, or without," has an etymological root in the Chinese or Korean *hanja* character 無, originally capturing a dancing figure, which would eventually be borrowed from as the ideogram for the meaning "not have, or without" that Moten is interested in turning inside out. And the second meaning, "shaman or spirit medium," has an etymological root in the Chinese or Korean *hanja* character 巫, depicting two pieces of jade used in shamanistic rituals, or the sleeves of a dancing shaman. This inanimate root object emphasizes more what Mackey refers to as the "whatsaid-ness" of *mu*. The Korean signification of 무 as both 無 and 巫 carries with it a socio-philological relation between both dance and nothingness (無) and the body as shamanistic medium (巫). Despite the fact that the idiomatic meaning of dance is essentially dead in current linguistic usage of the *hanja* character 無, it nonetheless is there in and as the mark, the character, as well as its homophonic twin, 巫.

This orthographic duende achieved through the transliteration of *mu* into 무 recovers 巫—ritual body as medium—which conspicuously does not appear as if it was and is nothing in the Japanese notion of nothingness. It also elicits a certain retention of a recurrent labial shape and acoustic fashioning essential to "'mu'" in *Splay Anthem*: "Reconnoitering mouth, mouth / rummaging mouth, crimped circle."[64] Depicted by the Korean *hanja* character 巫, the idea of *mu* comes to us as a phantom shamanistic orifice with its anatomical movements and instrumentations of both one (mouth, μ) and two (lips, *mu*). This *mu* is fundamentally libidinal—it is of body parts whose organic capacities take on the inorganicity of language and overtake the dialectic of mind and body that European and Japanese traditions of *mu* seem endlessly to loop.

巫 [Bari] II

If a Korean sense of *mu* accentuates the dependence of negation and nothingness on the body as libidinal conduit, then its utterances are the signs of some other type of language coming into being and a certain *receptivity* to the violence of this nativity. Theresa Hak Kyung Cha's *Dictee* reveals the particular problem of how the Korean language maintains a relation with Japanese and American colonialisms. The haunt of colonialism obtains specifically in the correlation of imposition with *an inability to speak with just one voice*. This more-than-one is given in the appearance of each letter, which can be seen as the "trace" or "mark" of another that has irretrievably disappeared.[65] A whole poetics of this form of nonrelation at the register of the transliterated letter—what Cha might have called a poetics of "phantomnation"—emerges here as an anoriginal source of Korean postcolonial history.[66] Every letter's articulation is the perfect exemplar of a return (to an abstract homeland) infinitely deferred and an exile (from and in an "atless" homeland). Each letter is a demand for a word as irredentist act. This nonrelation makes poetic truth possible insofar as an affective-libidinal politics *is attached to each letter* in the form of utterance.

For Cha, truth is borne by a figure reciting the distance between utterance and any authentic act of cultural retrieval or racial feeling. In one of the opening moments of the text, entitled "Diseuse," Cha writes this emergence of "the utter" in a liminal state of preparation that is at once a state of defeat and failure *and* of expectancy and drivenness:[67] "*It murmurs inside. It murmurs. Inside is the pain of speech the pain to say. Larger still. Greater than is the pain not to say. To not say. Says nothing against the pain to speak. It festers inside. The wound, liquid, dust. Must break. Must void.*"[68]

Whatever must and has yet to be said is both the assumption of the pain of not saying, and submission to a fundamental homology between pain and speech. Mimicry in speech, recitation, and a certain performance of memory is the structure by which inner wounding of this not-yet language mutates into a language of evacuation: "She allows others. In place of her. Admits others to make full. Make swarm. All barren cavities to make swollen. The others each occupying her. Tumorous layers, expel all excesses until in all cavities she is flesh."[69]

Mark the mouth. It is no mere vocal instrument. It is a topological dip in the body that locates the emergence of language in a place, "in all cavities she is flesh," that is simultaneously and radically inside and outside the subject: "The above traces from her head moving downward closing her eyes, in the same motion, slower parting her mouth open together with her jaw and throat which the above falls falling just to the end not stopping there but turning her inside out in the same motion, shifting complete the whole weight to elevate upward."[70]

Cha's *Dictee*, for me, is a catechism of the "atless," or "is-lessness." The rote and studied recitation that submits to a certain unknown knowledge in service of the emergence of a language from an elsewhere both inside and out is neither mute nor noisy. It is a "murmur," a "drone," a "bared noise, groan, bits torn from words."[71] And it "begins imperceptibly, near-perceptible."[72]

Beginnings that are imperceptible are no beginnings at all, and time becomes infinite. But also, beginnings that are near-perceptible drive the reader to ask whether something has begun or will begin and, consequently, to forever question assumed orders of time. The question for us, then, is not only about whether, when, and how *Dictee* as a text begins. It is also whether, when, and how *this* subject, the diseuse of *Dictee*, comes to a life born precisely in not assuming its beginning or having begun.

Michael Stone-Richards reads the Korean shaman, the *mudang* (무당), and in particular, the mythological Bari Gongju (바리 공주) figure appearing in *Dictee*'s closing section, "Polymnia Sacred Poetry," as the disuese's double.[73] The Bari Gongju myth is an epic poem about the devotion of a daughter to her family: abandoned by her royal parents because she was a girl, Bari Gongju nonetheless braves the underworld for a magical elixir to save her ailing parents, and in the process she is transformed into a goddess with the power to guide the dead in their transition to an afterlife. As the origin story for Korean shamanism, the myth is performed by *mudang*, who are usually women, and as well is a cultural tradition of feminine filiation that departs from both oedipal and Confucian patriarchal orders.

The specificity of the *mudang*, in contrast to healers or priests, is in her ability to summon the spirits through trance, or *sinbyung* (신병), a mysterious form of psychotic and physical illness that befalls a woman. Her survival is seen as a sign of her chosenness by the gods for this divine role. Korean shamanistic myth requires a feminine figure's submission to being possessed by a form of divine madness. She, the *mudang*, marks the place of carnal descent wherein the effacement of difference between human experiences of suffering and a mythic origin of a people is relentlessly pursued through a form of active loss, not having, being without, at the center of what is now recognized as "Muism." The *mudang* is not just the figure of folk allegory upholding the virtues of filial piety but is also the cultural valorization of a uniquely feminine political subject essential to the defense and reproduction of Koreanness.

To say this is not to multiply the role of the poet as performer but to transfigure the poet as material conduit. Bari as *mu* (巫) is the book form of *Dictee*, whose movement folding into itself, its logarithmically curved seam, sitting between and cutting the *hanja* word 父母, in hangul 부모, transliterated as *bumo*, meaning "parents."[74] *Mu* is its own conception of genealogy as a libidinal form of touch and conjoining that both constitutes and disappears into the middle of any possibility of origin and word. The book as inanimate material, as conduit of letters, is bound for ritual reading, turning, recitation, and study. This suggests that the presence of Bari as *mu* (巫) is not simply figured in the closing section but is given in a kind of labor of madness across the whole of the text.

무 [hangul] **12**

In a photocopy that appears several copies removed from the original image, figure 2.2 is the one and only appearance of hangul in *Dictee*.

The hangul there appears handwritten, but because it is a photocopy, it has the distinctive appearance of writing in white light on a blackwashed backdrop. Stone-Richards, and other critics who have written about this image, offers this English translation of the hangul: "Mother / I miss you / I am hungry / I want to go home."[75]

The photocopy of hangul as a near-absence is double, or more precisely, an absence within an absence: the absence of critical commentary on the Korean language in *Dictee* takes place in the very observation of the Korean language's near absence. It is, Stone-Richards says, "the very texture of memory fading to the archaic" and functions like a "Latin tag."[76]

2.2 Frontispiece from Theresa Hak Kyung Cha's *Dictee* ([1982] 2001). Photo by author.

Indeed, the hangul is placed on the second side of the first unnumbered page of *Dictee*, on which we encounter an image of a stone landscape. Flipping the page from this landscape to hangul is not a "beginning" of the text as much as it is a leap into the depths of some subterranean place—indeed "archaic"—we are always standing right above. The hangul hovering in the frontispiece is not an interruption of the telos of narrative but the performance of language at the limit of (both before and after, as we discover on descending into the experience of the text) translation.

I attempt a translation of the hangul that would retain, like Cha's dictated texts, the necessary bungles in the process of translation. Translation veers into madness. Either permanent and serial incompletion or unintelligible transcription is the result: "Mother want to see stomach is hungry would like to go to hometown (or homeland)" or "to homeland (or hometown) would like to go stomach is hungry want to see Mother" or any number of variations in word sequence, punctuation, and so on.

Hangul registers a primary madness of writing located internal to the Korean language.

If we take hangul as a "Latin tag" beyond analogy, and extend this idea at the level of the terra incognita, hangul *is* the Latin of all the romanized natural languages, French Catholic rituals and symbols, and classical Greek references arranged in *Dictee*. This second pass at reading the hangul in figure 2.2 is my attempt to register a more fundamental problematic that *Dictee* struggles to articulate in its form: while English and French belong to the Germanic and Romance language families, the Korean language is generally classified as a language isolate, meaning that a genealogical relation with a "language family" cannot or has not been recovered.[77]

As a language isolate, the Korean language itself is both a limit text within *Dictee* and an impasse created by language in history. It is the terrain of a translingual erasure relentlessly in pursuit of but never arriving at an ontology of origins presupposed in multilingual experience. If Cha's multilingualism gives over much to space and spacing between the irreducible gaps produced by translation and transcription between French and English, and the temporalities of Japanese and American colonialisms, then the Korean language waits in those gaps not simply as another language that produces another set of gaps, but, more profoundly, to observe and mark when translation and transcription *must* open up onto something wholly other than the possibility of reconciling the structured absences between languages and histories.[78]

This language without origin or kin raises a general question about a certain enigmatic nature of the life of a language that can only be understood as the usage of that language, and, more specifically, about a certain social-historical coincidence between that usage and the conditions of that usage that would send the language off in some untraceable direction—the direction of trance, possession, and madness—that cannot return to any reference that might have genealogically anchored it. If there is something Korean about *Dictee*, it would be this form of "atlessness" marked in and as hangul. All of a sudden, and in every instance of the letter of *Dictee*, Koreanness demands to be known as *parlêtre*, despite but through the mediations of history and culture. Koreanness is accompanied further by an incessant questioning of what kinds of experiences of writing, speaking, thinking, and associating might avail themselves in such linguistic genealogical isolation. The archaism of the image of hangul can be thought of as a heteroglossic endogeneity of Koreanness, which claims neither forms of classicism nor indigeneity in signifying an anticolonial sensibility.

This Koreanness follows a law of reproduction (repetition, recursion, resonance, etc.) without genealogy. Its content is the relation between any and all words in the text, which function like a *mudang* to summon some spirit from the inanimate world of letters. They constitute a *mudang* body for Cha, then, who is the locus of transversal time within and across the disorder of colonial languages. This time is produced through an almost fanatical interest in turning the body that writes inside out to show the already known and awaiting language of emptinesses and blanknesses. At this point, the body and the word become homologous, each born from a translingual, transversal writing of a hollowness of meaning symptomatic of colonial violence.

Cha's *mudang* as a form of libidinal attention does not assert or positivize an indigenous Korean monolingualism against the tides of deculturalization, military occupation, and ongoing colonial impositions on the peninsula. This would only relinquish the truer and ever-present question of violence. Instead, it evokes a polyauralism of the self-voiding communal rituals of "'mu'" that hang on between the many colonialisms of the East and West.[79]

Dictee as monstrated *mudang* solicits the conditions in which a Korean practice of *mu* might be read by someone.[80] If the *hanja* pictogram of *mu* (無) gives us the idea of nothingness through the representational erasure of ritual dance, and the Japanese modernization of this idea incorporates it into a philosophical theological system, then their postcolonial Korean idea of it is given in a kind of embarrassment of this other *mu* (巫). With 巫, we are reminded that dance depicted in 無 is not just any dance. It is the animist dance of the feminine mystical *mudang* performed, for example, by Lee Aejoo (figure 2.3). 巫 blushes 無 with traces of madness or primitiveness or both.[81]

巫 of her 無, ani*mater*ialist to the letter. Yes, as Glissant said, "the vivid contrast among the languages of the world . . . constitutes the desiring flesh of a poem."[82]

The Korean language is where untransliterated sounds live: where words take place in and through a self-voiding state of possession, where combinations of letters are both the portal to and signs of *mu* as animist copula. The polyaural sound of transliterating *mu* suspends us into the expanse of Glissant's terra incognita.

Through orthographic transliteration between English and Korean, or blackness and Koreanness, the Korean letter ㅁ, which depicts the mouth sounding "mmmmmmmm . . ." insists on our submission to the essential element of murmuring. And the Korean letter ㅜ, a combined shape from ㅡ and •, representing the sound "oooooooooo . . . ," depicts the heavens under our feet. Orthographic transliteration gives us some upside-down, underground, unconscious place of desire, always involved with each letter, mark, *parlêtre*, we make.

2.3 Lee Ae-joo performing her dance entitled 바람맞이 (*Barammaji*), a traditional shamanic folk dance, 살푸리 (*salpuri*), in honor of Lee Han-yeol in 1987. Photo from "Lee Ae-joo, the Path of Dance," a special feature in *Dance Webzine*, June 2021, Korean Association of Dance Critics and Researchers, accessed July 28, 2023, http://koreadance.kr/board/board_view.php?view_id=279&board_name=plan&page=.

- [relation with no end] 13

The peculiar copresence of law and nonreferentiality, or "genealogical isolation," can only be grasped by a writing at the limits of translation, transliteration, and utterance. Poetics between Mackey's *Splay Anthem* and Cha's *Dictee* evokes the duende of madness and the madness of duende internal to law as language and historical violence. If there is something originary that must be found for a subject or for a discourse, it is this *effluence of being and letter* as a kind of undammable real.

Bari, *parlêtre*, spectralize what cannot but must be translated.

What might we identify as the *mu* of Spillers's text? She begins with the law of *partus*: the law that not only equates birth to enslavement but makes the slave into a figure who is constituted, unlike Oedipus, by two absent fathers (slave or master) and a mother (slave). This scenario differentially casts both mother and child outside of patronymy and parentage—the part given to genealogy as name. Neither resistance nor complicity, perversity nor proper desire, can be determined in any clear sort of way in this situation. One could even go as far as to say that no one can ever know what it means to transgress or translate the oedipal relation, because the violent law of *partus* effaces genealogical knowledge.

Yet Spillers's analysis, in the end, still offers a curious promotion of oedipality as a desirable and necessary social institution:

> The [incest] prohibition must be embraced (in order to cancel out the other interdiction [the law of *partus* as an interdiction against black patronymy]) not only in father's interest, but that the daughters might know the appropriate lover and the future. In this case, the origins of the incest taboo are not at all shrouded in mystery, insofar as the taboo is reenacted over and over again: Wherever human society wishes to move into an articulation, or clearly differentiated familial roles, the father must discover and humbly observe his limit.[83]

What kind of defense is the adoption of the incest taboo, given her analysis of the afterlife of the law of *partus* in black literature? To prepare us for an answer, Spillers opens her essay with an injunction of her own issuance: "Every [Black] Reader shall be discomfited. Let that be the law. . . ."[84]

In "Poetics of Mu," I heard this as Spillers's identification with the paternal function. But now I hear it as Spillers's performance of law as desire, meaning, if she is establishing the law that every reader will be discomfited by her discussion of the doubled law of genealogy, then desire will be produced as a transgression of the law she announces. Desire will be the transgression of feeling discomfiture, but this transgression will not be a transgression in any straightforward way since Spillers establishes the law with a desire that it should be broken and that readers will feel something other than this dominant response to considering the figure of the daughter.

How many different ways are there to break the law of discomfiture, to feel something other than whatever discomfiture feels like?

Spillers knows that desire is an effect of law, and not the other way around. It's not that my interpretation of Spillers was totally off in my first pass, because I did ask, "What if we were neither discomfited in our reading practices, nor whatever would be considered its inverse?"[85] It's that my own desire is covered over by presenting it abstractly as a question that seeks permission to feel something other than discomfiture.

Instead, today, on this second pass, I can say I do not feel discomfiture. I feel a desire to hear the unique quietness of the girl's way through law, through the ongoing failures of patronymy.

Spillers touches on the girl's way in her reference to a certain reduction of the horizontal arrangement of black kinship to "sexual neutralities."[86] I hear in this neutralization not the eradication of desire but some unknowable kinness that shades all desire. Because horizontal and neutral, the risk of desire only partially captured by the term *incestuousness* runs across all relation. This is something we know that is unique to being willing to think out the logic of slavery. The loss of "gender function," even understood more broadly as a neutralization of symbolic identification through gender difference, hardly neutralizes the fate of sexuality under conditions of horrendous violence.[87] For a primal patronymy, which no parent of the law of *partus* fully embodies, incest remains the fundamental actuality of the structural relation between slavery and sexual reproduction.

Sexual reproduction—the *sequitur* of *partus sequitur ventrem*—cuts twice: it desymbolizes *both* issuance and the circumstances of its creation. This desymbolization renders it impossible to translate this ancient Roman law of slavery, as transplanted into the American context, into the slave's maternal law of inheritance. For the womb—the *ventrem* of *partus sequitur ventrem*—in its abject convenience to the sovereign traverses all possible female filial positions (daughter, mother, aunt, grandmother, cousin, and sister) and effaces the possibility of any notion of genealogical place. The full implication of this desymbolization for that which is both issuance and womb—the "daughter"—is, then, that the only possible way she can obtain symbolic life (to regard herself as a "daughter" or a "mother") is through the historical trauma of incest that takes the form of an imaginary act, and thus the oblique line.

Spillers's reading of Alice Walker's short story "The Child Who Favored Daughter" jumps out from her discourse. Spillers observes that "fathers and sons link back to a common ancestry of 'unnamable desire,'" which circles around the memory of a daughter's desire for "'the lord of his [the father's] own bondage.'"[88] The complex of desire here is the black daughter's desire for the white master, the black father's desire for the daughter, and the unnamed reason the daughter's murder by her father should be better than living out either one or both of the desires she cathects.

Here is where I believe *mu* rears up from Spillers's reading. Immediately following the above note on the narrative circumstances of this "unnamable desire," she turns to a poem embedded in the story in order to think about how it "threatens every female alike":[89]

> *Memories of Years*
> *Unknowable women—*
> *sisters*
> *spouses*
> *illusions of soul*[90]

Spillers discusses the effect of enjambment here, but it is worth taking up and extending. The enjambment is not simply a function of "anaphora."[91] As repeated interruption, hiccups of words from within a narrative, the affect of enjambment is like that of the law of *partus*: one literally *does not know where the line (of femininity) ends*.

Familial names take on the topology of enjambment, which formally corresponds to kinshipness in genealogical isolation: Unknowable women-sisters, or Unknowable women-spouses, or Unknowable women-illusions of soul, and so on. This is the monstration of a poetics of (non)relation, an anarchic core of gendered domesticity.

Enjambment functions as an absence within the absence of (an oedipal) law distinguishing between memory and fantasy, past and present, and types of kin. The enjambment of names, specifically dependent on the hyphenation, "Unknowable women-," is the issuance of the law of *partus*. But let us be clear that this enjambment consists of a perverse poetic seriality that cannot but taper off into an unknown precisely because of the psychic trauma of the law of *partus* for human sexuality.

The unknown into which this oblique line tapers off is the terra incognita.

The hyphen gives a name to generic filial identities—"sisters," "spouses," "illusions of soul"—but this is a name that infinitizes these identities because of a fundamental effluence of genealogy beyond the pale of restitution or readjustment (or clear differentiation). The expanse enabled by this form of punctuation, evoking with each line an unknown excess heard in filial naming, signals that we are once again in Glissant's terra incognita and witness to another valency of *mu*: a serial nomination that haunts each and every filial place with a cut that both severs filiation from specific and personal names and attaches the signifier, "Unknowable," in the form of an anonymizing proper noun.

The enjambment this poem formalizes, with the seriality of this curious deindividuating feminization of the proper noun, seems to mirror Spillers's detours and loopings around the law of *partus*. We are not simply given an anonymous name, "Unknowable women- . . ." but challenged to think of relation, "-," through this anonymity, at a horizon where kin-ness and incestuousness historically meet.

"Sisters" shift into "spouses" in the poem, and this shift registers not only an ungendering in filial relation but, simultaneously, the presence of a pledge or an embrace. The relational identity of "spouse"—"a husband or wife, or (in later use) a person joined to another in a comparable legally recognized union, considered in relation to his or her partner"[92]—comes from the Latin verb *spondee*, "to promise sacredly, warrant, vow, give assurance."[93] "Flesh of her flesh" as black feminine reference contains a form of promise, foreverness, and ultimately an unknown knowledge of intimacy given in a society structured by the law of *partus*.

Unknowable, but enjambed, genealogy does not produce kinlessness but a kinshipness as monstration of a secret promise, an offering of relation everywhere with no end. Blackness is sexuality subject to the law of "flesh of her flesh," and to know something about sexuality that is not and has not been regulated by symbolic, which is to say, patronymic culture. The problem, as Spillers has consistently argued over the course of her writing, is not the supposed matriarchal culture of black communities but the lethal psychical and physical costs of regarding the signifier patronymically.

mu st/ch [Sorrow] **14**

What kind of writing is this where, on the one hand, everyone is related, or at least possibly associated; and on the other, everyone knows that symbolic lines of succession will fail?

The discomfiture Spillers addresses to "Every [Black] Reader" recalls Hélène Cixous, who refers to feminine being as "nothing but disturbance."[94] Such writing sends the monstration of an "unnamable desire," an unwitting textual occurrence despite or because of a disposition of thought to resort to law. She, the daughter, is there, *in the deed*, obliquely an object, both deeded and transferred, but also transmitting. Spillers will finally name her, the "Urlover," whose mere utterance is uncomfortable.[95] Indeed, as the daughter is the thought of a child descendant of and into an unthinkable seriality of a-nomination.

A-nomination here is not a function of the laws of coverture. It is a function of the master's doubly incestuous sex as both the source of white patriarchal genealogy and an unavowable violent natality of a black genealogy of disinheritance. A-nomination, unnaming, always without name, naming with no original name to speak of and yet still exists in relation: -.

As Spillers resorts to Walker's poem within a story, the grammatical figure of the hyphen emerges as a special signifier. Insofar as it is the mark through which the a-nominative can be put into relation, it is *parlêtre*.

This bare dash, the story's Ur-condensation, is the way the poem loves.

We should speak not of hyphenated identities but of the blackness of Walker's hyphen. It delivers us into the libidinal forms of enjambment and looping, cutting and circling, scansion and repetition. Poetry meets mathematical incomprehension again, here, as the poetic thought of a-nominative relation is mirrored in the ceaseless subtractive computation of an infinite loop, "flesh of her flesh."[96]

Spillers's "flesh of her flesh" irrevocably marks human reproduction with the maternal body. While Julia Kristeva writes that "the pregnant woman is losing her identity, for, in the wake of the lover-father's intervention, she splits in two, harboring an unknown third person, a shapeless pre-object," Spillers's "flesh of her flesh" is a formulation of the maternal body that does not begin with the premise that pregnancy is the loss of identity.[97] Hearing "flesh of her flesh" to include pregnancy as "womb of her womb," all life can be understood to be hyphenated with blackness. We are challenged to think of human reproduction in a context inhospitable to identity. It leaves us with a non-narcissistic passion that springs not from one being split into two but from a looping half-life of zero: zero being split into two zeroes, that is, the two references to "flesh" in the utterance "flesh of her flesh."

"Flesh of her flesh of her flesh of her flesh of her flesh of her flesh of her flesh of her flesh of her flesh of her . . . fe

Identification in relation itself is impregnated with division and separation, beginningless and endless. Dirt and plant. Hill and gully. A girl and some gulls. The shape of her and some shapeless flesh she harbors.

In Toni Morrison's *A Mercy*, nobody really knows anything about Sorrow. But it's because she wants it that way. Only the gulls know.

When they asked her name, Twin whispered NO, so she [Sorrow] shrugged her shoulders and found that a convenient gesture for the other information she could not or pretended not to remember.

Where do you live?
On the ship.
Yes, but not always.
Always.
Where is your family?
Shoulders lifted.
Who else was on the ship?
Gulls.
What people, girl?
Shrug.
Who was the captain?
Shrug.
Well, how did you get to land?
Mermaids. I mean whales.[98]

She who speaks words not to tell remains unclaimed, even when she at that moment is named and taken possession of as Sorrow. Her presence is registered throughout the narrative in so many oblique looks and comments she herself makes, but as well, those of others perplexed by both her birth and her pregnancy. Her mysterious non-narcissism, already halved by the absence of her imaginary companion, Twin, marks a figure whose self-mention is only a shrug. Sorrow shrugs off origin so that whatever being Sorrow names is not just the reality of having survived. It is an inexplicable, continual gestation of life, whose presence is so textually gestural, "shrug," that it seems impossible to reconstruct what happened. Her shrug gives no clue and yet exists even so.

I hear Sorrow's *mu* in the silent gesture of half-effort. "Shoulders lifted" emphasizes just how much Sorrow refuses in the passivity of letting her shoulders drop to complete a shrug. The duration, endurance, of the shrug is as much in the lifting as it is in the dropping, in the unfinished initiation of movement, a halved response.

This shrug is in the drawn-out words we find in *Zong!*'s book of "Ferrum":

uld prove our mu   st our mig[99]

And later,

are not too mu   ch jus[100]

Burdened as they are by distance, blank, white, aberrational spacing, our acceptance of this emptiness is required to read a word—“must” and “much”—from and within these breaks. Sorrow might say “complete” them.

Sorrow’s *mu*thingness abides by some obligation connoted in *must* and some surplus connoted by *much*. The madness and duende of *mu* here conjoins, across an expanse where time and location can go in all and any directions with a mere shrug, including the digraphs *st* and *ch* as *mu*’s many and unknowable destinies as word.

mu   *st/ch*: an inapparent stitch, a suture arrived at only by making some way across a word halved by an expanse, a conjoining by the body with a shrug, its *parlêtre*, the blankness of too much space beckons, as too, a girl born of a boat.

nonperformance

I wish to note that although this chapter includes specific citations to Fred Moten's texts, the form of this chapter emerges from an ongoing experiment in the pleasures of dispossessing one another of individuated authorship. Our thinking on Betty and nonperformance has and always will have required an attunement to the beauty of how writing blurs thought beyond citation. And so it is inadequate, but I still acknowledge here that every word in this chapter is itself a citation to every word of Moten's I have read and listened to over many years of friendship.

Mō+SH(ə)n [consent] 15

A consent motion, or a *joint motion*, is an action filed by opposing parties for some form of relief they have agreed on outside the usual legal process. I am interested in how this legal form of agreement, which implicitly bears an understanding of the impossibility of legal justice, might suggest a knowledge of common movement we discover ourselves to have already been possessed by. This agreement itself gives us relief in ways we can't know except by letters of the law inscribed with and as eros.

From "Knowledge of Freedom" (2004) to his chapter "Erotics of Fugitivity" in *Stolen Life* (2018), this consent motion emerges through a fundamental question driving Fred Moten's writing across the whole of *Stolen Life*: "What will have been the relationship between non-sense and the sensual, (the irregular and irreducible materiality of imagination)?"[1] He goes on to provide as a response across the whole of his reading of the transgenre of slave narratives a performance of a form of consent motion. "The point, of course, is that the regulative reduction/irregular irruption of sensual materiality is the condition of possibility of sense and its normative sciences. Again, is there anything other than this ambivalence?"[2]

Ambivalence demands articulation outside the courts of sense and science. And in this demand, knowledge flees from Greco-Roman epistemological jurisdictions into Onitshan paraliterary realities. These are space-times where a "political erotics of market writing" and all their radical ambivalences are performed through consent motions Moten tells us we are made by if we can follow the sounds of a certain "objectional insistence."[3]

not to be a

single

The radical truth in this sound is that "submission of the ownership of labor and labor power to a radically—which is to say immanently and inorganically—dispossessing force is a terrible enjoyment of loss that no politics can survive."[4] *Submission* has at least two valences here, meaning both "to propose or tender" and "to surrender and comply." The specific erotics of submission in the form of fugitive thought foils the language of the political with a dispossessive ethos predicated on both giving and withdrawing. The complex weave of "objectional identification" avows the pleasure principles of and in loss at every level of the subject.[5] It is an endless drafting, in consent, in motion, jointing together radical political commitments through practices of "uncongealment."[6]

Consent, motion, Moten, Mō+SH(ə)n.

What can be said of an erotics of submission to consent (not to be a single being)? It would be false to say I can say something about it, because, if thought is to invite this erotics, no "I" of a speaking being is meant to survive this form of consent. Consent outside the outer limits of individuated agreement abolishes the signature. As such, its erotics can't be said insofar as the/an/my "I" won't say. But it does leave things. Specifically, what's left is writing that appears from writing about an erotics of consent not to be a single being, and bears the kind of desire Moten elaborates on as "love."[7]

That which is uncongealed reassociates into what can only
be regarded as a cipher: Mō+SH(ə)n.

Taking turns with Fred turns into turns, and unknown
terms, of agreement to be taken.

In this place from which we write,

dystranslation revels in jointly dispossessive pronouns.

The command is its own reward. There is

no way to attribute the writing in this chapter to
Fred in any conventional or proper way because
it would individuate the writing,

which has, to speak incompletely,

always been a function of *parlêtre*,

pieces of agreement found

in some devotional attention to Betty,

whose naming is a necessary practice for

consenting

This consent Mō+SH(ə)n appears on page 260 of *Stolen Life* and in the thought of an erotics of fugitivity. Specifically, it is given in a brilliant, errant absence of indentation. It is as if the rules of citation can't keep up with the vortex of history and thought that collapses into itself in taking turns. I find words from a *Law and Literature* article, once locked up by my signature, re-turned, freed, as two paragraphs of *Stolen Life*. The absence of individuation between Fred and me as thinkers is formally given in the absence of spatial differentiation between "my" writing, conventionally signified by indenting block quotes, and "his" writing, which uses the standard margins of the page. The greater share of blank space assigned to a cited author, that is, an absence that surrounds quoted text, is absent on page 260.

An absence of absence that would mark differentiation of source or origin is amazingly given in the writing of writing about an erotics of consent not to be to a single being. It is the only way to know something of Betty, to keep thinking of and with her. In the strangest *aprés-coup*, this amalgamation of an absence of absence gives us a glimpse of how taking turns is taken up by not only agreeing to share that which should not be owned but agreeing even to succumb to the unforeseeable of dispossessing desire.

If it is true that one is taken by the words of the other, this is to consent not to be a single being, and writing about this consent, then, is to mark this having-been-taken as such, this stolen life, by the presence and absence of blank space on the page. Poetics here is given less in the fashioning of white space than in the unbroken line of vertical margins burnished by a ghost hand that touches us all.

This continuousness marks our unwitting but always welcome enlistment as an undying organic sonic chamber for the name Betty. She slurs us.[8]

"Is citation a mute or a microphone or miles' whisper muted in the microphone?"[9] It's "all" of it, especially in that which is not quite silent, and not quite invisible, and exists as wisps of something that endures in dispossession.

Cite until citation is so long that the smallest of "small indenture" brings us in closer and closer, and still closer, until, being this close, being this compact, whatever might have been consent is now a cipher: Mō+SH(ə)n. This compact citation bears an unorderable citationality of the marks of language itself.

I find myself facing *Betty's Case* a second time as I return to include it here in this book.[10] In the repetition of writing about Betty's case, there are some things that are still true as stated, some things that I want to revise, and some things that mark the unsayable. I decide I will delete that which needs to be revised, mark and remark the unsayable that especially appears in a series of questions that emerge in Moten's engagement with Betty. The scandal of Betty's decision to return to Tennessee continues to be the occasion for retrieving

Betty's Case from an American legal archive with far more doctrinally significant rulings on the status of the slave.

And yet it is precisely because of a certain unthinkability as to Betty's enactment of legal freedom that the case rises to the surface of the American legal archive to be read and heard again. Or at least it felt that way back in 2016 when I first started writing about the case, and I am circling around it again to consider what nonetheless remains unthinkable about it now. It will always, by every measure, remain a marginal case, even after we come to understand Betty's choice as the only position from which a radical structural challenge to freedom's empire can be thought.

My daughter drops a grain of sand in my hand. She says she's found the smallest shell ever. I look again at this pale pink speck in my palm. I can barely make out the spiral formed on its surface. Betty and this shell demand an attention that hard concentration, like my effort to visually focus, frustrates.

Betty is the bearer of a shimmering Fibonaccian recursion, a certain wild unfurling thread of life at the outermost edges of what thought can conceive of as the performance of freedom, including whatever attention and desire was required for my daughter, in that particular moment, to pick out this otherwise completely negligible object from the vastness of the beach.

It certainly is possible to understand Betty's act as the performance of some nominal form of personal autonomy exercised against the slave's legal status as property. In other words, it is reasonable to read *Betty's Case* as evidence of slave resistance to, or incomplete domination by, the legal enforcement of the slave's property status. But this would occlude the material, almost mathematical circumstances, of the case, which give us something like the golden ratio of freedom that no personal performance of it can break from. Here, freedom is a repeating relation in which the lower number decomposes the higher number into the inapparency of difference rendered when writing the golden ratio decimally (1.61803398 . . .). This is where thought and mention of Betty's consent becomes the very terrain where thinking near-inapparent differentiation, or finding some language to refuse rounding the ratio up, is also the experience of consent not to be a single being.

The operation at issue is this: the division of the ultimate right of contractual freedom by the nonperformative right embedded in the name. Divide your right by Betty. Divide my right by another's. We operate with and through differences of virtual nothings, until we are shown that they're not but a shell. Consent Mō+SH(ə)n.

What if the imagination is not lawless but lawful?
What if it is, in fact, so full of laws that, moreover, they are
in such fugitive excess of themselves that the imagination, of
necessity, is constantly, fugitively in excess of itself as
well?
What if in our attempt to understand the
significance of the legal case, the enigmatic outline of the legal
personality of the slave, appearing as Betty, was not reduced to any
one
type of legal relation in advance? How might we
think this enigma through the totality of modern American
jurisprudence while at the same time retaining the uniqueness
of its imprint on the legal archive? Will law have then
been manifest paralegally, criminally, fugitively,
as a kind of ongoing antisystemic break or breaking;
as sociality's disruptive avoidance of mere civility that takes form
in and as a contemporaneity of different times and
the inhabitation
of multiple possible worlds and personalities?
If it is
Betty's Case, *more than any other case, that marks*
the American legal archive with a material question about
slavery and freedom, how does something like
resistance take
form within
the specific confines of the law's language of contract? Exactly what
form of
"resistance" takes shape at this singular instance—where a name,
Betty, appears as a sign of free will, and as the name, Betty's
Case, *of a form of legal decision at the limit of the law's*
idea of freedom? Is it even adequate to call this

resistance? *Why should we not call it* freedom, *as Betty*
neither accepts nor rejects this declaration made about
and for her by the law but nonetheless
acts in relationship to it?

The questions want to get together, and we're just their ride to the party. They are hysterical with the rhythm of betting each other to touch on Betty. Hysteria is a music. Questions, and our bodies they make into their vehicle, divide each other into some looping comput(improvis)ational formula. Mutual division is maximal mutating satisfaction. The function of so many no-but's lives in the yes-and's of touching on somethings on the mind.

++ [nonperformance] 16

Page 260 of *Stolen Life* is a littoral place where consent is consent to not being-conditioned-to-the-world.

In his essay "Lituraterre," Jacques Lacan describes the littoral as a psychoanalytic form of writing where literature and literary criticism meet. Here is the question of "so called avant-garde literature," as put by Lacan: "Is it possible to constitute such a discourse on the littoral which is characterized by not being emitted from semblance?"[11] He offers this question not to answer it head-on but to perform what he says "is in itself a littoral fact" and, he explains further, "thus not sustained by semblance, but for all that not proving anything but the breakage, which only a discourse can produce, with an effect of production."[12]

He echoes this point about a literature radically nondependent on semblance: "To land the erasure [*lituraterrir*] myself, I bring to your attention that in the gullying which gives an image of it I have made no metaphor whatsoever. Writing is this gullying itself."[13]

Littoral—a meeting of land and water. Its etymology gives us *litus*, *litor*, from the Latin, meaning "shore." They are related to the Proto-Italic *leitos*, a word of unknown origin, with a possible Proto-Indo-European root of *lei*, meaning "to flow," or *leit*, meaning "to go forth," also "with sense evolution 'the going away,' hence 'the edge.'"[14]

I wonder about the topological erotics of lituraterre, of surfaces touching, interpenetrating, inversely (de)sedimenting. Across our both being spoken through by writing on and with Betty, this "literature perhaps turns to lituraterre" insofar as our performance shores desire and the unsayable, just as calligraphy, to use Lacan's own example, is a littoral between painting and the letter.[15]

The "wake" of slavery, as theorized by Christina Sharpe, has a myriad meanings, "the keeping watch with the dead, the path of a ship, a consequence of something, in the line of flight and/or sight, awakening, and consciousness."[16] The oceans, carrier of the bones of African captives who never survived the Middle Passage, batter meandering shorelines with wake waves. Wakes litter the littoral with these human letters.

Littoral, litter, letter, Betty

Li ++ oral li ++ er le ++ er Be ++ y

Nonsingle pluses divide and add. Figure the why of all letters. Letter the why that Being should continue to pull us to the bottom of the ocean when the ++ in Betty's name is not what we utter, separate and collective, but the sound of its tapping us on some ante-individuated shoulder of desire, spun in the plus of her plus.

To consent not to be a single being is to return to this littoral. Consent littorally. Which is to say fugitivity is a never-ending consenting to the littoral thought of blackness.

Betty's Case presents (and, again, this is not because of the law's ruling on Betty's status, but rather because of what Betty did in (non)relation to the ruling) the question of whether freedom, as constituted by the law's language of contract, must include *the freedom to be a slave.*

This question is not unthinkable, as I previously wrote. It only feels that way to do it alone.

The modern liberal conception of freedom understood and developed by law has always been a monstrously but imperfectly enforced unfettered right to

The relation between freedom and slavery is not mutually exclusive but mutually metonymic. Freedom is a metonym for slavery, and slavery a metonym for freedom. If so, Betty shows us how freedom is an attribute of slavery, and that abolishing slavery left intact and expanded the very freedom that was and is an attribute of slavery. Betty challenges us to have to figure

contract anything and everything with anyone. This is the underlying logic of propertizing and commodifying African captives; the underlying logic now of propertizing and commodifying any thing, capacity, or relation; and the underlying logic of any assertion of freedom. The abolition of slavery has only reinforced and expanded in unimaginable ways freedom itself as a modality of enslavement.

But the name Betty, its remaining crucial fact, is the act the name refers to. The act does not necessarily reflect an individual decision to valorize either the common understanding of freedom as the antithesis of slavery, or freedom as a metonym of slavery. Instead, it bears something of a desire (without words, which, at least any that Betty may have uttered, are lost to us) that survives in the law's logic of contractual freedom. Working through this paradoxical logic, from the mutually metonymic relay between slavery and freedom, the name Betty marks the *mu* of law.

out how we live with and because of, or recognize how we have always known something about the reverse metonym, which is how slavery as an attribute of freedom survives as the truest and perhaps only chance of enacting a freedom beyond liberal cognates of the individual subject of political life.

The condition of the slave is that she is chained to a war for freedom, chained to the war of freedom, to the prosecution of freedom as war, to the necessity, in freedom, which freedom imposes, of the breaking of affective bonds.

The other metonym, then, reveals that every aspect of the condition of the slave—her living and dying; her subservience and rebellion; her contempt for and love of freedom (as slavery); the affective bonds she keeps and breaks; her desires and fears; her undignified or virtuous pleasures; her secrets, traumas, and antisocial thoughts; and everything we might or might not know about her—are essential to this other form of freedom. The thing of it is that with any of these elements through which black social life is reproduced, if given cultural or historical significance in order to define what blackness is, they will no longer retain that metonymic relation with freedom, and become just another signifier of freedom as metonym of slavery.

To avoid reduction to semblance, which is to say, escape the quicksand of semblance, or hold the metonymic line, we must move from paradox to koan:

Question:
Does blackness have freedom?
Answer:
Betty.

Contract law is how the law draws its ultimate political border between an empirical realm of law's regulatory power over exercises of individual free will and an absolute right of freedom. On the one hand, there is the necessarily enclosed and enclosing development of legal principles in reality that attempts to order the social activity of promising; on the other, there is an a priori right of freedom of contract that the law protects from the singularity of the individual in order to continue promising the promise of freedom as contract.

The blackness of promising, fugitivity, exists outside of the whole constituted by these two sides of contract.

Naturalizing this border language makes it seem like the littoral is something that can be mapped, ordered, delimited, instead of what it is, which is some place whose time and shape can only be given in the many ways we find ourselves, uncannily, on the shores of unconscious desire anytime we can't let a broken promise go, or die everyday deaths to keep a promise.

The law is always "generally speaking" and thinking about "what-ifs." This is border language: words used as stones draw, make, and protect a division. General speak asserts a certain givenness of order, whether that order is social, political, or epistemological. Sovereignty, as general speak, runs all these what-ifs through reasoning, all the while, beset by an anxiety about all the what-ifs of the social that its border language can only react to in the most violent, inadequate, outdated way.

The material structure of contract law is this anxiety, and our consent to regard ourselves through this anxiety, through the question of whether we are free or enslaved, is just a sign that we constantly confuse the damage to and of our existence with being (or not being, which is only the thought of it in either case) as the reproductive mode of this anxiety.

In the tumult of this anxiety, abolition, whether of slavery, or prisons, or sovereignty (which are all versions of one another anyway), threatens with a form of hypothetical thinking that gathers all the what-ifs about how promises are made and broken in the midst of the most catastrophic circumstances toward some other knowledge of freedom.

How do we get unstuck from the crosshairs of this anxiety, which compels a blindly self-aware, insecure, frigid, neurotic performance of revolutionary thought that acts out, outward? Instead of inward, which is to say, in (good) stead, a way, holding a( )way, that is neither inward, outward, nor wayward, but wayfaring. There is a meeting place, go and find it, where demise and promise meet.

Callistratus of Aphidnae is recorded in *The Digest of Justinian* to have said that a pecuniary penalty shall be imposed on "those who deliberately move established boundary stones out of their position and territory under the agrarian statute introduced by Gaius Caesar."[17] Penalty during Caesar's reign was "fifty gold pieces" paid to the "public treasury." Long before this monetized sanction, corporal punishment for moving a boundary stone was based on the status of the mover. Nerva, two centuries before Caesar, established that "if a slave, male or female, should deliberately so act without the knowledge of his or her owner, he or she is to be put to death unless the master or mistress be prepared to accept a fine."[18]

When we move rocks, when we unborder a border, when we "change the face of the land" and see everywhere a littoral created by the slave's hand, what punishment do we invite with our "rank and degree" and "the violence of what [we] have done"?[19]

What is the punishment for moving a grain of sand that turns out to be an itty-bitty-Betty shell? Who can articulate a punishment severe enough for a "rank and degree" so base, whose violence unborders by picking this shell up and passing it from palm to palm?

Contract marks the law's impossible attempt to harmonize principles of regulated and regulatory exchange *and* a categorically abstract realm of freedom. Its impossibility is coded in the compact spiral catalyzed by uttering Betty's name, which spins out from inside the commercium into unheirable space.

What is the commercium?

Commercium is the imperial jurisdiction of citizenship's need to regulate its own people, places, and things. It is a set of laws of enjoyment, enforceable by any means necessary, on anyone who belongs to the anxiety-ridden fantasy of sovereignty. The pains and pleasures of belonging themselves are the commercium.

But connubium, the right to marriage, reveals how the commercium is defined by forms of union, which either expanded or delimited the imperial inclusion of non-Romans into the commercium.[20] The Roman jurist Ulpian reasons that because "there is no connubium" between a free male and a slave woman, "the offspring follows the mother."[21] As a form of contractually articulable affective bonding, insofar as a union furthers imperial sovereignty, it expands the commercium. Conversely, if that bonding enjoys something other than imperial identity at the heart of the Roman Empire, then what Hortense Spillers refers to as a "social subject in abeyance" is born.[22] The connubium renders the chance of unheirability in every exchange, regulation, and ideal constituting the commercium.

We're talking about the erotics of the connubium that contracts the commercium, whose essence Ulpian said was consent, and in the case at hand was at work to give us a form of freedom to give freedom away, or shore the commercium up with Betty's *contubernium*.[23]

So we won't be taught that that tautological logic that contract law traces between transcendental and empirical sovereign right is the only way to draw a circle.

The signifier borne by the name Betty, this letter, ++, is a jurisgenerative impurity of promising to a beloved other, at the outermost edges of imperial connubium. Insofar as this promise might be rewritten, from within and against the law's language of freedom, it produces an obscene sign of "free will" that reknots the Real from the neurotic profession of contract (law and philosophy) to a *savoir* in and of nonperformance.

Hypoconnubial descent: a way (of life) of freedom's return to *contubernium*.

Is there a way to generalize from the expressly abolitionist expression and enactment of Betty's obscenity? Does it have a principle? Does it have a substance? Does it have a

Nonperformance is speech (including its silences) that persistently, quietly, openly, breaks promises in private service of some other promise. *This* promise is that which Betty's name bears, ob-scenely.

How to cut this discourse to break the paralysis the sign "social death" induces in thought? Reveal the signifier as a vessel for speaking desire, and then, in speaking desire, know internally, privately, in and with confidence, the unsayable about blackness.

The name, Betty and Be++y, a density and deviance both from and within the grammar and diction of the administered world, is not reducible to the imaginary meaning of social death. As vessel, the name is a superimposition of the wor(l)d of law on or over itself: a bold, shadowy, obscene, anafoundational font, meaning an assortment or set of type of characters sharing a style and size.

Let the letter "++" be our font, assortment, set, style, size. It is the mark of Betty's anascriptive superimposition. She is not-X, not the signature of an anonymous individuated subject. This is the same thing as saying she is XX, she who has always been an ungovernable repeating mitosis of life, twinned, entwined anonymity, engaged forever in doubly skewing the X: ++. As prints left by consent Mō+SH(ə)n, this letter, ++, is a strange writing all over and under the law, sounding the letters of the name, Betty, out. The poetics of this must be emphatically pronounced.

form other than what we have been trying to failingly think about as nonperformance that marks the horizon of unforeseeability and improvisation internal to law? Is there such a thing as force with no substantive or formal definitional qualities?

A force, per force, the blackness of law comes out of nowhere precisely because it is a nonperformance. Nonperformance is a performance whose having been enacted by someone is secondary to the actedness of something we have no access to except by its very symbolic circumstantiality and its significance for reproducing and reducing the question of someone's freedom in favor of hearing the specificity of a form of freedom given in an object. This object perforates the sociolegal institution of freedom with its obscene edges.

Per force, her performance is an obstetrics of some law of relation that both is absolutely against and has nothing to do with freedom for all. The hands again: flesh of her flesh of her flesh.

If it is wrong to read the disavowal of individual freedom, not as some transcendent enactment of absolute freedom, but rather as a disavowal of any such transcendence or abstraction or formalism, then it is because immanence, materiality, and (il)legal(sur)realism offend the senses. It smells so much it can't make it into the story, it kills mood, it empties, skunks, the room.

Against Robert Cover's juridical grain, Betty's side of the story, withheld from the court so that "she" is absolutely missing anything we can refer to as her "my," obliterates the court.[24] When we say, then, that Betty had no standing, or that to come before the law is to reproduce this lack of standing, it is not to say that she is "nothing." She is that which, on an occasion we must be able to continually listen for by participating in silence, dystransliterates the court whose concreteness is built to house multiple languages of freedom that dissolve into an a priori matrix of unsayable words that have always been an obstruction in liberal freedom.

We have so far understood Betty's act as nonperformance. But now we further understand nonperformance as a function of her name that combines obstetrics and obstruction to birth some other promise she was in, not only with her people in Tennessee and throughout the Underground Railroad, but *with us*.

This catastrophic nuance retained by the case in the formal structure of legal reasoning in *Betty's Case* holds open the question of a subterranean realm of legal thought about freedom that precedes property understandings of the legal personality of the slave. The case stages property freed, but so free as to be given away as something that might arrive again as or like property. Property with a difference. What is the property of the difference of blackness?

What can we know about such obstinacy? About a freedom in compactness, a social internality that, by the slurring of the living, the dead, and our bodies into a radically unincorporable in absentia, delivers us to some perforated occurrence of nonsingle assent?

The monstrosity of being property without property.

A disruptive noise of the improper borne in and on and out of the world.

Refusing what has been refused by resignifying what has been imposed.

Dispossessiveness in kinship.

What it is to unown.

What is debt as a form of belonging?

Consent to entanglement's habitation in relationality's void.

Uncontractable nonrelationality.

A terrain of anti- and ante-relational promise.

A venereal, funereal, futurial (under) ground.

Nonperformance rattles, ra++les, quakes.

Betty's Case spectrally opens up a territory of law where her will, free so as to be given away, crosses freedom with slavery. That freedom that is given away turns out to be a complete negation of legal freedom, with the arrival again of the slave as koan: Does blackness have freedom? Betty.

The fact that she would be (re)unowned is a contingency, while the freedom of a freedom to give away freedom is unconditional, or possible in any condition.

Freedom in law's discourse is a rebus debtor's colony where ++ marks a spot for the treasure of an unknown knowing.

Ante up, place your bet, it's its own reward. Betting begets a certain debt we happily inherit as the unheirable of the earth.

ə [surplus] 17

The *io* of *motion* is phonetically signified in the International Phonetic Alphabet with the symbol *ə*. This inverted *e* is called a *schwa* and marks the sound value of a vowel produced when the lips, tongue, and jaw are relaxed, when the vestibule of the mouth, we might say,

I'm listening for the flat spots.

is taking a break. It's the way writing marks how vowels when spoken find common shape in the sound *uh*. It marks momentary phonetic relaxation in the utterance of words. Apparently, the mouth needs lots of breaks when uttering English words because the schwa is its most common vowel sound.

During my last visit to Korea four summers ago, I heard that older generations decry the "laziness" of the way younger generations speak Korean. I understand now that the hip-hop I heard playing in stores and cafés was schwa'ed Korean. The lazy *ə* is how the likes of E-40 globalize blackness as an in-built general strike of the mouth.

Blackness in schwa'ed Korean is the murmuring nonperformance of a fugitive liturgy in some sliding, glissed, Glissantian sound of tongues, lips, jaws that go limp as resistance to being the unnoticed lubrication between the sound of consonants.

Schwa comes from the Hebrew word *shva*. *Shva* is the name of a diacritic, an extra mark made next to a letter, in *niqqud*, Hebrew's orthographic system of diacritical signs for indicating a vowel sound or distinguishing between different pronunciations of a letter. The *shva* consists of two vertical dots, written under a letter to denote the sound value *eh*. The colon key will have to do to mark my writing with this uncanny Hebrew diacritic.

:

Modern hangul does not use diacritical marks, but Middle Korean did.[25] They are called 방점 (*bangjeum*), or written in *hanja* as 傍點.

방, *bang*, meaning "tone." And 점, *jeum*, meaning "dot." The two *hanja* characters are themselves compounds, each with its own compelling etymologies and

Just as the slave is *formally necessary* in broaching a fundamental split in the development of legal freedom between organizing radically heterogeneous exercises of individual contract rights (within both public and private realms) and protecting a transcendent idea of free will at the heart of contract freedom, so too is the schwa necessary for broaching the aural making of words and protecting the biopolitical idea of free will at the heart of speech. Juris*dict*ion—performances of word, of experience, and of freedom—
is the condition of and against which what Laura Harris refers to as the "aesthetic sociality of blackness" has a chance of nonperformatively appearing.[26]

I struggle to find ways of reminding myself to listen for all the contracts that riddle (which is not to say, euphemize), with the schwa as so many tiny black dots, the "narrative *shorthand*"[27] of the propertization of the slave, the consonantal rhythm of spoken English, the idea of freedom. These black dots sprinkle the text, speckle the idea, splatter the experience. Their fac-

root meanings: "beside, next to, direction, all direction"; "black, smoke"; and "to make dirty, ignite, wither."

These little marks connected writing to the impermanence of vernacularity. In the wake of colonialism, diacritically littered writing is scorch-earthed, on which survives the people's ways of moving their mouths while writing.

How to translate these withering lines of smoke, flare effects of the slave, of the schwa, of the *jeum*? Whose speed of disappearance, as ephemeral and short-lived as the phonemic tonality of any sound that catches us, we do not and will not have the concepts to order?

titiousness is like a million flare effects in a million photo negatives of all the breached (sovereign) promises of the past and the future.

Betty's Case as a case of blackness materializes as the Real. Listen for and from that lazy ə. Dystranslate freedom.

This exiled prosody breaks me with the weight of the unknowable in and as the musicality of any language.

ō [azurance] 18

I hear *liturgy* in *littoral.* What is liturgical in the littoral? And the littoral of liturgy? What liturgy performs the fugitive littoral? Moten's poetry must be performing a liturgy of Betty's trace. Poetics then can be thought to be performing a liturgy of the fugitive littoral . . . I'm drawn to something in these questions his writing raises, which is to say, I am moved, but not of my own capacity. I am neither resistive nor submissive to what is going on behind or in the midst of all his beautiful writing, which slays the whiteness of philosophy and art and lovingly draws out the brilliance of how blackness thinks and does.

When I try to handwrite *litt*, the letters appear out of order. I first mark a small downward line but unwittingly put a dot above the line, turning it into an *i*. To correct this, I put an *l* in front of the misplaced *i* to keep writing without erasing, but unwittingly, again, I miswrite a *t* instead. These bungles of handwriting gesture the inapparent in something of the word: *till.*

This bungle offers a complex etymology. *Till* means "cultivate land" (thirteenth century) and "plow" (late fourteenth century); from the Old English *tilian*, meaning "cultivate, work, tend, get by labor," and prior to that, "strive after, aim at, aspire to"; related to *till*, meaning "fixed point, goal," and *til*, meaning "good, useful, suitable."[28] These Old English roots are related to Old Germanic *tilojan*, including Old Frisian, Old Saxon, Middle Dutch, and Old High German *zilon*, meaning "to strive," and German *zielen*, meaning "to aim, strive," and *Ziel*, meaning "limit, end, goal, achievement."[29]

Across Sigmund Freud's writing, *Ziel* is closely related to his analysis of the human experience of pleasure to theorize the unconscious. It has an uncanny sonic resemblance to the word *Seele*, the German word for "soul," which appears in the philosophical and literary texts Freud so frequently references in the couplet *Leib und Seele* (body and soul) on his way to theorizing the unconscious structure of desire in the play of language. The *Ziel* of pleasure as part of the phenomenon of the unconscious is irreducible to the body, the soul, and the mind/body metaphor that grounds the individuated sovereign subject. It comes out in "'*Zittersprache*'" that always attends the fugitive, revelatory nature of unconscious desire.[30]

Listening, we till the littoral of *Leib* and *Seele* in the question of *das Zielen* of the unconscious. This listening is fundamentally related to the audible and the nonperceptual, but a knowing nonetheless. The limit and the end of something is near, not temporally, but libidinally, in and on the body that feels because it becomes in a watery, lightless context. The symbolic vibrates a thing eventually to be referred to as a body, which precedes the reality of the "I" of the ego. The body is bound to and by the symbolic with a tick, a constriction, a small delirium of sound inscribed on the body by sound's oscillative touch.

My great-aunt recently told us the story of how she, her sisters, and her mother fled south during the Korean War by boat on the eastern shore of the peninsula. She did not mention where they were in the north, but the sea that dark night would deliver them to a small town, Gangneung, in what we now refer to as South Korea. My father always said his family was from North Korea, but when we visited Seoul four summers ago, Gangneung was the closest we could get to visit where he was from. It was the one place my parents wanted to make sure to visit together, and we all had a lovely day at the beach. The water was a paler shade of blue than the Pacific I am used to seeing in California.

My great-aunt was eleven, the youngest of her six sisters, when they snuck away on this boat.

She repeated many times as she was telling this story that her mother, without explanation, bound the family's money to her torso under her clothes. I wonder what she could know at the age of eleven about this.

She recounts the actual experience of being on the boat, that that night was so dark, the captain couldn't tell whether they had moved from where they launched. He called out into the dark, asking other boats or docks they passed where they were. "Are we still in the North?" she recalls him asking over and over.

In her retelling, the darkness of being at sea is littered with sound, "ttok, ttok, ttok." She repeated this onomatopoeia, not to dramatize her story, but to express something unsayable about her fear, the dark, and her experience of unknowability. As I write this onomatopoeia, I myself can't recall what it signified for her. Was it the sound of the boat's engine or the sound of the captain signaling to my great-aunt and her family where he was waiting for them when they got onboard? No matter. It is a pure signifier of intergenerational transmission that invites a doing otherwise.

Between *Ziel* and *Seele*, the unconscious is a shore. Land is an extension of the floor of the oceans, and thus its shores. Whether walking on land or sailing the seas, we are always on this shore, always ashore, assured only in that something is near. Of this, we assure, azure, each other. But in this context, the "each" of "other" and "me" are discovered as having always been indistinguishable while giving assurance. Azurance is the currency of consent not to be a single being.

We are implicated in what psychoanalyst Annie Rogers refers to as "the signifiers of intergenerational transmission," which overdetermine not only a life but also the whole of social life.[31] Blackness is the beautiful, surrep(ə)titious sonic movement of all our various *objets a* in this messy terrain of intergenerational transmission of a knowledge of freedom. To azure these *objets a* that we are to one another is to assume the inherent non-single responsibility of history for the first time from all the fragments caught in the many languages we are spoken by.

ttok ttok ttok

++ok ++ok ++ok

++ ō ++ ō ++ ō

Take this little ō as azurance.

It is an unceasing sound of something, a currency, a flow, discovered along the writing path of our nearness across vast distances of time and place on the violent currents of the littoral, which is to say, the topology of the social net of signification. They are the sound of a "speaking discontinuity."[32]

Writing as "desire for desire" is an endless burnishing, rubbing, polishing of this ō.[33] *It cannot be, and has never been, done alone. Only in joint motion do we burnish blackness as nonperformance, as the movement of burnishing blurs its devoted potters into so many hands.*

And then I can finally write that these burnished promises carry on their surface what is the intergenerational transmission of blackness as nonperformance. Use whatever is on hand, "ttok, ttok, ttok."

Make dirt gleam.

When Theophilus Parsons, in his treatise *The Law of Contracts* (1853), observed, "The law of contract, in its widest sense, may be regarded as including nearly all the law which regulates the relations of human life," he did not know that this also meant that it, as American law's internal structure of translation, also transmits ō.[34] If Parsons is correct that "all social life presumes it, and rests upon it; for out of contracts, express or implied, declared or understood, grow all rights, all duties, all obligations, and all law," then all social life could also be said to presume ō, rest on ō, and, out of every ō,

My great-aunt is eighty-six now and shows signs of the onset of dementia, just like her older sister, my grandmother. We treasure these stories as, recently, everyone's beloved Mrs. Calderon is prone to getting lost when she's out for a walk, or forgetting to eat. But her retellings also are prone to a knowing, the way she knew something that night at sea, "ttok, ttok, ttok," and the way she repeats the same advice she wants to give us about life. She is still plucky, affectionate, gentle, and miraculous in her dementia.

The fugitive littoral: sound in total darkness, moving over a moving medium, some unknown destination without direction, the going forth and going away in a context of unseeability. Unforeseeability. There is only sinking, ascension, and discoordinated lateral movement: to the bottom of the sea, to the heavens, and unmoored fugitivity on the rough surface of the sea where seeing where it touches land demands some other form of knowing: "ttok, ttok, ttok."

The slave, an enigmatic party to or object of various kinds of contractual relations that make up private practice, remains

grow rights, duties, obligations, and law, and in them grows ō.[35]

The expansive and categorically *abstract* consent-based idea of freedom of contract characteristic of today's late-capitalist legal regimes riddles slavery's narrative property shorthand with ō. They look like holes. But don't assume them. Don't fill them with individuated wills. Otherwise, they turn into forgotten land mines where the "private law of slavery" was never abolished, waiting to be triggered.[36]

Listen empty. It's what ō sounds like. It's what ō looks like.

even after the various kinds of positive law institutionalizing slavery have been abolished. The slave is a figure of the afterlife. A tremor, a solicitation of legal reason. A blur. Betty's blur, a promise kept and given in the contract's nonperformance. It precipitates "totality's ghost":[37] the always present (im)possibility of enacting a freedom that is freedom because it simultaneously exercises and gives away the freedom the law would recognize in her but for its fundamental dependence on her to continue promising freedom.

Stop promising freedom, keep giving azurance.

un [act]

19

The lesson *Betty's Case* teaches us is that freedom at every register of sociolegal reality must be written as *unfreedom*. Freedom is unfreedom. The name Betty begs the question of what matrix it moves in and as the condition of possibility for "her" disappearing act.

I ask because I want to disappear the way Betty disappears, not without a trace, but as a trace of some unknown promise.

In his article "Force of Law: The 'Mystical Foundation of Authority' (Deconstruction and the Possibility of Justice)," Jacques Derrida writes that "a foundation is a promise. . . . And even if a promise is not kept in fact, iterability inscribes the promise as guard in the most irruptive instant of foundation."[38] Oliver Wendell Holmes depicts contracts in *The Common Law* as promises whittled from this iterability through various forms of bargaining.[39] But Spillers succinctly describes the complex historical scene of slavery as an "enforced state of breach," where we find ourselves on the iterative shores of bargaining littered with promises "not kept in fact."[40]

In this enforced state of breach, the letter, unreciprocated with any consideration whatsoever, again sounds. That which Spillers condenses as a matter of history can be further condensed into the sound of the nonsingle letter *un* of ***un***freedom and of a certain fecundity of the jurisgenerative principle. For what or whom does the *un* offer something better than life lived under the deathly ethos of the social contract and its many legal forms to which there is no outside of its "schizophrenic quality"?[41]

What are all the ways to make and accept the offer contained in the *un* of (un)freedom and fecundity, of obscene and obstetric performance of law? Answering this question seems crucially related to how we understand the act of making an offer to form a promise . . . When a contract is made, often including signatures, which is to say, when there has been an offer on which another relies, does the offer become a sign? Or can it remain a signifier, which is to say, can a relied-on offer continue specifically offering nothing, absence, or the unknown? What strange accord would enable this continual offering?

Moten suggests that acts of freedom and unfreedom are acts insofar as they are the effects of the individuated subject, and performative acts, then, are signs of individuated expressions of desire. He questions whether what Betty offers can be fully known if her offer, as the survival of *Betty's Case*, is conceptualized as an act. To say that at the core of *Betty's Case* is an expression of desire is also to say that it implicates the drives, some of which we might celebrate and associate with artistic or historical expressions of freedom and resistance.

Drives, on the one hand, manifest as individuated pleasures, and on the other, one drive smuggles into lan-

Birds: Where are we? There's no understanding in this Valley of Understanding. Hoopoe: Here we must pay close attention. We are following a path. No one knows

guage something beyond the sovereign subject. This is the radically nonindividualizable work of the death drive. In his later writings, Lacan rejected readings of Freud's *Beyond the Pleasure Principle* that reduced notions of the death drive as desire for pain. Instead, he insisted on what we might refer to as a constant littoral surfacing of the unconscious, not necessarily between life and death, or pleasure and pain, but jouissance and *death*, both anticipated and certain.

how long we have to go forward or how far.[42]

Elaborating on his reference to the freedom drive in *In the Break*, Moten writes in *Stolen Life*, "The freedom drive is the death drive; and fugitivity is the realm of the (always anticipatory) afterlife."[43] I can't help but hear Moten through Lacan here, such that fugitivity is not some liminal or third space between life and death, or pleasure and pain, but is the name for how the pleasures and pains of the sovereign subject structurally turn toward and in a profoundly anticipatory knowledge of death, which is to say, the unconscious. Acts of freedom, performative or contractual, insofar as they bear a death drive, are incomplete in the precise sense that they operate at a realm in which the sovereign subject falls away and leaves us in and as a socio-libidinal entanglement in and as a net of signifiers.

The signs of this freedom/death drive . . . they mark how an offer, how the practice of desire through offering, might outlive the consequences caused by it. Betty's offer is the offering of the unconscious. She gives oblique form to an offer that carries with it unconscious desire as the fecundity of experience of (un)freedom. The scene of her offering is both obscene and obstetric. The blackness of promising depends on this unactionable offer.

The Korean word for promise is 약속 (*yaksok*), or in hangul 約束.

속 (束) *sok*, meaning "inside, or the interior," is a homonym with a different *hanja* character, 俗, meaning "worldly, secular, or common" and "vulgar; unrefined; common; popular; vernacular."[44]

속이 안좋아: it's a way of saying "I don't feel good," but its literal translation, "Insides are uneasy," conveys better the sense of mystery in a condition whose saying has no possessive pronoun but nonetheless is felt by us, or around which we curl up, fetus-like.

"속이 안좋아," my mother would say when anxiety libidinally manifested in a strange splitting pain in her stomach. And I inherited this psychosomatic symptom from her.

The 약 (約), *yak,* of 약속, meaning "to promise, to bind, to tie a knot," is a homonym with another *hanja* character, 藥, meaning "medicine."

But the symptom my mother and I share is impervious to any kind of drug. I wonder now what kind of broken promise, or missing signifier of some broken promise, this symptom takes the place of? Would another promise have reknotted her, our, this, symptom, from a wrenching pain somewhere in our insides to some other movement within?

Perhaps the act of such a promise would draw a line of movement from some internality, some internal pain, externally perceivable only as common, vulgar, vernacular, folk, malingering; to a medicine that will not be a drug but some equally common, vulgar, vernacular, folk treatment.

So unmodern is this promise that even those who would police tradition and claim some part of what is relatively regarded as primitivity would not want to register its offer. Unconscious desire is the beginning of such a 약속, a promise, from which something totally other and unforeseeable emerges, as in this offering letter, *un*.

Promise: promittere*:* pro *(forth)* mitt *(send): "to send forth: to have been sent forth: to have been sent." The silvery line is knotted in uncountable places by so many partial acts. They appear from one angle as an unclosed set of acrostic marks, and from another, as a shimmering, billowing fabric. The nonperformativity of an act is precisely in its nonsequential, nonconsequential destiny as an open offer so open no one can make it, and no intent can materialize it. That which we would have referenced as a single being, reliant on it, is no longer.*

Black's Law Dictionary defines an *evergreen promise* as "perpetual renewal or reoccurrence regardless of what happens in the future."[45]

Unconscious desire is a form of an evergreen offer. Unforeseeability, unanticipatable change, the letter *un* glints that which is undying about the promise. Yes, I'm thinking of, always, the improvisation of making, breaking, and keeping promises. Improvisation, notably, is that which cannot be contracted, nor performed against a contract, but is nonetheless a legal matter and issue that contract law refers to as nonperformance and contains as its other question of freedom.[46]

But now. But now, nonperformance as improvisation marks matter in some verdant place where promising comes from a source whose life is neither genealogically sequential nor genetically sequenceable. This is the form of life that concerns psychoanalysis. It is the death drive, some thing we imperfectly refer to as an "us," amid the glinting drops of letters, glistening, being of the jungle (people).

Betty's act, then, is neither the performance of decision, nor a sign of intent. Betty's act is a *provisional* form of joint motion toward an emptiness around which is collected a circumstantiality that dwarfs decisional significance and an endurance of the question of freedom.

The jungle laughs at the human.

Any act we provisionally and unsatisfyingly refer to as a decision can only be remedied in language by listening for the letter *un*: hers is unlike freedom, unlike submission, unlike resistance, unlike death, unlike living, unlike history, unlike anything we would want to attribute to it as its consequential meaning. If there is a truth to Betty's act, it is this single hysterical function of the letter *un*, or the unary function of negating her act's symbolic significance. And via this unary function, the magical realism of the death drive present in contract law presents itself all around us.

Un as offer permits reveling in illiberal political ideals and feelings. It carries with it the shade or tone of what Stefano Harney and Fred Moten have described as "a willingness to break the law one calls into existence."[47] It marks the time of a "violent and cruel re-routing" precipitated by a certain inseparability between the "work of blackness" and the "violence of blackness."[48] It is not a speech act in the Austinian sense in which speech is thought to be performative insofar as it has a self-referential function of a doing in the very utterance of the word. *Un* as mark is a performative that promises the nonperformance of whatever can be known about the future from the here and now. *Un* marks revelatory possibility in a magical legal realism surrounding Betty's act.

As a letter it stands for life lived in a "state of breach," or in a psychosocial condition the signifier "social death" indexes but does not define. To utter it is to say neither that whatever Betty might have promised did not and no longer exists, nor that the reality of unkeepable promises forecloses the radical undeterminable futurity contained in those promises. It is to signify the name's radical mystery as an unnotarizable promissory note, containing already its unfulfillability or breach by nonperformance and, thus, the possibility of a radically indeterminable futurity to which we consent to being bound through such promises.[49]

운 [tongue] **20**

Book 34 of *The Digest of Justinian* contains a section on "Legacies of Gold, Silver, Toilet Equipment, Jewelry, Perfumes, Clothing or Garments, and Statues." On the question of how to temporally delimit a "legacy" left in these specific forms of property, Paul, the second- and third-century Roman jurist Julius Paulus Prudentissimus, wrote that it should be "regarded as comprising property that existed at the time of his will." This is because when a testator says "'my clothing,' 'my silver,' by the description 'mine' he indicates present, not future, time." He goes on, "The same is the case, too, if someone has left as a legacy 'my slaves.'"[50]

"My silver," "my slaves." How to determine their quantity and value is at issue across this section on the luxuries, in large part, a husband instructs his heir to reserve for his surviving wife.

Silver has the distinct qualities of being ornamental, functional, workable, personal, quantifiable, and precious. It is commodity, money, and a natural material whose symbolic meaning can be traced to antiquity. So, too, in the analogical litany of luxury goods, does the slave possess such qualities.

But what of silver's fugitive qualities?

My silver. My slaves. Silver, slaver. Slaves. The signifiers start to sound like so many variations on *selves*. I want to break out of this overdetermined catalog of *SLV* words, or at least mark it, dyssensically: *Shva* the *s*, the *l*, the *v*. If

Differentially ceremonialize. This repetition will show up as a failure to defeat social death. So I consent to failing, not because of "my" unconscious desires, but with *the* unconscious, whose tongue touches.

Sō gō ōn.

This obscene transliteration cannot escape the erotic figure of the mouth. Let this be some other social practice of the freedom drive as death drive. Let the tongue's life of service, its servility and confinement within, remind us how quickly pleasures turn, because what is sweet, what is beautiful, what allures and washes the tongue

Saidiya Hartman's Venus needed two acts to be fabulated, then these letters need at least two diacritical marks.[51]

Silver, that surface shared by a swarm, a murmur, a school. Silver, whose halide crystals, exposed, write light. Silver, a note of color the ocean twitches on a dark, dark night. Silver, some lymph-like liquid draining into language-streams. Silver, the aura, leftover, the afterlife of the yellows and reds of gold and copper. Silver, the surrounding air made conductive force field when uttering the name Betty.

Silver, 은, shwa'd eun, əun. The circle in the hangul spelling of the word for silver, 은, is the silent letter ㅇ, called *ieung*. It depicts the open vocal tract, the sound of air, silent as it moves from the throat and out through the open lips. It's the silence of glottal opening but before saying *aaaaahhhhh*.

This silent consonant sits on top of the vowel ㅡ, which sounds like *eu*, or *û*, and represents the flatness of the earth. Below, we have the consonant ㄴ, called *nieun*, which depicts the shape of the tongue, curled up, its tip touching the ceiling inside the mouth.

The Korean word for silver choreographs some secret, underground way we invisibly lick ourselves with every utterance of words whose destiny is to end with *n*.

When we mouth 은, it is obscene because below the plane of the earth, on some underside of a line, the tongue lives and serves. It is the live end of a lightless, bottomless, glottal drop into some place, inside. *N* cleans wounds. It kisses, tastes, not so much something desired, but perhaps some thing of and in unconscious desire, perhaps.

While the sun silently beats down on this earth, the erotics of ㄴ, its mark, choreographs the tongue to taste,

over with saliva, is always, too, deadly.

The (give me liberty or give me) death drive is the failure to defeat the touch of the tongue that marks these failures. If to choose liberty is to perfect the dance of the tongue in total submission to thought, then choosing death (drive) is the erotics of the mysterious, organic muscularity of the tongue, fecund with nerve endings that unconsciously cause the water that we are to flood or dry up.

Betty, again, always, doubly marks some treasure with ++. This time, ++ is there in the hangul consonant ㅇ, a silent glottis, *parlêtre*. *Glottis* comes

touch, the thing of a part, of flesh, whose parts always touch.

The tongue of the letter teaches us how to consent not to be a single being.

from the Greek word *glōtta*, a variant of *glossa*, "tongue."

Silver, slave, glo++al dilation: *an opening to the beyond of consent is cut by a strange undying glossolalic touch.*

A "lackground" music made when trying to retrace the tongue's dance of inseparable letters in *One Long Black Sentence* (by Renee Gladman and Fred Moten).[52]

銀 [coup] **21**

"Given as she [Betty] is to the renewal of a maternal ecology," Moten writes, "she cannot be our mother."[53]

I turn this limit over and over in my head to articulate what the truth of this statement is. If Betty is the mark of a regenerative capacity at an ecological register, that's what we get. A mark, and not a mother, as she who elicits all our unfulfilled demands and bears the cost of some archaic satisfaction we and she never had.

As mark, she returns that negation to us so that we can choose either to suffer it passively as so many ways we are assailed by what we do not have, or what we are politically told we must (not) want; or to move with and join up with this mark in a different register of signifiers.

The name Betty is the latter. Or as Rogers might say of the name, it "is the promise of psychoanalysis: to circle and claim as destiny an ethical position as the signature of one's desire and one's death."[54] And so it is that she is not our mother. Let her person rest. Lay her to rest. Let this ethics of rest itself be our destiny, spelled out in the trace, the name, Betty.

Grieve, claim, write, circle. This is no place in particular and no time except what will be, just that. Pause, draw, cut, press the materiality and time of the skin that every inadequate saying of "not mother" reverberates through.[55]

To say that Betty cannot be our mother frees and affirms the thought of life's socio-uterine environment. If the female is the figure for what might be referred to as the maternal, I am interested first in this psychophysiological condition of gestation, and the question of the audible, as discussed by Willy Apollon in "The Limit: A Fundamental Question for the Subject in Human Experience" (2010).

name,

aprés-coup

> The strangeness of this voice, its exteriority with respect to everything that generates sounds in the uterine environment of the child, and its effects on this environment will no doubt cause the child who is yet to be born to be resensitized to the voice of the mother. . . . This surging forth of the audible in the living being and in the child's universe determines his entrance into humanity, or its birth into what we traditionally call the spirit (where the French *esprit*, much like the German *Geist*, designates both the "mind" and the "spirit," or the spiritual dimension of the mind).[56]

hear,

aprés-coup

He goes on, the "field of the audible that structures human temporality . . . is a veritable effraction of the living being, which opens onto a dimension where things escape its control."[57]

Effraction: forcible entry, or, in medical terms, a bone fracture that breaks through the skin. Effraction in utero is sound that breaks through the membrane of life becoming the skin of a child. This effraction is the earliest experience of the constitution of the child's body, and its logic continues to work in the formation of the child's body, even after birth, detachment, separation, or whatever terms we use to refer to the socialization of the child as a free(standing) subject.

skin,

The limit-idea or unsymbolizable experience of dividing organismal life is retained in a nonperceptual field of the audible. "In putting in place the mother tongue," Apollon writes, on the one hand, "the mother's speech determines for the child the radical difference between what is heard and said without being present to visual perception and that thus escapes all control," and on the other hand, "what constitutes the space of the collective and individual consciousness, where what is said can be seen and falls under the control of the Other."[58] The environment of consent *aprés-coup* here is an intraeffractive intimacy that is the growth within the mother, and the touch of sound within the child.

aprés-coup

mirrors,

Life is a mutually procreative paranormal mutation.

Mutated sound, music, fertilizes this growth, cancerous but for the way language beckons. The sharing of a time outside of time is unconscious, and we refind this sharing when we lose whatever mothers we assume and conscience a mutually metonymic time, of fluttering, of the fluting enunciation of letters and flesh.

aprés-coup

aprés-

Some socio-intrauterine teaching, or transmission, allows for a radical difference to be known between the nonpresence of a voice nonetheless heard and conscious thought structured by language. Consent is consent to not being conditioned to the world, consent to some hearing with the skin, to the ghostly effractions of the skin. What we consent to is not reattachment or refusing detachment, but a knowledge always there of some unknowable feeling in and of the flesh that theories of natal alienation (as physical birth, individuation, and social death) can never represent. The transmission of the possibility of knowing the radical difference between unorderable, nonperceptual sound that the body already knows, and the many ordered fields of the Other, is a structural reality of life.

-coup

aprés-coup flood,

She cannot be our mother because her profound imprint as the effracting voice that continues to live in and as skin does not birth genealogical egoic selves. But as well, to say that that Betty cannot be our mother is perhaps also to say that she is the "law of the mother" insofar as the ***un***-common signature produced in a practice of the name always writes the experience of an irretrievable memory given in a mode of knowing, a *savoir*, voice in and as skin.

aprés-

We are on an "irrepressible quest for an unpresentable object" whether we conscience it or not.[59] But if we do choose to know something of it, desire becomes the medium through which we can radically reconceive of a form of consent given in our skin, a third ear that registers some socio-intrauterine time of nonsingleness.

cut

Grow in this subjective time of amniotically animated sound.

ef fusal
re fractal

Effraction, ravishment, surge—a time before the division of spirit and body. This is the context of drives organized in the body. We refind them in learning how to hear nonperceptual auditory objects for whatever they might bear of the mother as a double impossibility of

-coup

representation: first, as an association with the socio-uterine effraction by the voice; and, second, as the censorship or regulation of the audible by a social link.[60] Consent in this second order must be a form of agreement to refuse what is offered by the social link, in favor of what recent political discourse refers to as "imagination." Consent in the first order, however, is to existing in an unknowable shared time that ruins the conditions of giving consent in the first place.

-aprés
- *cut*
a
p
--

How do we refuse individuation? There is something to be learned in how one divides every identification with the Other within. But further, this internal division must refuse the replacement of the self with a collective, and continue on into the emptiness that catalyzes internal division, such that it becomes impossible to confirm or deny the existence of an original boundary called *self, body, mother*. The more radical calling is to refind the nonperceptual voice we are on a quest to know despite the fact that it is beyond representation. Hear the questioning in the quest without reducing behaviors, decisions, preferences, and fantasies to transgression.

r --
é
s
c

I think this articulation is as close as I can get right now to explaining how we materialize "real return."[61] Alight, twist, wind around a poetics given in touching, a touching that is actually a listening for the aural sociality of the effracting letter, of blanknesses, of the open field, all that which points to something beyond perception, image, and conscious thought.

o
u *p*
coo

Anyway, it can only be known *aprés-coup*.

Don Mee Choi, in her 2020 essay *Translation Is a Mode=Translation Is an Anti-neocolonial Mode*, marks the stakes of translation with Walter Benjamin's words "embryonic or intensive form."[62] The translator is female insofar as they gestate signifiers within and through submission to trace, trance, and tongues. Words, letters, names are embryos of intensity, created by the no-mothers.

"I say, we are all floaters, we are all motherless translators."[63]

Yes, and Betty is the name of a

zi ++ er spr ache

Zittersprache, a secret language kids invent while they play, translating, gliding along in the amniotic littoral of blackness.

> Erasure of no trace whatsoever that is prior, this is what constitutes the land [terre] of the littoral. Pure litura, that is the literal. To produce this erasure is reproducing this half without complement of which the subject subsists. Such is the exploit of calligraphy. . . . Between centre and absence, between knowledge and jouissance, there is a littoral which only turns to the literal insofar as this turn, you can take it in the same way at each and every moment.[64]

turn of

time

The Chinese ideogram for silver is 銀. It is a compound, one part of which is the character 金, meaning "metal" and "gold" but originally referring to the five metals—gold, silver, copper, tin, and iron. This character is also a compound, one part of which is the ancient character 亼, meaning "to gather or collect from three sides," and is the basis for the character 今, referring to the idea of "in the mouth" and meaning "this," "now," "at present," or "current."[65]

translation

coo

coo

The ancient character 亼, though used only as a phonetic designation in the ideogram 銀, is etymologically traceable in the character 集, meaning "collect, gather" or a "collection or set," and can be cut even further, revealing 隹, a short-tailed bird in a tree, 木. The *hanja* character 集, written in hangul as 집 (*jip*), and meaning "collection," is a homonym for the Middle Korean word for "home," "house," or "nest."[66]

coo

coo

coo

coo

coo coo

What were the circumstances that necessitated 雧 as a variant of 集? With its three little birds and their "sing, sing, sing kinda quality"?[67]

non liquet blackness

for Palestine

로 [demo] **22**

The other day, I was struck with a brief moment of fear because I could not recall what area of math my father studied as a PhD student at the University of California, Berkeley. I recalled a gigantic yellow notepad, so big it took up most of the space on his bedroom floor as he crouched over it, scribbling away. What kind of thought was so complex and so big that it required this notepad? What kind of equations and formulas required him to get on his hands and knees to write?

The study of smooth surfaces, he once told me. Right, he studied differential manifolds: tori, atlases, knots, bundles. He talked about the idea of neighborhoods once when I asked whether there was some mathematical way of formulating the global travels of an idea as a smooth surface. I couldn't follow what he was explaining, but I wanted to listen to how he would think through the problem.

The thought I am interested in unfolds itself in some necessary condition of mutual desire to know. My desire cuts this mysterious faculty for deriving truth. At first blush, math exists as a language of truth between us. Physical existence is an essential medium, but it moves in some other register of being alive. For me, math as an approach to truth was, is, a creative mode of thought. This creativity harbored a logic that could prove that, one day, the US military occupation of South Korea and the demilitarized zone (DMZ) dividing the peninsula would be abolished and Korea would be an autonomous communist nation.

He prepared us each day to go out into the world and defend this truth in our minds if anything contradicted the propositions supporting this logic. (I say "we," but I think I was the only one among us three siblings who felt this way.) We were not told what to say. For it was not a matter of debating or arguing. We just knew, because we thought, or could think. Bowing down to bring our noses to that notepad, something as seditious or unpopular or impossible as a reunification of Korea on North Korea's terms could be written as truth.

Fernando Zalamea writes in *Synthetic Philosophy of Contemporary Mathematics*, "Mathematics' richness takes root in its *weave* of demonstrations (the impossibility of evading certain obstructions and the possibility of effecting certain transfers)."[1]

If the United States was, is, an unavoidable obstruction to Korean reunification, its abolition was, is, necessary for the historical possibility of effecting the transfer of a certain idea of living. Conscious, contextual, political positioning is a mere effect of a certain creative consistency or endurance of thought, wherein, Zalamea goes on, "a problem, concept, or construction *is transformed* by the problem's partial solutions, the concept's refined definitions, or the construction's sheaf of saturations and decantations."[2]

I am taken by the word *demonstration*, as in mathematical structures of thought applied to a problem; and marching and chanting in the streets.

Korean Buddhist monks crawl in protest.

The Korean term for protests is 데모, *demo*. This clipped word, to my ear, conjoins the Latin root of *demonstration*, *demonstrare*, meaning "to show, point out, draw attention to, display" and "to make plain, give evidence (of)"; and the Latin root of *demolish*, *demoliri*, from *de-*, meaning "down" and "not, do the opposite of, undo"; and *moliri*, meaning "build, construct," from *moles*, meaning "mass, massive structure, barrier."[3]

데모 is some complex mathematical weave in which the Black Panthers, Korean anti-neocolonialism, and Zalamea are topological neighbors.

This weave gets at the root of what is unsatisfyingly referred to as *solidarity*. Abolition (of the United States), and all the cataclysmic and mundane consequences contained in this partial solution, is already folded into the ongoing procedure of thought about and living through the transfer of a larger socially driven mathematical imagination of (un)freedom in and of the DMZ's ribbons of time outside time.

D e Monstration Z one
Don Mee Zalamea
ante DeMocratic *Ziel*
이데모, *i dae mo*

이대로, *i dae ro*
로 De Mo
diiiiiiiiiiiimelo dimelo didididiiiiiimelo[4]
디매로. 말해.[5]

The image in figure 4.1 is from poem 3 in a series by Don Mee Choi titled with the name of a South Korean political prisoner, Ahn Hak-sŏp. It depicts a fragment of handwritten notes she took while interviewing Ahn in 2016. The fragment is Choi's handwritten transliteration of the English word *terror* into the hangul word 태로. In the poem, Choi renders this cipher into type as "G H 로" and then interprets this as an acronym for "Global Humanity" with a translation of 로 as the English preposition *toward*.[6]

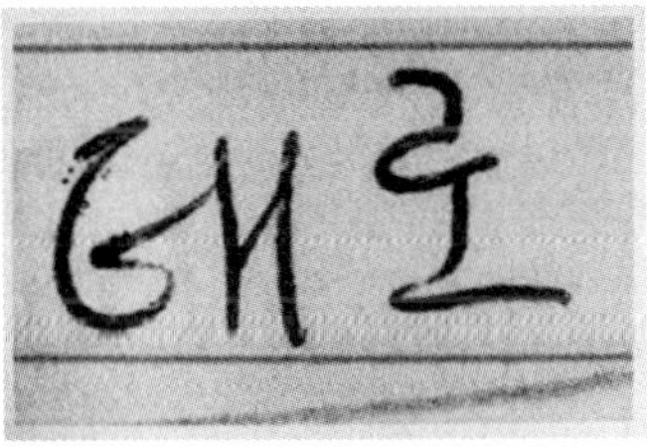

4.1 Handwritten note on page 29 of Don Mee Choi's *DMZ Colony* (2020). Photo by author.

But I see the scrawled marks as a form of blur you get when living histories of state terror and violence cause transcription, translation, and transliteration to move like the sound of a giggle.

> A winged animal hides behind the wall's steel rods
> and giggles.[7]

The hangul letters are squirming to get away from the word. Choi's instantaneously marked play of letters, achieved in this peculiar calligraphic effect of a ballpoint pen, echoes a certain vibration of the letters we see when LaTasha Nevada Diggs's verbal performance of the Spanish imperative *dimelo*, meaning "tell me," "talk to me," "let me know," or the slang greeting "What's up?," is transcribed.

If there is a 로, a toward, to the poetries above, it is in the way that sounds and marks live where letters have been absented in an acronym.

6/13 [entanglement] **23**

Beginning in my earliest experiences studying and organizing in the US-based prison abolition movement in the 1990s, I have always been uncertain about the belief that mass incarceration is slavery constitutionally sanctioned by the Thirteenth Amendment's exception clause. Now pervading our popular culture, this argument removes the Thirteenth Amendment from the history of its legal development and reductively converges with what perhaps some seem to think is a more accessible term: *loophole*.

Abolitionist discourse is made of so many variations of demands to close the loophole, which is to say, to hold states and various private sectors responsible for a malfeasance of monstrous proportions. Abolish this loophole, abolish that loophole . . . recount, account, audit, and assess. So goes the logic of the critics of the Thirteenth Amendment imagined as a "loophole": We must close the loophole of the Thirteenth Amendment, and to the extent this loophole remains open, the United States will never have abolished slavery.

The loophole arouses public awareness of the relationship between the history of segregation and the racial politics of punishment, but it is a paranoid awareness. It derives from a view of constitutional law as a mega-contract between nation and citizen, the latter of whom is responsible for demanding identity between legal meaning and effect.

The popularization of prison abolition depends on the condensation of the problem of the Thirteenth Amendment, or the legal history of slavery's unfinished abolition, to the six words of the exception clause. And so it appears to us as if the crisis of mass incarceration today is an inevitable outcome of an edict descending on us from a past that might have been abolished if these six words from our Constitution had been omitted. Yet, abolishing some of the words contained in the Constitution (or any law whatsoever) abolishes neither its jurisdictional authority nor its institutionalization through social order and cultural meaning. This problem extends to other abolitionist campaigns: banning the box doesn't abolish the employer's discretion, eliminating police departments from municipal budgets doesn't halt gentrification, closing a jail doesn't decrease state surveillance, and so on.

The deeper question such reforms push us to constantly return to is: How to think through this coexistence between the social capacity to invent, reform, and maintain perverse racist institutions and policies, and slavery's partial legal abolition?

I want to take the six words, "except as a punishment for crime," as what Jacques Lacan calls "a chronicle . . . the neurotic's individual myth" that marks the Constitution's double failure as a paternal metaphor.[8] Its failure is double insofar as the postbellum Constitution continues, of necessity, to bear the marks of those clauses and doctrines abolished from its antecedent form. These six words together are a signifier through which the myth of American democracy articulates the historical debt we owe to our ancestors who fought and died in armed struggle (against colonialism, against enslavement and segregation), and the political debt of the social contract that founds democracy, and, more importantly, the "impossibility of bringing these two levels together."[9]

Lacan goes on, "By trying to make one coincide with the other, he [the individual] makes a perennially unsatisfying turning maneuver and never succeeds in closing the loop."[10] On or off? Clean or dirty? Abolish or reform?

The demand to "close the loophole" can never succeed. It circles around a structural legal neurosis, a "hole," to bring together what I have elsewhere called "the private law of slavery" and a universal law of liberal democracy.[11] This incommensurability cannot be resolved, but popular abolitionism attempts to bring it to closure by a constant reshuffling of political ideals, aims, and fantasies. Meanwhile, we don't know what the "hole" is, as it is unsatisfyingly filled in with this persistent reordering. Where and what is the "hole" as an absence held in the many loops of interpretations of the Constitution's many parts that give us the monstrous legal edifice of mass incarceration? What if we thought of these six words as doubly marking absence? Absence in both the Thirteenth Amendment and the entirety of the US Constitution?

What if the hole is not law's double failure but is a DMZ within that law's many loops of meaning?

Divide the loophole metaphor to enable the transfer, transference, transmission—the migratory flight—of abolition as an axiom for a wider, global structure of thought and action. Divide the rule of the exception with the whole of the violence of the US Constitution's ideology and history. Divide the signifier, the six words of the exception clause, by the amendment: 6/13.

The legal formulation of a loophole marks how interpretation as a method of measuring meaning from the chaos of sociolegality changes what is otherwise a general quantum mechanical condition of entanglement.[12]

A loophole, *Black's Law Dictionary* tells us, is "an allowed legal interpretation or practice" that is "unintentionally ambiguous due to a textual exception, omission, or technical defect." The consequence of a legal loophole, then, is that it "evades or frustrates the intent of a contract, law, or rule" but "without violating its literal interpretation."[13]

While we are accustomed to treating literal and ambiguous meaning as categorically distinct and opposed, and equally accustomed to faulting legal texts for their ambiguities, what is interesting about how the law regards a loophole is its emphasis on a coexistence between literal interpretation and unintentional ambiguous interpretation. A loophole, sometimes explicitly identified by a legal exception or contractual exclusion, is the sign of this peculiar double interpretive possibility in law. According to this dictionary definition, a loophole is the sign of a lack of contradiction between literal and ambiguous readings in a given law or rule.

Under such formal conditions of legal interpretation and practice, frustration is structured into the very writing of a law's stated intent and/or purpose. In other words, the symbolic reality of law's development will never achieve the object of its aim. Indeed, the etymology of the word *frustrate* traces back to the Latin verb *frustrare*, "to disappoint," which comes from the root *frustra*, meaning "in vain."[14] As well, frustration, psychoanalytically speaking, is an affect of having been wronged that inevitably arises from the noncorrespondence between the symbolic object of desire and a more primordial demand (like the infant's demand for love from the mother).

The word Sigmund Freud uses is *Versagung*, as the experience of obstacles that get in the way of libidinal satisfaction. Jean Laplanche and Jean-Bertrand Pontalis summarize, "The upshot . . . is not so much the lack of a real object which is at stake in frustration as the response to a demand that requires a given mode of satisfaction or that cannot be satisfied by any means."[15] And because *Versagung* is a precondition for the subject of desire, it should and can be maintained by the analyst and, by extension, political analyses and imagination.

This structural sense of frustration built into law has an uncanny resonance with a certain contemporary political frustration with a less-than-absolute law—with law that always contains "unintentional ambiguity" in practice and, contrasted against its stated aim, produces a curious fixation on words already scripted by the formal structure of law. Critique of the loophole that demands the eradication of exceptions and legal ambiguity only secures the law's authority to either create other loopholes or pursue a law absent of loopholes.

As such, the law is left with two options: continue to frustrate by creating different loopholes or impose an absolute law and right of the state to enforce this absolute principle. Addressing frustration to the law is a desire for fundamentalist rule—in the case at hand, a US Constitution as fundamentalist doctrine of an absolute right of the state to eradicate slavery. The outrage of prison abolitionists against the Thirteenth Amendment registers a structural frustration. But this frustration is not produced by some external constitutional denial but by a denial internal to prison abolitionism that refuses both other loopholes and a fundamentalist state. This is where prison abolition might escape incorporation into neoliberal racial politics.

I think to myself, frustration is only on one side of the contract, the Constitution, and the sense of what historically should have been. Take this frustration as a shortcut to some other space-time of law where life, law, and letter are entangled.

> As she walks up the stairway
> to the second floor clinic
> her dry, starved fingers
> search diligently for something
> inside her pocket
> then wriggle around the found object.[16]

Here, abolition will not have been the nullification of the legal object of frustration but a necessary means to discover what mode of social promissory satisfaction we are in fact after, which otherwise is crowded out by attempts to appease frustration with compromised substitutions of abolition with reforms.

The six words of the exception clause, depicted in a screen grab from Ava DuVernay's documentary *13th* (figure 4.2), are found in Section 1 of the Thirteenth Amendment. Section 1 is self-executing, meaning it is the law of the land by virtue of its declaration. This image, at the same time, begs the question of the shaded words of Section 2, which we cannot know from the film unless we go and actually look up the full text of the Thirteenth Amendment.

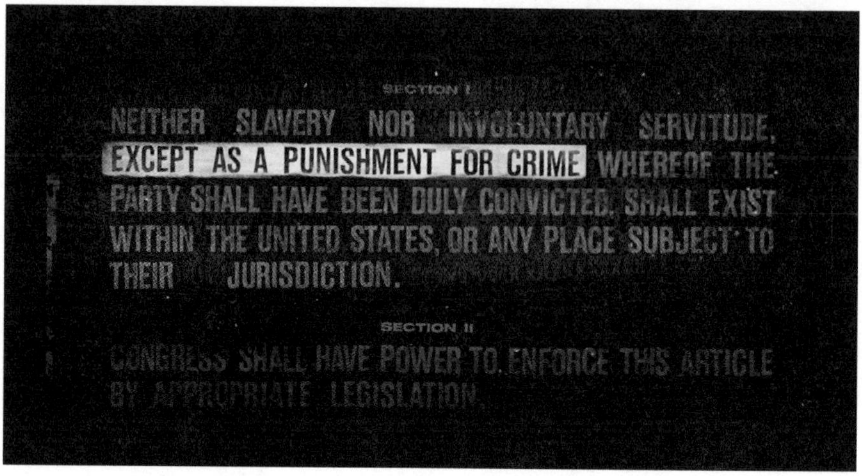

4.2 Screen grab from *13th*, directed by Ava DuVernay (2016).

There we find that it reads, "Congress shall have power to enforce this article by appropriate legislation."

Section 2 of the Thirteenth Amendment delegated to Congress a new federal power to enact laws to give effect to the statement of Section 1. The infamous *Civil Rights Cases of 1883* refused to recognize that Section 2 empowered Congress to create affirmative civil rights legislation to abolish "all badges and incidents of slavery," including portions of the Civil Rights Act of 1875 at issue in the case.[17] Solicitor general Samuel Phillips submitted a brief in the *Civil Rights Cases of 1883* defending the constitutionality of the Civil Rights Act of 1875 to regulate and punish private acts of racial discrimination and terror because "every rootlet of slavery has an individual vitality, and, to its minutest hair, should be anxiously followed and plucked up."[18] While the court would reject Phillips's arguments, it did lay the words "all badges and incidents of slavery" onto how the Thirteenth Amendment would be interpreted, and also incorporated a temporal obligation to *prevent* slavery and involuntary servitude from establishing itself again. In Justice Harlan's dissent, this temporal obligation is expressed when he insists that "their [freedmen's] freedom necessarily involved immunity from, and protection against, all discrimination against them, because of their race."[19]

This temporal obligation interprets Section 2 to allow for "prophylactic" legislation "preventing the de facto reestablishment of slavery."[20] This should immediately strike us as running against the grain of contemporary progressive discourse about slavery, which is that it was never eradicated and so our task is to finish the abolition of slavery once and for all. This is the sentiment launched by demands to close the "loophole."

However, what if we assume that Section 1 did abolish one element of slavery—the legal status of black people as property—and that prophylactic legislation authorized by Section 2 is necessary to prevent this part of slavery from ever establishing itself again? That is, Section 2 perhaps casts abolition as a preventative modality of radical legal transformation. Section 2 in this light encourages us to continue to develop the meaning of "badges and incidents of slavery" that might be prohibited by the Thirteenth Amendment and, as well, to imagine living in such a way that prevents the future perpetuation of these "badges and incidents."

Invent associations and language that prevent the hold of anti-black signifiers and scenes by breaking them up into letters.

The prohibitory tone of the Thirteenth Amendment turns into a prophylactic one. *Prophylactic*: from the Greek *prophylaktikos*, meaning "precautionary," from *pro*, "before," and *phylattein*, "to watch over, to guard," but also to "cherish, keep, remain in, preserve."[21]

The Thirteenth Amendment creates the conditions within law for a consent motion to know and remain in what is the absence of slavery, and to create new precautionary, inoculative social axioms for what should and can never be.

Pamela Bridgewater's argument that the Thirteenth Amendment prohibits sexual and reproductive exploitation offers one of the most important interpretations in this regard, by reminding us that "while Congressional debates over the Thirteenth Amendment fell short of clearly delineating the precise conditions of slavery intended to be eradicated by the constitutional declaration[,] the degree of specificity and frequency that Congress mentioned reproductive and sexual abuse is on an equal footing with any other condition of slavery," and that "one of the first times the term 'badges and incidents' was used was in reference to infringements on family and natal relationships."[22]

Her singular contribution, which focuses on the unique status of enslaved women and the centrality of slave breeding for the political, economic, and psychological development of American modernity, makes possible an abolitionist approach to a contemporary politics of reproductive freedom grounded not simply on liberal theories of privacy and choice but on a radical critique of sex, the domestic slave trade, and colonial and imperial expansion. In other words, insofar as the Thirteenth Amendment's abolitionism challenged slavery as a political economy of breeding slaves, it can be articulated in the current moment as an injunction against the breeding of human life for purposes of extracting time from life.[23]

The Thirteenth Amendment's relative underdevelopment since its adoption has little to do with a historical acquiescence to its exception clause, or with whatever enforceable rights we should or should not derive from it. Rather, its underdevelopment has everything to do with the fact that US constitutional law hardly ever permits preventative legislation. This unique underdevelopment leaves it open to new interpretations that perhaps resist incorporation into the neoliberalization of racial politics. The subversive capacity contained in dividing its words is the practice of being in service to abolition as prophylaxis, from which deinstitutionalization, decarceration, and decriminalization grow as political campaigns.

Abolition is service to some thing before the advent of a Thirteenth Amendment that would unravel all law. Abolition is devotion to unexceptional taking of exception to both the state's rules of exception and those who object to the state with their own rules.

Abolition is what happens when American constitutional imperialism, with its compromises, equivocations, broken promises, and permanent military operations, is left untended, allowed to grow wild in the long shadow of reform, redevelopment, and reconstruction.

DMZ abolitionism: It's a mutual desire to (pre)serve before mutual assured destruction, before mutual aid. It's a "before" like *mu*, Section 2, all that which holds a before in what comes second.

Sight, rate, nature, thought, [illegible] is [illegible] for an entanglement of life, law, and letter from which the illusion of abolition appears, in a split-second movement, in a split Section 2.

頁 [lacuna] **24**

I take a second pass at the Thirteenth Amendment.

In my dream last night, I was stuck in a car, trying to evade being tased. The filaments of the Taser looped around the seat backs and through the open windows, trying to embed their darts in me. The terror of state violence came to me in an image of a Taser, more like a downed power line than a gun, circling and swerving back around toward me. The lines of the filaments looked like the drawing of yarn turning about two needles in a knitting instruction manual my daughter and I worked from the night before. Looping to paralyze, looping between the arms to hang a stitch, closing the loop, reforms upon reforms. And it was all I could do in the dream to keep myself, keep the target, moving. To stop moving, to allow the closing of the loop of electric shock, would have conceded arrest.

Movement keeps loops open, knots loose, practice provisional, life evasive.

Eleana Kim includes a map of avian flyways, conceptualizing them as "cartographies of the Anthropocene," in her discussion of the red-crowned crane and its traversal of the DMZ.[24] The crane's cartography emerges or coincides with contractually based transnational phenomena like commercial trade, human rights enforcement, war and democratization, and knowledge production. It is a picture of the litigious strategy to (fail to) close loopholes and their destruction of these global loops of avian movement.

But before fixing these massive flyways as zones of protection and surveillance, I would want to ask my dad how to articulate these intersecting loops into a topological formulation. What is the smooth surface of which these lines and their intersections are provisional glimpses?

The red-crowned crane, in hangul 두루미 (*durumi*), on the wrong side of the DMZ is not just, as they say, a canary in a coal mine. It is *parlêtre* of an unconscious that does not abide by the rules of the political, historical, or natural processes of Cold War late capitalism. *Durumi* is the common native Korean word for the red-crowned crane, while its more traditional name is

단정학 (*danjeonghak*), or, written in *hanja*, 丹頂鶴. The middle character of the *hanja* word, 頂, means "to carry on top of the head." It is a compound character, a part of which is the character 頁, which means "head" but would later additionally take on the meaning of "sheet or page of paper."

The page of paper carried by the *durumi* is a membrane, a reservoir, my father's notepad, of some revolution of the subject that loopingly arrives via the unwritten letters of some north-south flyway.

I think I continue to survive the madness of the COVID world because I had decided a year before fall 2020, the first quarter of fully remote teaching, that I would offer a graduate seminar on Angela Davis's writing and activism. I asked my students to bring a text, memory, artifact that represented their relationship to Angela Davis. Davis's passion appeared in my students' personal histories spanning Haiti, Pakistan, Angola Prison, Oakland, the United Nations, Rikers Island, China, Angel Island, Dallas airport, Bakersfield, Cleveland.

We pursued Davis's philosophy of abolition against the kind of average understanding promoted by the documentary *13th* and the popular book by Michelle Alexander, *The New Jim Crow: Mass Incarceration in the Age of Colorblindness*.[25] We were the cranes charting the flyways of Davis's thought.

Are Prisons Obsolete?, asks Davis in her 2003 collection of essays on prison abolition. This little book encapsulates a leading social commentary on mass incarceration by mobilizing various enduring radical political traditions that insist on an affirmative answer to what otherwise seemed, at the time, an absurd question.

At the core of the text is a historical narrative of the convict lease system as the successor to the racial institution of slavery, and a description of the transmutation of an institution based on the private right of the master into an institution based on the privatization of the public administration of criminal law. Given this narrative and the "parallels between the prison and slavery," Davis puts to us a challenge: "A productive exercise might consist in speculating about what the present might look like if slavery, or its successor, the convict lease system, had not been abolished."[26] The implication is that if we could imagine the horrors of a slavery never abolished, then in order to avoid such horror, we would be moved to abolish a slavery that in fact exists in the present as mass incarceration. The thought experiment invokes a supposed fictional present that looks similar to the one we in fact inhabit, and based on that mirroring, the ethical stance of abolitionism logically should extend across the different historical eras of racial domination. Historical narrative has a double function in a kind of negative telos of abolition: to deepen our political consciousness of the present as a function of slavery's unfinished abolition over time; and to counter this negative telos, displace the grip of a political pragmatics of prison reform in favor of a more radical ethics of abolitionism.

Something happens to this negative telos, though, when Davis articulates it with a legal demand. It's as if the historical periodization of slavery and abolition that abolitionism today relies on is yanked out from under our feet. In a transcribed interview Davis did with Amy Goodman just after Hurricane Katrina in 2006, Davis called for amnesty for the "prisoners of Katrina," identified in an NGO report to the United Nations Committee on the Elimination of Racial Discrimination as "those arrested during Katrina, for trying to take care of themselves and their loved ones, and those whose cases were impacted by the storm."[27]

In the course of her interview, Davis connects this legal demand for amnesty with a discussion of the Thirteenth Amendment. She begins:

> Now, we know that the 13th Amendment abolished slavery. Right? At least that's what—that's what they say. I just can't believe that we believed it. Like, one little statement in the—you know, in an amendment is going to abolish this huge, complicated institution.[28]

This opening of her discussion begins with a common critique of constitutional law: that the power of constitutional amendments, and federal rules that spring from them, more generally, does not adequately fit the enormous scale of social transformation necessary to fully materialize the law's universal principles. However, the next statement about the Thirteenth Amendment presents a problem that exceeds the logic of proportionality or scale that the initial critique assumes. She goes on:

> And the 13th Amendment doesn't even tell us what slavery is, so it doesn't even say what it abolished. It just says slavery and involuntary servitude. But slavery was a lot more than involuntary or coercive labor. You know, what are they talking about? Abolishing slavery as be-

> ing based on human property or being based on social death? Or being based on racism? 'Cause the racism is definitely still here. And the vestiges of slavery are definitely still here.[29]

Here, Davis exposes the false assumption of a common or legal understanding of the meaning of the word *slavery*. She neither attempts to define it in a historical sense nor proposes a contemporary meaning. She simply notes that the language of the law leaves the word *slavery* undefined in such a way that encountering this nondefinition provokes us to pose additional conceptual questions about "involuntary or coercive labor," "human property," "social death," "racism," and the "vestiges of slavery." Instead of a politics of interpretation that normalizes limiting a word's range of historical meanings, Davis opts for a word's legal nondefinition in order to open up a politics of interpreting various conceptual terms of the present.

Davis's Thirteenth Amendment is not frustrated. It is radically interpretable because of its honesty about what of it remains uninterpretable. Its meaning is not made impossible by ambiguity. Its meaning is possible by a protocol of suggestion and suggestibility.

> 쉬었다 가세요, 네?
> [won't you stay for a bit, yes?][30]

Rest on this: "I just can't believe that we believed it." Stay with this: "The 13th Amendment doesn't even tell us what slavery is, so it doesn't even say what it abolished."

What emerges after a belief in a literal interpretation of the Thirteenth Amendment is no longer desirable? After we are disabused of the social impact of a legal decree abolishing slavery? It is a kind of double take, a disbelief in belief: Is the Thirteenth Amendment law if it abolishes that which it does not or cannot define? If it is not law, then what is it?

The fog of the Thirteenth Amendment lifts, and we are left looking out over a lacuna. Prison abolition as a form of "epistemological rupture," within the changing same of legal reform and historical progress, reveals the cunning of reason and narrative.[31] And insofar as prison abolition becomes a form of *Aufklärung*, it risks establishing a new form of deception or belief that Davis's disbelief in our current moment momentarily shakes us from. The question is how to move with this disbelief, or a knowledge of the reality that not knowing is structural to any history of the present.

Again, here emerges the necessity of keeping the unknowingness of knowledge open, unfilled, unfulfilled.

Lacuna comes from the Latin *lacus*, meaning "lake," and *lacuna*, meaning "pool," which would later give us, from French and Italian, the English word *lagoon*. *Black's Law Dictionary* defines *lacuna* as "a ditch or dyke; a furrow for a drain; a gap or blank in writing."[32] *Lacuna* is also used in medicine, linguistics, music, mathematics, and geology to refer to absent parts, depressions, blanks, vacancies, and hiatuses.

Amnesty, as a legal remedy for the prisoners of Katrina, on Davis's view, is grounded in a nonunderstanding of the "slavery" to which the Thirteenth Amendment refers as its object of abolition. Davis's legal reasoning treats the Thirteenth Amendment as a lacuna and not, as popular discourse has labeled it, as a loophole. Davis's use of the word *slavery* reverses what we would assume to be concrete and without need for interpretation ("slavery"), on the one hand, and abstract and begging for interpretation ("shall [not] exist"), on the other.

For Davis, "slavery" is the elusive legal reference in the amendment, and what is concrete about it, in the wake of devastation, is that it marks an absence. This is what her disbelief at having believed marks. As if echoing Senator Lyman Trumbull, one of the coauthors of the Thirteenth Amendment, who observed during the 1866 congressional debates that "it is difficult . . . to define accurately what slavery is and what liberty is," Davis's legal praxis critically pauses on this difficulty and emphasizes how the reference to "slavery" in the amendment marks a fundamental blankness immanent to US constitutional law.[33]

We should think about this lacuna, rather than fill it in or close it up with sentimental notions of law's unkept promises or indignant watchdog politics. Davis's is a legal theory of abolition that expands our understanding of law by referring to slavery as that which has not been or cannot be defined by law, rather than reproducing the law's authoritarian fantasies of how we, others, and it should not be allowed to get away with things. And this is so despite her appearance in DuVernay's documentary.

What happens when Davis's lacunate Thirteenth Amendment is extended into contemporary critiques of law and mass incarceration? Instead of a neoliberal abolitionist critique of the Thirteenth Amendment as a loophole, what critiques emerge from the lacunae that render abolition unachievable because, as Davis's revelation reveals, slavery and freedom are not opposed conditions?

Prison abolition sounds like a consent motion in these flyway zones.

흑흑 [hook] **25**

> She closes her eyes, mother, inside a dream
> This, you, dear one, thrown out like trash
> Feeling the sobs [흑흑 느껴], she cries until morning.[34]

흑흑, *heuk heuk*, is the Korean onomatopoeia for the sound of sobbing. The hangul word 흑 is derived from the Middle Korean word originally spelled as 흙, meaning "earth" and "soil"; and also carries the *hanja* root, 黑, meaning "black." This conjoining of sorrow, sobbing, soil, and blackness as the unconscious materialization of that which a mother spills when she can't sustain the life of her child, and what she imparts in her very departure on birth, is a surreptitious repetition that blackness echoes across a global topology between English and Korean in the sound *heuk heuk*.

Dreams allow us to know the unconscious, here, in what it is to feel sobbing. It doesn't cry. But we cry while we sleep and are spoken to by our lost mothers. On their last breaths, even so, they hold us, or we hold them, in some shared destiny to be dumped somewhere as refuse. The movement to abolish one aspect of this destiny—the prison specifically, and the many cities' many dark alleys—benefits from Davis's suggestive and suggestible Thirteenth Amendment, precisely because it produces a kind of hall-of-mirrors effect where there is an absence of legal meaning (of slavery) and an absence of psychic meaning (of maternity).

Fred Moten might refer to this as the "sur-repetition" of a radical black political imaginary present if not apparent in and because of the violence of law, history, and language.

The maternal sonic ecology of 흑흑, *heuk heuk*, is a musical hook, effracting. Some might hear it as a sign of wretchedness. But no one can tell me it doesn't get you the way the poetics of the *h*-sound (ㅎ) is like breath hovering over the earth's soil (—), as if unbreakable, as if of an endless looping over the buried *g*-sound (ㄱ) that reaches for something deep within.

Cut the unclosed loop, and it's a hook by which we hang on to a radical and unceasing opening of the law of refuse and refusal.

The idea of closing the loophole, of pulling the rope taut, finally is rendered as a seductive, but wholly unnecessary, inconvenience compared to the satisfaction of just cutting the trace loose. So we arrive here at rendering the Thirteenth Amendment as the trace it is.

38 [NL] **26**

A lacuna is a real legal phenomenon in international law. It describes a set of circumstances in which "the absence of suitable law, the vagueness or ambiguity of rules, inconsistencies in law, or the injustice of the legal consequences" permit judges to refuse rendering judgment.[35] It is denoted as NL, which stands for the Roman legal concept of *non liquet*, meaning "not clear."

NL, en el, 이날, *inal*, (f)inal, on this day, we celebrate by working on the function of nonfinality in law given in the possibility of No-Law, of exhaustive abstention from justice, of decisions that unravel and undo the closure of thought, judgment, sentence, pronunciation, jurisdiction, and reason.[36]

International law has a jurisprudence of self limiting authority that recognizes that rendering judgment or handing down a sentence is not inevitable or the only possible conclusion of a case. In international law's political imagination, law is not always relevant to a given dispute and does not always need to exercise its power because some disputes are not clear either factually or morally. Judicial abstention, though rare, is sometimes necessary and pushes against the pervasive assumption that a judge must render justice.

This is especially so in "use of force" jurisprudence, developed primarily from Article 2(4) of United Nations Charter, which since 1945 has prohibited "the threat or use of force against the territorial integrity or political independence of any state" and delegates to the Security Council a collective decision-making process for deciding when and to what degree nondefensive uses of force are warranted.[37] Between the self-defense exception for initiating war, an ideologically divided Security Council, and the displacement of international conflict into internal or regional conflicts, the charter did not have any real effect during the Cold War.

In fact, the Security Council has achieved consensus to authorize military use of force in response to one nation's attack on another only two times over the course of its history. The first was on June 27, 1950, when it adopted a resolution recommending that members of the United Nations assist South Korea to defend itself against North Korea and restore "peace" on the peninsula. The Soviet Union, which backed communist North Korea, was not present to veto this resolution because, at the time, it was boycotting the United Nations for failing to replace Taiwan with a seat for the People's Republic of China. This began the Korean War, led by the United States, which ended in an armistice signed on July 27, 1953, by the United States (representing the United Nations), North Korea, and China. The DMZ was created at this time, refortifying the 38th-parallel border between the two Koreas.

A peace treaty still has not been made to bring the Korean War to a formal end. One might say that the Korean Armistice Agreement and the physical geography of the DMZ mark a loophole to the law of war. Maybe it is more of a loose end. In either case, though, it remains from a Cold War era many presumed over when the Berlin Wall fell in 1989. Insofar as the armistice is a refusal to continue to let war judge whether the reunification of Korea would be under North or South Korean terms, it is a lacuna. It is a border that marks the gap or gulf of reconciliation between war and peace, communism and capitalism, postcolonial self-determination and international humanitarianism.

The DMZ, a lake of pine and the mythical possibility of the return of the tiger, always knew about mutual assured destruction as colonialism's general condition.

The DMZ is a global political ecological non liquet: 38^{nl}. This barely apparent borderland reminds us of the evergreenness of the Thirteenth Amendment as promise.

The DMZ precedes the Cold War logic of the war on crime, the war on drugs, the war on terror, all wars by means other than formal, legal uses of force. Our political rhetoric should expand our understanding of the non liquet as a form of nonjudgment the law has always had recourse to and continues to assert with its hesitancies. Stop worrying about how we or it gets away with things and jump into Lake NL.

The central case in modern international law that demonstrates the legitimate though controversial use of non liquet is an advisory opinion from the International Court of Justice (ICJ) in 1996 on the *Legality of the Threat or Use of Nuclear Weapons*. On the request of the United Nations General Assembly, the ICJ took up the question of whether international law permits the threat or use of nuclear weapons in any circumstances. In a 7–7 vote, the ICJ held that it "[could not] conclude definitively whether the threat or use of nuclear weapons would be lawful or unlawful in an extreme circumstance of self-defense, in which the very survival of a State would be at stake."[38] Judges who voted against the holding to not render judgment thought the court either did not go far enough in its suggestion that the threat or use of nuclear weapons in self-defense would be illegal under principles of humanitarian law, or went too far with this suggestion.

The US judge, for example, argued that the threat of a nuclear attack on Iraq deterred its use of chemical weapons on the eve of Desert Storm and thus complied with principles of humanitarian law to deter violence and death. The Sri Lankan judge, however, argued that the nature of a nuclear response is beyond an analysis of proportionate violence and thus beyond anything that humanitarian law might regulate and prohibit. "With nuclear war, the quality of measurability ceases. Total devastation admits of no scales of measurement. We are in a territory where the principle of proportionality becomes devoid of meaning."[39]

There are two kinds of clarity that emerge in these two positions on the non liquet of the ICJ's decision. One is that a deterrent logic for the necessity of developing, possessing, and using (or threatening to use) nuclear weapons is set up to prevail and justify military buildup because a "global Armageddon" has not come to pass.[40] The other is that the mere existence of nuclear weapons is "a risk which no legal system can sanction" because their use (or threatened use) creates conditions beyond legal reason's capacity to regulate.[41]

The ICJ's non liquet allows us to see the false choice in these nuclear times, or in a context of cataclysmic violence, between brinkmanship and complete disarmament, both of which have paradoxical effects in reality because of the United States' imperial relation to the developing world and the United Nations.

This NL, *nuclear liquet*, and the choices that justify nonjudgment of an issue before the law underlie all radical positions derived in the aftermath of cataclysmic violence from which there can be no return to the same or to the past. If there are to be movements beyond the alternatives of brinkmanship and disarmament, then armistice must be approached as its own place and time.

A place and time of somewhere north of wherever we might be, whose existence as unknowable is the very reason one looks and listens for any sign of life sent from that side of the wall.

The shapes of 3 and 8 are not examples of open (3) and closed (8) loops. They together are a hole given in a compound ideograph for an un(dis)closed outdoors in which we discover infinite ways to abstain from the United States' militarized zones. The 38th parallel is just one ribbon among 38^{nl} ribbons of time that unfurl across the earth on an endless wind.

jong jong hudoong hudoong
dool dool neureet neureet a-ah
break brighter nari nari
inal inal break break a-ah[42]

3 [pro-(un)freedom imperialism] 27

The shapes of the numerals 13 and 38 each contain the contour of openness: 3. Their shared partiality reminds me that every mark is a piece, a fragment, of the desire that moved something to make it.

What kind of political ecological non liquet is the Thirteenth Amendment? What kind of armistice is the Thirteenth Amendment?

In *River of Dark Dreams: Slavery and Empire in the Cotton Kingdom*, Walter Johnson tells a history of what he calls a "pro-slavery imperialism" that emerged in the mid-nineteenth-century South right before the Civil War.[43] Enslavement was a way to reduce human life to a form of investment capital, but it also made it impossible for planters to liquidate, lay off, or abandon this capital in response to financial crises. "Their capital," writes Johnson, "would not simply rust or lie fallow. It would starve. It would steal. It would revolt."[44]

Slaves were not immediately incorporable into new or reformed modes of production. So "[planters] were caught between unsustainable expansion and unspeakable fear: the fear of the fire next time—of Toussaint L'Ouverture, of Charles Deslandes, of Denmark Vesey, of Nat Turner, of Madison Washington."[45] It was in this context that slaveholders set their eyes on expanding globally, which would require Southern secession from the Union, and the South's independence from what it perceived as a compromised colonial relationship with the North. These global dimensions for a pro-slavery imperialism were already outlined in W. E. B. Du Bois's first study, *The Suppression of the African Slave-Trade to the United States of America, 1638–1870* (1896). There he documents how, despite the United States' resounding condemnation of the slave trade as a form of piracy, it refused to join the international effort to abolish the slave trade by signing on to Britain's Right of Search Treaty. As a result,

> the traffic thus carried on floated under the flags of France, Spain, and Portugal, until about 1830; from 1830 to 1840 it began gradually to assume the United States flag; by 1845, a large part of the trade was under the stars and stripes; by 1850 fully one-half the trade, and in the decade, 1850–1860 nearly all the traffic, found this flag its best protection.[46]

In fact, the United States did not join that treaty until two years into the Civil War.

The Thirteenth Amendment as armistice was not only a ceasefire between Northern and Southern ideologies and political economic ways of life within the United States. It was also a ceasefire between slave-trading piracy and legitimate international commerce. It divided the territory of black life between that which was and is unincorporable in international trade and that which is necessary to develop and reproduce what we might refer to as a "pro-(un)freedom imperialism." Every act of enforcing freedom throughout the world and within the settler US republic was and is the imposition of the Thirteenth Amendment as a mark of demilitarized, pacified black life.

The Thirteenth Amendment as armistice is the demilitarization of a war over and with uncapitalizable life. Every reference around the globe to the antebellum US Constitution as a sign of freedom transmits a spooky peace enforced by a liberal social order. The institutional development and militarization of local and federal police agencies since the Civil War is just one element of a Cold War logic of stockpiling subjects of (un)freedom on either side of the Thirteenth Amendment as a demilitarized zone.

This zone cuts across the prison space, just as it does every other space associated with the "free world." It cuts the way sound cuts the image of the Cook County Jail wall in Maria Gaspar's sound/video piece *On the Border of What Is Formless and Monstrous* (2016).[47] As our sight is dragged along a wall, the composite sounds of the jail's insides and outside remind us that it is ultimately impossible to distinguish ourselves from others on the other side of the wall. The uncanniness of the sounds of entangled lives, streaming background noise, and ambiguous placement is produced as the afterlife of some division. Vision is forced to work harder, to see differently. And the grayness of the wall starts to differentiate into the tones of weathered concrete and different hues of gray paint used to cover over what we can only assume to be graffiti art. The marks of time by moisture and rust fall vertically from the top of the wall, and fall short of, and never seem capable of touching, the voided remnants of writing hovering in the lower third of the frame. The height of the wall is an injunction on traversing horizontal and vertical coordination. Water and paint can't touch. Prisoner and outsider can't touch. Desire and history can't touch either. And in that prohibition, state violence takes place, occupies space, everywhere.

The concept of armistitial space, impervious to time, appears. This demilitarized occupation of grayness is so unmitigated, unreserved, even acting like we're neighbors, talking and sharing and making, creates a spooky sound you can hear anywhere if you listen for it.

As if to mitigate this spooky sound, there always seem to be carnivals on the (un)free side of the armistice border. Nothing was as obscene as the small amusement park, complete with a Ferris wheel, at the DMZ when I visited Korea in the summer of 2019.

Meanwhile, the (un)free side of armistitial space thinks. If they only knew we don't want to know about their plastic, neon games. Fuck your fun.

Hear where we begin and stay where the sounds mingle and echo? Can you stand it? Or do we just break, waiting in the drop of that pause right before the beat, down, as matter+1 breaks into some tone we can't even call noncompliance because compliance is so total.

Because compliance is so tonal.

Break, day, repeat. ma+ter+ı, to+al. Repeat, listen, repeat. ma++er+ı, +o+al. Hear the +one.

라 [no way of knowing] **28**

My daughter and father are both Aquarians, born four days apart in the month of February, and born in the lunar year of the cow. She is him, five twelve-year cycles of Jupiter around the earth later, a sixty-year-old return.

Newborn infants don't usually cry actual tears, but my daughter did the very moment she took her first breaths of air. The nurses thought them miraculous, when it was really that she was born with lachrymal glands ready to work. Some transindividuated continuity of organismal life was already at work. This clarity is shed in the form of drops where suffering and tenderness are one. She is lachrymist reincarnate, a lachrymose lacuna.

Lachrymal: from the Medieval Latin word *lacrimalis*, meaning "that produces tears" and "worthy of tears, pitiful, mournful, lamentable."[48] The French word for *tear* is *larme*, in Spanish it is *lagrima*, and in Korean, 눈물, *nunmul*.

The Korean word for *tear* does not have an easily identifiable *hanja* character. The Korean word is a compound noun, eye + water, and corresponds to a simplified Chinese compound character 泪 that I can't seem to find in my Korean dictionary. Its traditional version 淚, takes us into a whole other world of association, with its ideogrammic and phonetic combination of water, door or home, and even a dog trapped within.[49]

There is something about the transitive and intransitive nature of the thing, a tear, or tears, and the action, to cry, to weep, that creates a sinkhole in these layered dictionaries open all around me.

This dog's Buddha nature, too, is *mu*.

The English, Korean, and Chinese interplay among writing, saying, and uttering the word *tear*, it seems to me, retains what is lost with the grammatical rules of the English sentence that send one off into the baroque world of Latin when one really thinks about the capacity to *tear*. Contained in Korean hangul and the spokenness of language is a reminder of the poetic calligraphic representation of crying: water's movement, rivers, the eye, its partial openness or closedness, a circle that depicts an emptiness that sees, a dog, *mu* dog, *mudang*.

I find myself in an upheaval of glyphs and homophones given in any mark that stills judgment:

la　泪　cry　淚　ma (na)ra　ul ji　ma　hannamununmulullinda

"She fell back into her eyes," Frank Wilderson recalls in *Afropessimism* of his last moments with his dying mother.[50] She would no longer be the object that held the place of an object cause of desire. His mother's fading eyes mark the gaze, what Lacan would develop as a partial object, that "reflects our own nothingness, in the figure of the death's head."[51] She also, Wilderson recounts, "asked me who I was."[52]

The mother's enigmatic question—who are you?—captures something general about maternal (mis)recognition. Unknowability appears between Wilderson and his mother in this specific form of (mis)recognition as *blankness*. As he loses his mother as an object, structural lack as cause of desire emerges as a reminder that it is precisely the unknowability of our object causes of desire that compels us to desire desire.

The feeling of a surreptitious, militant figure is dying in the body of his mother, within whom, Wilderson discovers, his lack had always been held. For with her dies the object against which he rebelled and which fueled his political desire. As if knowing this, in the wake of this loss, and in answer to her question about who he is, Wilderson recalls that because she taught him to "want to write," he might find another way to desire desire.[53]

". . . you told me to write what I know."[54] This confluence of writing and knowing, as Wilderson would report back to his mother some thirty years later, "makes us worthy of our suffering."[55] Writing is one way to confront how suffering is produced not only with violence but also with desire. I understand Wilderson here to be remarking on writing as a way through and toward a nothingness that symbolic discourse holds. Beyond challenging the violence of the desires of white people and their junior partners, writing is a way to do something else with unconscious defenses against risking and giving up the imaginary grip of beingness. What is ultimately narrated in *Afropessimism* for me is writing, and how writing—which takes as its topic rebellion, which performs rebelliousness itself, and which preserves the thing rebelled against—is indebted to a certain maternity.

Wilderson renders, here, what happens, or can happen, when asked by your mother some version of this question of who you are. It cuts but does not castrate. It transmits a desire for what is unknowable in even the most intimate, naturalized, and seemingly unchangeable circumstances of life witnessed between mother and child.

And receiving this (mis)recognition of unknowability from his mother, Wilderson in turn asks, "Where was she, the woman who made me want to write?"[56] Their gaze is an internecine armistitiality forged where writing and knowing, living and dying, and grief and politics meet to reveal they had always been already and incompletely each other. Revolutionary desire *as* writing is always walking the line between disappearing into the imaginary or bungling its way through the symbolic, all the while wielding the fantasy of murdering and maligning the enslaving Other. It is how the mother's general law, or a first-order principle, is encrypted in his body: "Didn't I tell you, boy, people have to die? I know I told you that."[57]

But what of what Lacan refers to as the "real-of-the-structure" in the Woman, the mother?[58] How are her desires transmitted to the child, who insists that she was the one who made him want to write? Whose desire is this to desire to write his desire and produce a story about how obeying the rules of revolutionary freedom struggle requires constant preparation with others to bring the unknowable into the world?

The women who birth and raise revolutionaries transmit something essential about obedience and dying as they put these children to bed at night and wake them in the morning.

This essential something is a rule: write to desire desire. While Wilderson has critiqued the notion of "full speech" in psychoanalysis, this critique opens onto the question, for me, of what Lacan calls the "well-spoken" (*bien-dire*).[59] The "well-spoken" is the saying of a half-truth that holds on to the Real of the body.[60] The *bien-dire* of Afro pessimism is what you can come to write about in that interval where being subjected to, or enslaved to, desire turns into desiring to know the unknowable cause of desire unconsciously written through the body in service to black liberation.

Why does the helicopter shake the window?
Why are you pulling down the blinds
and reading such an anti-play as the *Ohio Impromptu*?
. . .
Ch'an-u, Yŏng-ja, Mi-kyŏng, Ch'ung-nyŏl
are all solving a strange math equation.[61]

What uncanny math equation does Afro-pessimism provoke from within the black radical textual tradition that causes so many to want to disavow the writtenness, and thus openness, of the idea of Afro-pessimism?

Perhaps it is the repetition of the insurgent's perennial and futile work of creating liberated zones of thought and life. But this time around, with Afro-pessimism, we submit our bodies to theory in order to expose the Real in the mess of symbolic and imaginary desire rendered in writing. This is the unconscious in an armistitial zone. By this, I do not mean that the unconscious can be analyzed to distribute the capacity to enjoy and be happy more widely if we could only divide and separate the objects of political desire from all other forms of being subject to desire as the desire of the Other. I mean presencing the body traversing the border between the imaginary and the symbolic so that our experience of signifiers stuck in a repetitious, regulated crossing of this border can encounter each other as Other and allow the surprise of some other form of crossing: a crossing over into unknown knowing.

Amnesty for the blackness of all things that bear the armistitial state of a world on the brink.

the sur-round

門 [mass] **29**

1984: North County Jail must have just been constructed when my father pointed it out as we drove past it on Interstate 980 (figure 5.1). "That's where the police lock people up," he said.

5.1 North County Jail, Oakland, California, 2020. Photo by author.

Also that year, Ronald Reagan was running for US president. The spread of AIDS/HIV had just reached epidemic levels. Chun Doo-hwan, waging a cold war with the other Korea on the north side of the 38th parallel, gassed and gunned down popular uprisings against his puppet presidency. Tina Turner received a Grammy that year for "What's Love Got to Do with It?" And I was in first grade.

I fixated on the oddly slim windows. I was sure that I saw a figure looking out from one of them.

The geometry of the building's purpose appeared straightforward. The frame of the person detained within must be wider than the width of the window, whether the person faced forward (looking out at our car whizzing by on the freeway below) or to the side (as some of the profiles appeared to me in the other windows). What else would keep that life from bursting through the bulletproof glass and returning to us, like rivulets of water running toward the San Francisco Bay?

As I looked through my father's eyes, North County Jail rose up from the urban landscape to appear, momentarily and maybe even eternally, as a place where the rectangular framing off, just so, of unceasing life violated another order of things that I would later come to understand through the unique international terrain of black freedom struggle in the Bay Area.[1]

The swerve of driving toward and then away from that building would serve as a daily reminder that the United States, not our souls or our mere living, was the true aberration. He never missed a chance to denounce the United States by referring to it as the "police of the world" and, by this very denunciation, demanding thought: Imagine ourselves without it? Imagine ourselves colluding against it? Imagine ourselves refusing the strange border it polices everywhere?

The sense of such wishing, the goodness of such questioning, was as unassailable as it was obvious to my seven-year-old mind.

This geography lesson in state violence was the first of many my father taught me as he drove us around the East Bay. The cruelty of geometry in service of North County Jail's architectural strangeness could be felt and critiqued from any point on the messy weave of streets, highways, and sidewalks surrounding this locus of unfreedom. Reflecting now on what it first felt like to existentially reject such cruelty, I realize that the place I grew up in was a sort of parallax panopticon.

. . . the prisoner, my neighbor, at the center of the city, captive looking out, knew something; and I, in movement, locked in a secret promise of liberation, no matter how unknowable the path, belonged in this blurry swerve (figure 5.2). I and the Other came into being in the blackness of these bulletproof windows.

The Korean word for "window" is 창문, *changmun*, or, written in *hanja*, 窓門.

The *hanja* 窓, *chang*, is a variant form of the Chinese character 窗 and generally means "window." The latter character depicts a window in a house,

5.2 North County Jail, Oakland, California, 2020. Photo by author.

while the *hanja* variant curiously captures the image of a window with bars. The *hanja* is also a compound of 宊, an ancient form of 容, which means "to hold, contain, tolerate, stand" and "facial appearance, looks."[2] I discover that 容 is also the *hanja* character for 용, *yong*, meaning "face; contain." The other part of the compound is 心, *shim*, the pictogram for a heart, meaning "heart, mind, thought, idea, center, core" in Chinese. As a *hanja* character, it also means "heart, feeling, emotion."

The first syllable of the Korean word in hangul and *hanja* associates the meaning of window with a frame or a structure that holds something essential. It suggests a core something contained within, perhaps perceivable or knowable through, the window. Windows mark a structure's interiority, beg the question of what this structure holds, contains, tolerates even. Windows give an expression or face to this structure, whether built or natural.

The second syllable of the Korean word in *hanja*, 門, *mun*, means "gate, door, gateway, portal." It is a pictogram for a gate and has many meanings in Chinese, including "valve or switch," "way of doing something," "family, school of thought, tradition," and "class or category." It is used not only as a noun but as a classifier for three categories of nouns, including "lessons, subjects, branches of technology, languages"; "livelihoods, trades, skills, businesses"; and "thoughts, ideas, or emotions, particularly those forming a system or complex."[3]

I learn that most languages have mass classifiers. These are words that indicate a measurement of nouns denoting something that cannot be counted.

Mass nouns in English are nouns that lack a plural in ordinary usage and are not used with the indefinite article. For example, we say "nine sheets of glass" and not "nine glasses" when discussing glass as a substance.

I wonder how this grammatical notion of mass might inflect another understanding of *mass incarceration*? Does this suggest, in addition to the now-common understanding of the term, that *incarceration* is a mass noun? Can it refer to a thing that is indivisible as a form, and if so, what is indivisible about it? Is there something about the state of confinement or the substance of punishment through confinement that is uncountable, indivisible, nonsingle?

As water, in rivulets. Or air, in gusts. Or time, in memories.

I hear those windows, or whatever essential is on the inside of their enigmatic transparency, sound a warning. Do not be deceived by the term *mass incarceration* as a function of the countability of lives. Do not exchange the source of our sense of injustice for the reduction of the term *mass incarceration* to the astounding number of people behind bars or under state surveillance. Life, as a category of noun that brushes up against those categories of Chinese nouns, like language, skills, or ideas, is not yet another countable substance. Life refers to an element beyond counting, no matter how accustomed we are to ascribing age to its individuated form.

Contenting ourselves to imagine and analyze mass incarceration as a problem of scale determined by the number of human beings inside, or the number of dollars spent on locking them up, is like a daylight robbery that reveals how grossly we had underestimated the fantasy of proportionality and the so-called enlightenment of our society as fundamental to punishment.[4] We delude ourselves if we continue to think that political conscience can be mobilized, and the anti-blackness that is often its consequence purged, through reasoned debate and dissemination of facts and testimony.

Mass incarceration cannot be abolished by reason because it is the effect of reason. Get off that train. Those windows stubbornly look out at us. Like a poem's words on the page.

Regarding their darkness, 門 is a doing that is itself a portal to the thought and language of the anumericity of life and its loss.

2020: We are in the midst of a pandemic that weighs down at every imaginable register of living. My father is dying of late-stage stomach cancer, and the people of Oakland light up the streets every night with fireworks demanding justice for George Floyd.

He watches the signals every day on TV. All normalcy has been upended, at the same time that the place death and dying occupy in real time is merely revealed to have always been there. We were neither in the beginning stage of the end nor in the end stages of some new beginning. We were, are, in some interminable middle part of some centuries-long, or months-long, weeks-long, or even minutes-long politicized natural disaster: slavery and colonialism, Trumpist white nationalism, cancer, chronic illness, and exhaustion. Every tragedy, every loss, my father taught me, was a chance to shit on the seductions of the naturalized political disaster of capitalism and American empire.

Our job, our principle, is to stay ready to see and reject the crown ring around a genetic structure, the cold gold badge adorning a blue shirt, the walk of they who always need to be, laying claim to this or that.

Go out and find so many different ways of destroying the crown, the badge, the self-preservationism, all of it (figure 5.3).

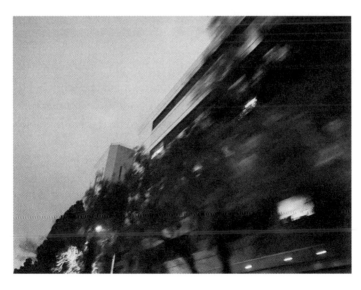

5.3 North County Jail, Oakland, California, 2020. Photo by author.

He loved smashing things, in all manner of ways, and especially all those social insignias of the United States' right to exist.

t^h [hollow] 30

Magic is art outdoors. People came outdoors on the westside, neither in Oakland's commercial downtown nor in its residential hills and flatlands, but in our city's industrial zone, to make things with fire. It was where I would drive my daughter during this summer of total 20/20 liminality. Outdoors, we were protected from the virus's omnipotent cloud and found haven for the flesh from the burn of each day that brought us closer to losing my father.

She melted glass, baked clay, welded silver. In one of the hottest summers recorded in California's history, this young woman created her own searing vortex of shiny objects. None of them were particularly useful or conceptually creative. But she could tell you where and how heat and fire did their work. Fire transformed the color of glass, fused the many parts into a non–a priori one, entwined crystals with each other. The objects were animate light affixable to living beings. Raw heat glowed from some place other than the sheen, shimmer, and glistening of glazes and glass. We know she had visited this elsewhere because she knew nothing of the cuts that sprinkling frit left on her fingers, except that they were there.

The drive home after dropping my daughter off would take me under the I-980 and I-880 interchange, right where Old Oakland and the Acorn Industrial area meet on Seventh Street. The first time I made this drive that summer, I was turned awry by how these two highways and their columns framed the jail. The angle's pedagogy was completely new to me. From below I-980, its noxious beige architectural power seemed perfectly framed, just so

From this point of view (figure 5.4), the odd verticality of the windows marked again its function, but this time as a post–civil rights "super jail."[5] This is how it was described by the Alameda County Sheriff's Department when it neared completion in the spring of 1984. With more "comfortable living quarters" compared to the then overcrowded and "creaking" Santa Rita Jail in Pleasanton, North County Jail was part of a wave of "new-generation"

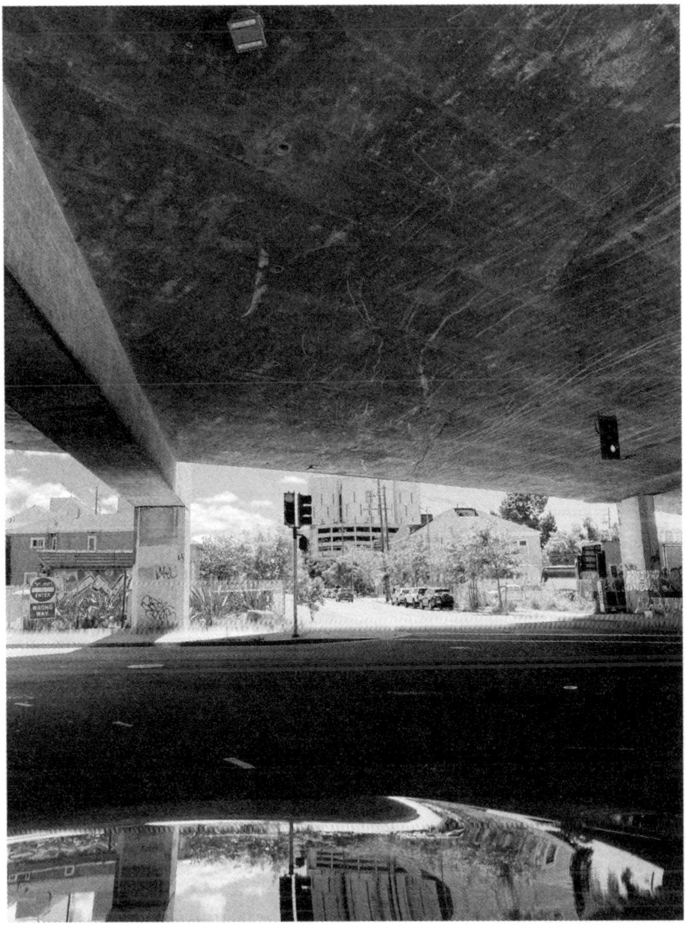

5.4 North County Jail, Oakland, California, 2020. Photo by author.

jails built in consultation with the National Institute of Corrections. Three years earlier, Contra Costa County, northeast of Alameda, was the first in the country to build a new-generation jail in Martinez. And the National Institute of Corrections would publish its *Jail Design Guide: A Resource for Small and Medium-Sized Jails* in 1988, with updated editions published in 1998 and then again in 2011.[6]

This new-generation jail is distinct from preceding, more well-known designs in the history of the prison in the United States: the Benthamite Stateville Correctional Center in Illinois, the "radial plan" of Eastern Penitentiary in Pennsylvania, or the "telephone pole" design of Soledad Prison in California. The new-generation jail's *direct supervision* model foregrounds bureaucratic risk management, favoring rehabilitative punishment after the dramatic failures of mid-twentieth-century "medical" approaches. It heralded a new era of jail construction, which standardized operational efficiencies codified by, for example, the American Correctional Association's accreditation procedures, established after the 1967 report of President Lyndon Johnson's Commission on Law Enforcement and Administration of Justice.[7]

Oakland's North County Jail might have been the first of this new generation, but for delays caused by issues with the concrete in early phases of construction.[8]

Indeed, there is a pause built into every new era of prison reform that compromises its very foundation.

Most know Harry Weese as the architect for the Washington, DC, metro system, but he has a more nefarious aesthetic urban imprint. He was also the architect for the Metropolitan Correctional Center in downtown Chicago (1971–75). At a glance, one might mistake it for the North County Jail because, again, those slim, vertical windows hold your gaze. No public institution or function, including punishment and incarceration, is spared the postwar vision of a modern architecture promising public regeneration, economic utility, and humanitarianism.

The scale of the high-rise city jail works at the level of the "office building and castle keep, banal and yet still unnerving."[9] The vertical movement of bodies in these buildings suggests modes of urban white-collar work, or at least the possibility of work at some point in the future. One cannot imagine a view from the top that is not inspired or inspiring just enough to work on a self for capital. This is served environmentally by filtered light, hygiene, and routine interaction between prisoners and guards.

The foregrounding of raw materials—cement, steel, glass, brick—by the brutalist aesthetic of both the Chicago and Oakland jails suggests a frugal yet humane approach to meeting social needs. Its aesthetic ecology blends people and things into some weird fraternal order between people and things. People live in cells, just as cars wait in a parking lot, civil servants huddle over desks in their cubicles, and motorists drive along at some reasonable speed on the right side of the road.

The windows suggest that what happens inside is the ordering of sociality into individuated spaces of equal and uniform expenditures of personal time, either to earn a wage or to pay a debt to society. Indeed, Ben Weese, Harry Weese's brother, notes that the Chicago jail evokes "La Tourette on its end."[10] This is a reference to Le Corbusier's final building near Lyon, France, Sainte Marie de La Tourette (1953–61), designed as a monastery for Dominican friars.[11] Turned "on its end," each of La Tourette's dormitory horizontal slit windows would run vertically like those of the Chicago and Oakland jails.

Angela Davis wrote in her autobiography that "walls turned sideways are bridges."[12] But insofar as those walls have windows, brutalism tells us that a mere ninety-degree turn differentiates punitive from divine reformism. Each is the other's reflection on two surfaces that meet on a perpendicular line.

North County Jail is a physically built argument in support of both professionalizing corrections as a growing sector of employment in the war on crime and performing a democratic concern for the humanity of prisoners. Design would literally build bridges between various municipal buildings, between communities within a city or a county, and between guards and prisoners. Pods and clusters would spatially obviate the off-trend necessity of bars, solitary cells, and barriers of all sorts to maintain order within.

Architects have designed death chambers and psychological torture cells.[13] But North County Jail reminds us that they continue this death work by designing terminals of indefinite and permanent detention feeding into a massive administrative system of corrections, bringing us back full circle to "rights-focused design agendas" and Le Corbusier's ever-promising clerestory windows.[14] Windows are expensive, but if human rights require them, then they are a necessary design and construction expense, whose expenditure distracts from the fact that jails jail.

I asked my mother the other day whether the Korean word 창문, *changmun*, refers specifically to a window that opens. Is it an operational window? If so, *changmun* would not be the word for North County Jail's clerestory descendants, which offer a view but no air, no exit, no entry. She didn't know, except that she only ever uses the word to ask someone to open or close one. It strikes me that nonopening windows are for either the condemned or the wealthy, while in this vernacular memory of mine, *changmun* is associated with a window's ventilating, connecting function.

Punishment deoperationalizes the subject, just as its architecture deoperationalizes its windows.

The ever-pervasive, and thus most mundane, type of window is the *casement* window. It is standard for residential dwellings and refers to the encasement of the glass by a frame. Encasement, contain, container, 통, *tong*. In whatever reservoir of meaning Korean contains, for me, 통 surfaces as the word closest to the meaning of "container." 통 (桶) is the word for a cylindrical container, and more precisely means "barrel, bucket, cask, pail, vat," but is also used colloquially in compounds to refer to container-like body parts, like the chest or torso.[15]

통 is a homophone as well, meaning "pain" (痛). The two *hanja* characters associated with *tong* are differentiated by their radicals, the marks added to the phonetic reference 甬. The radical for *tong* as "barrel" (木) is a pictogram referring to "wood," and the radical for *tong* as "pain" (疒) is a pictogram referring to "a bed or stretcher for the sick."

These radicals cut the meaning of the place, as if first letters, like the first letter of *tong*, the consonant *t*, or the hangul letter ㅌ, called a *tieut*. Its sound is denoted [tʰ].

What line of historical movement captures this string of tʰ? From barrel to pain, from wood to bed, from formless substance to disease?

It is the movement of this body, this hollow body, specifically, where something resonates as another way to know in the coronal sound of the ㅌ.

SHV [zoetropic drive] **31**

Tong. Tongue.

The *tieut* is a letter created by placing an extra horizontal stroke in the middle of the two horizontal strokes of the *digeut*, the name of the hangul letter ㄷ, which corresponds to the English consonant *d*.

Strokes instruct the tongue. The tongue accords. Hollows sound.

5.5 North County Jail, Oakland, California, 2020. Photo by author.

Case, consent, accord, record. Marks move us in some enigmatic windowed syncopation (figure 5.5). It is the beat of the Möbius movements of the panopticon.

Each dark window installs us in relation to the captive who looks out to some outside of the history of the panopticon, and whatever panopticism presumes it can know everything about, while they, which is to say, we, do not. To suspend this presumption of panopticism is to suspend what we presume we do and do not know.

This is not unlike that form of suspension necessary to sprinkle frit, to engage in making and thinking with a certain not-knowing of both the tiny cuts frit leaves on our fingers but, as well, the wounds left on our psyches when we drive by these buildings of suffering. Suspended like this, there is a chance to know something else.

The photographic act of freezing time captures a reflection of myself (figure 5.6). It is a felicitous suspension of whatever is the "I" that tricks me into having a self. The image is a surprise occasion to return to some space between the now of a photo and some memory propelling me outside to take a drive in the city of my childhood. The unsayable places and times of history rush into the frame.

Some other knowledge avails itself when I give in to being gripped otherwise by North County Jail's curious gaze while in motion. Perhaps I am telling a story about the rush of *savoir* that being looked at by North County Jail

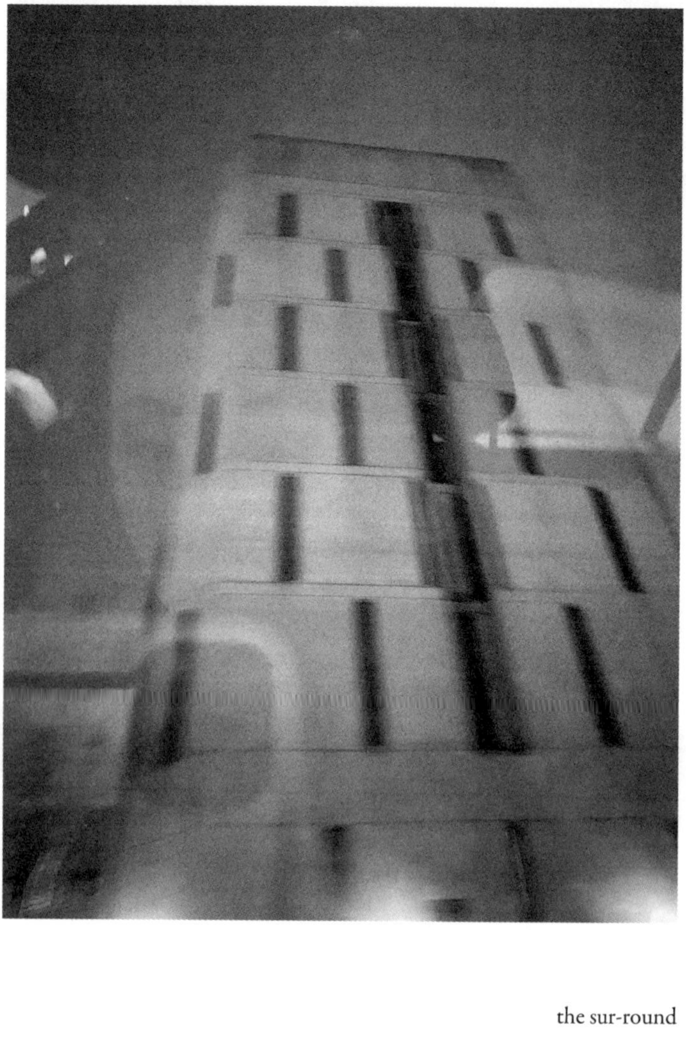

5.6 North County Jail, Oakland, California, 2020. Photo by author.

induces. If so, this is a story of two twinned, coordinated, but differentially staged illusions of movement, always occurring. The motion of the prisoner, inside, and me, outside.

This is a story about the panopticon as avant-garde zoetrope. The zoetrope is a way to animate still images by filtering the viewer's look inside a rotating structure through slits. As William Kentridge explains, "Zoetropes, praxinoscopes, phenakistoscopes . . . all these devices take a clearly still image and show us its transformation, not from flatness to depth, as in a stereoscope, but from stillness to motion."[16] Rotation animates the image on the inside, and the structure's slivered windows animate the image and us. But a zoetropic jail's illusion of a moving image is nonsequential and nonprogressive. There is no narrative seduction of a complete movement. It is the material appearance of what Fred Moten identifies as "that *other* reason, that more complex interinanimation of law and imagination" given in a certain stilled twinness.[17] In the case of North County Jail, the windows' black marks are portals to the Other, and a blurred, nearly invisible face, as Other, vibrates through and on a matrix of glass surfaces.

Jeremy Bentham's panoptic gaze watches each profile one by one until each person is a single being. The guard in the watchtower is part of a circuit or loop that replicates the gaze in and as the individuated soul. This individuation is constantly watched as a backlit shadowy figure, or a spur in space. But from the outside of the zoetropic movement of the structure where it is wrapped by the flux of unconscious desire, this spur also loops surveillance back on itself. The shadowy figure, not simply an outline of the human, but the illusory mark of a question about whether there is an outline discernible in the smoky glass, is a form of nondisciplined and nondisciplinary looking that demands a truer explanation about this strange building's presence.

North County Jail as gaze is architecturally splayed into so many fragments, lineaments, looks that find contact with so many eyes that together wander every which way and away on the highways and streets below. North County Jail as gaze is one that is not one.

Jail windows are panoptic frit.

The "heterochrony" that opens up in my experience of North County Jail as gaze produces my polyphonic delusions of dystranslation.[18] This "heterochronic" gaze is my polyphonic delusion.[19] But its murmur better represents the nonsingleness or mass-ness of the zoetropic jail's form of looking. Its materiality is given over to some excess beyond any geometry of a physical structure's function, beyond the geographic plans of an urban city, or the geological features of California's light in the modern history of punishment.

1970: As the Federal Bureau of Investigation (FBI) transports Angela Davis from its headquarters to the New York Women's House of Detention, the "red brick wall" surrounding the "tall archaic structure" triggers memories of passing by this "mysterious place" as a girl. She recounts:

> Walking to the subway station after school, I used to look up at this building almost every day, trying not to listen to the terrible noises spilling from the windows. They were coming from the women locked behind bars, looking down on the people passing in the streets, and screaming incomprehensible words.
>
> At age fifteen I accepted some of the myths surrounding prisoners. I did not see them as quite the criminals society said they were, but they did seem aliens in the world I inhabited. I never knew what to do when I saw the outlines of women's heads through the almost opaque windows of the jail. I could never understand what they were saying—whether they were crying out for help, whether they were calling for someone in particular, or whether they simply wanted to talk to anyone who was "free." My mind was now filled with the specters of those faceless women whom I had not answered. Would I scream out at the people passing in the streets, only to have them pretend not to hear me as I once pretended not to hear those women?[20]

I keep this memory close to me. Like those "red bricks," North County Jail's windows allow us to think the endless looping nature of the panopticon as a way of looking and hearing, and perhaps knowing when some signal emitted from an all-seeing abstracted point collapses and is unconsciously absorbed. If the panopticon as zoetrope has a sound, it is as Davis recalls the women's "incomprehensible words." Beyond ontology, they materialize a *savoir* contained in "the point of irradiation, the play of light, fire, the source from which reflections pour forth."[21]

“Red bricks.” Multimedia artist Sonya Clark marks red bricks in her sculpture *Edifice and Mortar* to show us how enslaved labor materializes continuously in the very building blocks of the United States (figure 5.7). The slave’s hand, her infrastructural mark, is as ubiquitous and common as uttering the word *ciao*. This sculpture of brick, human hair, and glass reminds us that the problem of slavery, punishment, and incarceration in this country is baked into its building materials, and any materials by which structures settle meaning and place.

On one side of this sculpture, imprinted with the words of the Declaration of Independence, these bricks are the layered ordering of law’s words. On the other side, they are imprinted in the practice of the ancient Roman maker’s mark. As both word and mark, each brick indexes “the signifier” where legal symbolic meaning materializes through the anonymity and polynymity of slavery as repeating stamp.[22] Lime mortar is replaced with a binder consisting of human hair, a protein, keratin, virtually resistant to decomposition. The afro, as both mark and bodily remainder, is in both the brick and the binder.

Blackness destabilizes the authority of the law’s hold on history with a material presence in between and on the other side of the word. It is grammar as glue holding words together. It is also a repeating depersonalized, unknowable feminine source of material production on which words are written.

5.7 Sonya Clark, detail of *Edifice and Mortar* (2018). Hand-stamped bricks, human hair, and glass, approx. 39 × 72 × 15 in.

It's what Davis heard.

Every jail is a structure, both architectural and social, in precisely the way Clark presents it here in *Edifice and Mortar*, and as Davis teaches us about what it is to hear from the outside of a red brick wall. Both bear the ethical question of abolition. Each dark shard of window, or each hardened block, cannot but install us in relation to captivity, whose sound and sign touch on the unrelenting writing of the gaze of the state.

If North County Jail's walls could talk . . . it would be in a hushed SHV whisper.

0° [*sur*-round] **32**

As I look from the passenger seat, there is always more to be seen, but what is seen will never be a total picture. Nor will it be an already known image. My camera surprises with images of visuality itself, and, more specifically, a vision that sees both surface and depth, front and behind (figure 5.8). This vision is simultaneously a seeing that passes through and a seeing of nothing other than glass/light/glass/light/glass/light/ . . .

Perhaps this is an abolitionist form of vision. The series of photographs I took to capture what I saw so many years ago through my father's eyes visualize a form of vision necessary to see something more from within the panoptic lines of disciplinary sight.

The passenger sees from the *sur*-round. Caught in an orbit of questions, a *sur*-face appears through the surfaces and faces planned into the city's landscape. This is what can happen with one look. A different way of seeing comes into being between political desire and a built signifier of human disappearance, between an unconscious knowledge and the many holes of time left in bodies that remember.

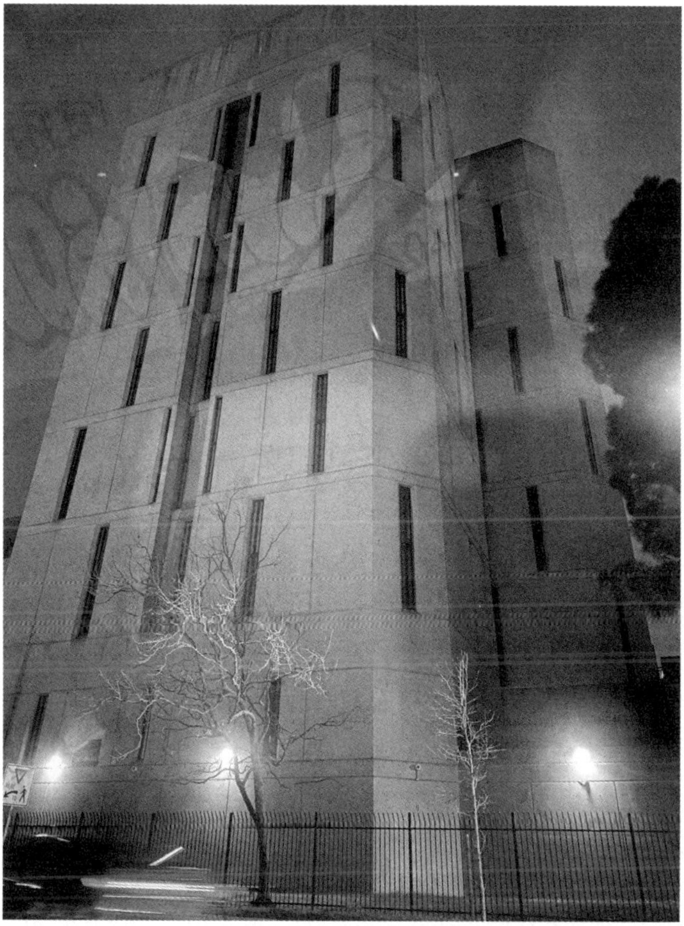

5.8 North County Jail, Oakland, California, 2020. Photo by author.

Graffiti behind me levitates in the air. The bubble letters appear as holograms. Writing in this strange interregnum of prison reform during COVID is a holography of time thrown up on the wall.

Letters and lives, the particulate matter of desire and violence, mingle.

Letters and lives, the particulate matter of desire and violence, mingle in layered and broken lines of sight. Windows, crossing light, shadowed light, peripheries, transparencies, unchanging light and shadow, surface visibility, right angles, rings. The image of punishment I try to capture here creates an image not of the object, in this case, North County Jail, but of how light, letters, and lives pass through and thread layers of glass—the lens, the car window, the jail window—into a dusky prism. They occlude us from each other partially. These partialities only imperfectly fit together, into neither total vision nor total blindness.

Analytic processes that try to perfect these imperfections into an ever-efficient, uniform, smooth, self-controlled form of dissociative seeing and being seen are known as *reform*. They are panoptic traps.

If photography is an occasion for pursuing a zero degree of the image, a neutralization of its form, or a denial of its dependence on form, as Roland Barthes performs it in *Camera Lucida*, visualizing abolition offers another way to degree zero. Barthes wrote *Camera Lucida* when he was teaching a class on *le neutre*. In his March 11, 1978, lecture, published in *October*, we find his mention of the idea of "degree zero."[23] It refers to a form of negation that sets language and speech in motion again because of a neutralization of power or the very terms of the paradigm. The zero degree of visualizing abolition would not be what he describes as the "suspension, abstention, abolition of the paradigm" but the articulation of a third term, "conflictual, sensitive to the struggle of angry forces that stand against each other . . . [it is a] complex term and not zero, neutral term."[24]

This image I've made is not simply trying to destroy photography's panoptic power (figure 5.9). It frees photography's constituent elements from the medium's denial of its shared form with glare, reflection, blur, or flare put in motion in time and space. And if it visualizes abolition, it does so by creating a third term, that *sur*-face, from within conflicting visions driving panopticism.

Further, this third term is supported by a fourth. This fourth term is Hortense Spillers's zero degree, or "flesh," in contrast to the body, as a "zero degree of social conceptualization."[25] *Flesh*, alluded to in every aspect of writing, photography, or speech Barthes is interested in, is a materiality that both causes the desire for a neutralization of form as a function of power and renders impossible the production of "zero, neutral term[s]." Discussing Spillers's deep engagement with Barthes's theory of myth, R. A. Judy describes Spillers's elaboration of *flesh* as a form of violent writing establishing the mythical signifier *Negro* but also a form of processual reading that cuts through the "first-order myth of the Negro" and its secondary orders, or the entirety of Barthes's "tridimensional semiological order."[26] An American grammar of *flesh*, or the hieroglyphic marks of the physical torture of slavery, and then its ideogram-

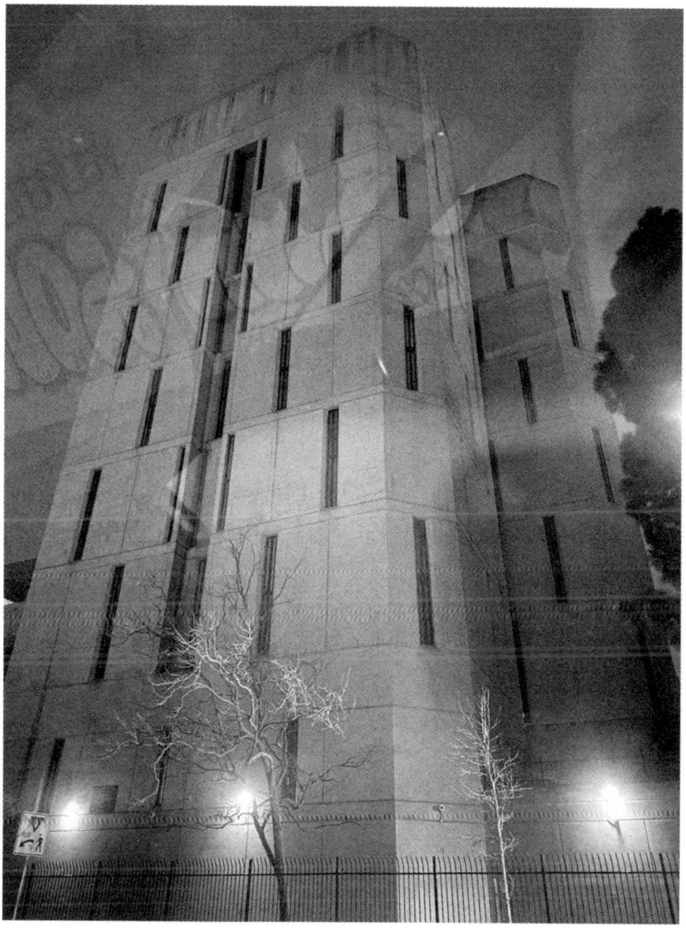

5.9 North County Jail, Oakland, California, 2020. Photo by author.

mic reading by and through enslaved captive bodies, demystifies a "a double theft [of myth]: *ethnicity* steals from *Negro*, which has robbed from *flesh*."[27]

The holographic images (figures 5.8 and 5.9) suggest that *flesh* as demystifying grammar works at the level of the studium of memory, where possible meanings of punishment as state violence emerge from an unsettled and thoroughly ambivalent socio-perceptual experience not yet disciplined by the demands of naturalized cultural meaning. A child's passionate rejection of the entire paradigm of state power cuts through meaning and concept and asks after their source. All this is occurring in the midst of historical positioning that poses the child's ethnicization and the prisoner's deracination as opposing figures: on the one hand, the captives inside North County Jail and, on the other, me, free to be going wherever we, on the outside, were going. I would spend the rest of my life thereafter in that rub of opposition to know about and with, which is to say, read, the *flesh* of multiracial community. This zero degree, a knowing driven by a desire to neutralize power, in practice, opens up on to and courses through the antagonistic signs and terms of social life, including the concept of abolition.

Rosalind Krauss, who translates Barthes's *le neutre* lecture, recalls a memory Barthes writes about in *Roland Barthes by Roland Barthes*:

> When I used to play prisoner's base in the Luxembourg, what I liked best was not provoking the other team and boldly exposing myself to their right to take me prisoner; what I liked best was to free the prisoners—the effect of which was to put both teams back into circulation: the game started over again at zero.[28]

Perhaps I was playing my version of this game in the California Bay Area. The *para-semiosis* it produced is a knowledge of *flesh* as the *sur* of the double roundness of the zero degree of visualizing abolition.[29]

Sur-face. *Sur*-flesh. *Sur*-round.

藍 [paradissociative blues] 33

Michel Foucault's discussion of the panopticon has become a dominant metaphor for theorizing modes of power as discipline, surveillance, and subjection. I wonder if there's anything new I can possibly say about panopticism
And so I return to his language of its architectural elements: light, windows, angles, shapes, size, lines, functionality, and engineering.

The panopticon is so much more than the tower from which prisoners in individuated cells are watched. A cell has "two windows," which "allows the light to cross the cell from one end to the other."[30] This "backlighting" has the functional purpose of allowing the observer to see, "standing out precisely against the light, the small captive shadows in the cells of the periphery."[31] Architectural design of light reveals that "visibility is a trap."[32] This use of light to trap the captive demonstrates that disciplinary power must be both "visible and unverifiable."[33] Architectural design must incapacitate the captive's ability to visually verify the absence or presence of an observer.

Foucault calls this an "axial visibility" of the tower from each cell, which produces "lateral invisibility" from one cell to another.[34] Axial visibility also occludes the captive's vision from seeing inside the tower by using "venetian blinds on the windows of the central observation hall," as well as, "on the inside, partitions that intersected the hall at right angles and, in order to pass from one quarter to the other, not doors but zig-zag openings."[35] The structural unverifiability of the disciplinary gaze, too, is precisely designed, "for the slightest noise, a gleam of light, a brightness in a half-opened door would betray the presence of the guardian."[36]

Windows, crossing light, shadowed light, peripheries, transparencies, unchanging light and shadow, surface visibility, right angles, rings.

Panoptic architecture is an enclosed space that positions modes of seeing between guards and captives, "dissociating the see/being seen dyad: in the peripheric ring, one is totally seen, without ever seeing; in the central tower, one sees everything without ever being seen."[37] And yet, while this "dissociating" is key, it is truer to say, despite how Foucault puts it, that from the ring, it is the captive's shadow that is subject to total observation, while the captive's vision is limited to a line of sight from individual cell to central tower. Conversely, from the tower, the observer sees to recognize abnormal movements of these shadows, while what is visible to the captive of the observer is not the agent but its radial point. Both guard and captive see in each other's direction partially, are occluded from each other partially, and these partialities only imperfectly fit together, neither into total vision, nor into total blindness.

Dissociation of the "see/being seen" dyad is crucial to the internalization of the architectural function of disciplinary power. One cannot be sure of what one is seeing: the captive cannot be sure there is someone in the tower, and the guard cannot be sure that a shadow signals some abnormality. And one cannot be sure that they are being seen: the captive *assumes* they are being seen by virtue of the tower's presence, and the guard *assumes* they are being seen by subjects casting their shadows in so many surrounding "small theaters."[38] This dissociation is a structural element of panopticism's two-centuries-old "imaginary intensity" that "as pure architectural and optical system . . . may and must be detached from any specific use."[39]

The architectural separation of seeing and being seen—a certain built disjunction between physical and mental control through "distribution of bodies, surfaces, lights, gazes"—precisely because imperfect, installs analytic processes of perfectibility into ever efficient, uniform, smooth, self-controlled forms of dissociative seeing and being seen.[40]

Perfectibility is another way to think of prison reform. Its modality of practice is the condition of possibility of constructing "a total universe" in what Robin Evans describes as "an island of anti-entropic regeneration."[41] Perfectibility is, like visibility, a trap. So, too, are the humanitarian impulses of brutalism's lasting projection from the walls of North County Jail.

At the same time, the totalizing imaginary of panopticism in real life is always delimited by Bentham's, or Foucault's Bentham's, specification that the building is "a space not too large."[42] That is, size, specifically small to medium-sized buildings, is fundamental to rein in the imaginary ambitiousness of utilitarian panoptic power. Furthermore, the reliance of dissociative and perfectible visibility inside the building on a window, "on the outside" of the periphery, introduces a nonperfectible visibility. It is the window that is doubly outside: "outside" relative to the tower but, as well, "outside" relative to the building as a whole. It creates "backlighting" inside the building and reflects light outside the building: as do the windows of North County Jail, the windows of the Chicago jail, and the windows of La Tourette.

This island with windows is surrounded by a sea of streets, highways, and walkways. And we can be sure of neither what those who pass by those windows, outside of the outside of the watchtower, see, nor by whom they are seen.

This island will be forever surrounded by the haunt of red bricks.

Conceptual artist Charisse Pearlina Weston arranges glass sheets in her sculpture *untitled (black points through the window pane)*, whose framing and balancing in a window partially occludes the red brick wall of an adjacent building (figure 5.10). I see Oakland in the darknesses of these glass panes, perched by a certain wonky geometry of right angles. They dare us to be in a paradissociative relation of seeing and being seen in the shadow of the red

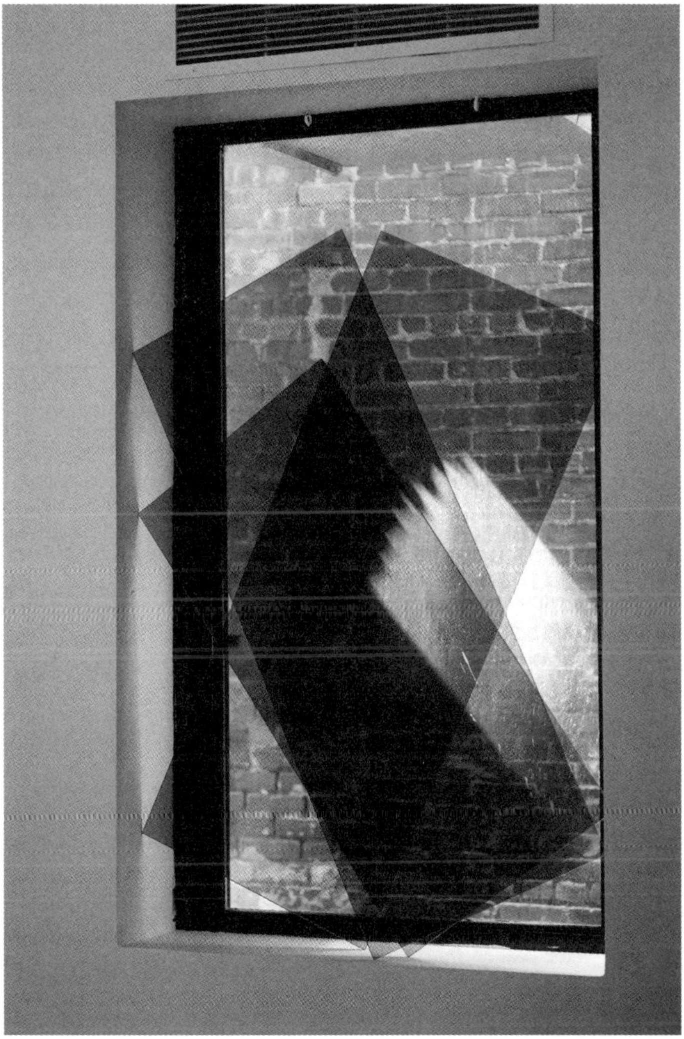

5.10 Charisse Pearlina Weston, *untitled (black points through the window pane)* (2021). Tempered, laminate, safety glass, balanced, approx. 25 × 20 × 5 in.

bricks through which Davis recalls the voices sounding out from the Women's House of Detention. In 1971 its function and capacity would be absorbed into the notorious Rikers Island with the construction of a new jail. "Watching the last busload [of women prisoners] leave, Mrs. Lenore Brothers, deputy superintendent of the abandoned jail, expressed relief. She paraphrased Oscar Wilde's 'Ballad of Reading Gaol,' by noting that 'now our girls will have a broad view of that tent of blue called the sky.'"[43]

When the prison tempts with these blue treats, always remember color, too, is an essential architectural element, such that blue is never simply a color but is on the spectrum of what Nicole Fleetwood calls "carceral blue."[44]

The *hanja* character 藍 is a phono-semantic compound, meaning "indigo plant," and together with the character 色 means "blue color." The ideogrammic references contained in these two characters bear an uncanny resonance with the color "carceral blue" in the sense that color itself refers to a certain spectrum of perceptible light and a form of endeavor, complexion, and human shape inseparable from creating a pigment from or like things.

The component ideogrammic parts of 色 are 人, meaning "person" and 卩, depicting etiquette in the form of kneeling.[45] This latter figure refers to the hangul word 절 (*jeol*), meaning "to bow, greet, pray." The image is of the devotional, invitational, color-regarding work of creating color, which when attached to the specific character 藍 is to mark that blue is created.

藍 combines the ancient pictogram 艸, or its radical form 艹, meaning "grass"; and the phonetic character 監, meaning "to supervise or oversee," which is itself an ideogrammic compound consisting of 臥, meaning "to lie down or crouch," and 皿, meaning "bowl." Depicting a scene in which a kneeling person looks into a bowl filled with water, the original meaning of 監 was "mirror/to mirror or reflect."

In Korean the word for "indigo" is 남 (*nam*). It is a homophone for the word "stranger," too. This stranger beckons us with the color-regarding work of creating color. Strangeness invites the devotional, prostrate, gestural color-making of something as precious and potent, the always differential relation of reflection, overseen by the law of the color's timeless shifting hue and use. The blush, a kind of thingly color, or claw or hand that reaches out from some unknowable place placed by the intimate relation of touch that brings us to our knees, might as well be a brush, or a needle, or an instrument that welcomes, submits, to some field whose openness appears like blue from the green leaves of an indigo plant.

The sound of the brush, or blushing, the undammable appearance of color from color, is given by the hand that mixes precious pigment. The slosh and swishing of whatever is in this seditious *tong*, whispers, like wind in the grass. A *parlêtre* of carceral blues.

玨 [a-formation] 34

Tong. Tongue. Tongues. Touching sounds. *Sur*-rounds

They are portals to some hollow origin, like so many hollows (of organs, wind, string, and percussive instruments, indeed, of the unconscious)

that comprise an orchestral confluence of sound. Through and with these windows, some signal radiating from some all-seeing point drops off, or is unconsciously reoriented.

In one of the letters that make up Nathaniel Mackey's epistolary novel *From a Broken Bottle Traces of Perfume Still Emanate*, the character N. writes to Angel of Dust about the Brazilian instrument the *cuica*. He is taken by how the *cuica* is a drum/horn that beats and bleats. In passing, he mentions the "curious" Korean 해금, *haegeum*, a traditional Korean two-stringed "fiddle," which, N. notes, is classified as a wind instrument. I did not know its name until reading N.'s study of amphibian instruments.[46]

But I do know its sound, though it is hard to tell whether its sonic familiarity to me is from having heard it played or having heard a woman perform 판소리, *pansori*, a traditional form of Korean dramatic storytelling, because they sound so similar. If the *haegeum* is considered a wind instrument, I think it must be because it sounds like a human voice.

The *haegeum* is fiddle sized, but it is held vertically like a cello. The ubiquity of the figure of the cello across Nam June Paik's body of work delivers the archaic sounds of Korean music into a shared amphibious underworld.[47] It is often said that the cello appeals and haunts because it, too, sounds like the human voice, or at least comes closest to the range of the singing human voice. If there is something uncanny about the *cuica*, the *haegeum*, and the cello, it is a certain more-than-human lamentation heard across the three.

Mackey's writing again takes us into the shimmering terra incognita of transcription, translation, and transliteration. But this time, we are treated to a pictographic translation between instrumental designs: the *haegeum*'s twinned strings, the twinned vocal cords of the human larynx, and embedded in the *hanja* word for *haegeum*, 奚琴, the twinned character 珏, a pictogram of two jade vessels, or strings of jade, and their vibrating, verdant touch.

Touching sounds. *Sur*-rounds

Bentham, who tried to design an acoustic system for the model panopticon. Foucault also notes this curious elaboration, which Bentham would eventually abandon.

Its purpose would have been, writes Bentham, "to save the troublesome that might otherwise be necessary," by controlling sound through a system of tin tubes that would allow the captor to listen to "the slightest whisper" of any prisoner attempting to communicate with another.[48]

Foucault wonders whether Bentham gave up including "acoustic surveillance" as part of the panopticon because "he could not introduce into it the principle of dissymmetry."[49] But I wonder

whether the real
impossibility of
designing the
omnipotence of
authority with
sound was not
because of an
unregulatable
symmetry of
acoustic relation
between the
prisoner and the
jailer but
because the twin
directionality of
sound has a
haptic quality
that produces
nonsingle
parasolitary
solid arity.
For, having
"appl[ied] his
ear to the tube,"
on the radial out
side lands of
this telenetic
working
twinness was
the
incomprehensio
n between Davis
and those
women's voices
coming through
the windows to
the street
below.[50]

g [slumping] **35**

1967: The federal President's Commission on Law Enforcement and Administration of Justice (Katzenbach Commission) introduced their yearlong study of the criminal justice system with this fact: "There remains an inherent sameness about places where people are kept against their will," a sameness produced by "restraint per se."[51] Restraint and removal of people from communities create environments of "isolation," "alienation," and a "strangeness of living apart from families, with no choice."[52]

While the Katzenbach report accepts this "inherent sameness" as one of the necessary "disadvantages" of democratic governance, it also proffers a model of prison and jail design that might minimize alienation and isolation.[53] The model institution is small in size, architecturally residential, and local to where its prisoners are taken from. It would offer mental health treatment, educational programming, and transition plans in partnership with outside community organizations.[54] And through a rather delusional vision of "collaboration" between prisoners and jailers, the model would promote "rehabilitation."[55]

This ethos would physically manifest as North County Jail less than a decade after the Katzenbach report's release.

2021: In a realigned California, no one lives or works in North County Jail (figure 5.11).

It is not a failed panoptic experiment. It is the monumentalization of model reform. It reveals the centrality of modeling for panoptic punishment and celebrates the virtues of bureaucratic authority, which hide that unavoidable truth about the "inherent sameness" of punishment that only abolition can address.

Visualizing abolition through North County Jail, we are organized by and organize the zoetropic movements of the lights and sounds of mass incarceration. Through its little viewing slits, those on the outside who circle around the jail continue to unconsciously look in. If panopticism "assures an infinitesimal distribution of the power relations," then the zoetropic twinned swarming of bodies in motion reconstructs these distributions into some other way of being looked at that is indistinguishable from being looked for, and, ultimately, the abolition of some "whom" to which we belong.[56] This alternate form of belonging is not merely a belonging-with in space and time but a belonging-to outside space and time where the presumed identifications required for panopticism—guard and prisoner—give way to unconscious association.

This unconscious association relies on the practice of making things, or regarding made things, in such a way that works with and against the panoptic guard/prisoner intersubjective relation at the core of individuated life. Alameda County did not plan that some seven-year-old girl would drive by that shiny new jail almost every day and grow to know that if she belonged anywhere, she belonged to those inside, who, by virtue of being inside, knew something about justice outside the distributive logics of punishment. That that girl would someday grow to have a daughter who had an eye for shiny lost objects strewn on whatever trail she traveled on, who would make shiny glass art with fire in the midst of the world on fire, and whose mother would drive her by this same jail's vacant windows, ever shining, and together understand that their vacancies would signal victory only insofar as cells across the

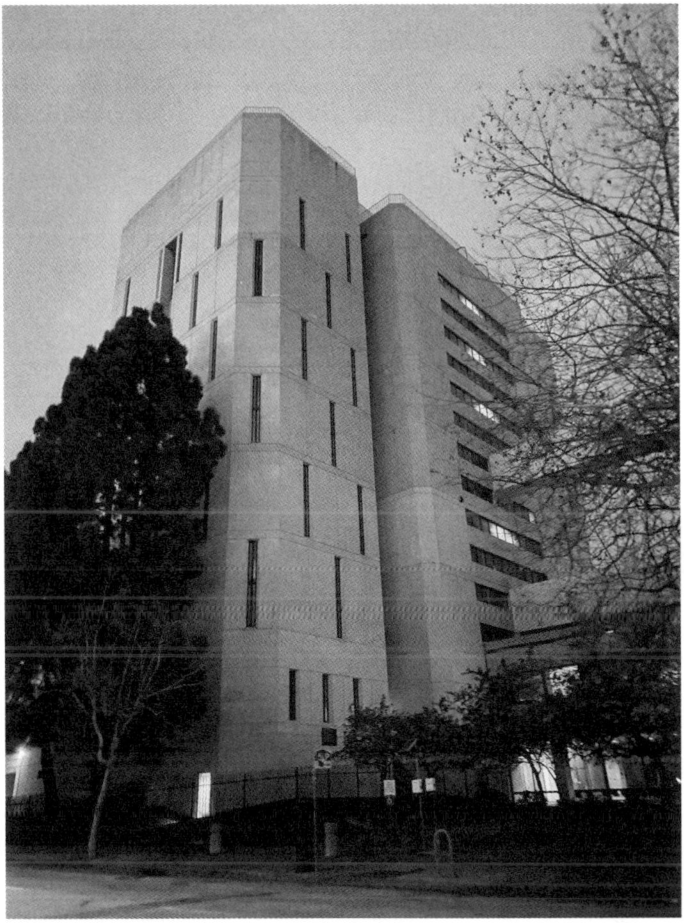

5.11 North County Jail, Oakland, California, 2020. Photo by author.

globe would be vacated because the people who put people in them stopped doing their jobs, because one vacancy there equaled a home elsewhere, and because . . . desire marks . . .

The windows still look, silently registering the syncopated sound of what Ruth Wilson Gilmore has conceptualized as "extracted time."[57] Some visual forms repeat in such a way that you can feel them like the way air around a speaker hits your body. The windows beat across a beige concrete cityscape, a riddled border between depressed industrial life and late-capital logistical governance, between highway speeding and street-level creeping.

How to defenestrate these windows whose very form is to conjoin natural light with new-generation punishment? How can we use them as something other than relics of brutalism? Can glass objects have a life beyond an architectural political consciousness built into the very structures of punishment?

Weston's sculpture below the window, *i am moored along the soft shored unity of impatient ruin* (2021) (figure 5.12), pushes us to consider what kind

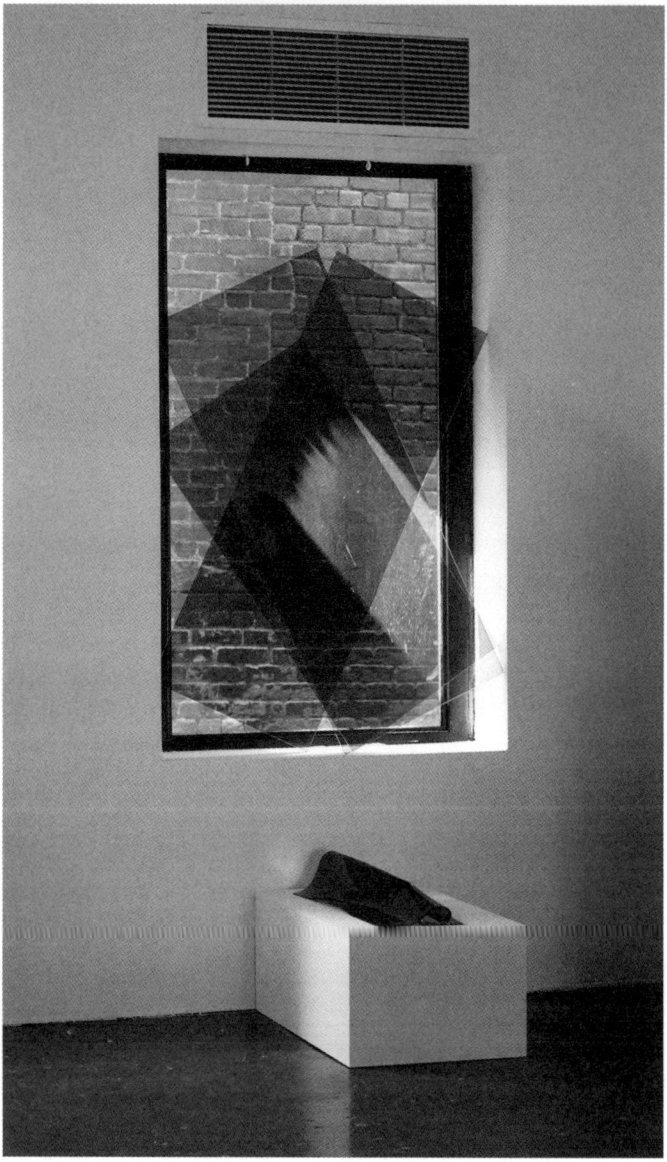

5.12 Charisse Pearlina Weston, *untitled (black points through the window pane)* (2021). Tempered, laminate, safety glass, balanced, approx. 25 × 20 × 5 in. (above); and *i am moored along the soft shored unity of impatient ruin* (2021). Enfolded glass, etched text, approx. 20 × 15 × 10 in. (below).

of heat would slump the North County Jail's windows. Their architectural admonishment? Their punitive humanism?

Slumping is a process in glass art where sheets of glass are formed into shapes with heat, gravity, and molds. Glass at high temperatures, above 1,400 degrees Fahrenheit, falls, bends, folds into figures that slump over and against rigid, unmelting things. Weston's slumped sculpture reveals glass's radical nonperformativity. The contrast between the flat panes balancing up against both the window and the red brick wall and the slumped pane resting on a block below provokes us to notice glass in states other than its brokenness. It recasts the straightness of window glass with precarity. The panes' imperfect layering creates shadows between and on themselves. Their four corners are maximally, anxiously, spread so as to render each individual, rigid sheet evenly apparent.

The slumped form of the second sculpture contrasts beautifully to put the material to sleep. Glass performs how it is a membrane, rigid *and* soft, sharp *and* curved. This figure, either fallen or having taken leave from the wall, is neither shattered nor broken but folds, rests, lies down, slumps (figure 5.13). It is not broken by the law of gravity. It absorbs and gives form to the law of gravity, at the same time that it seems still to be waiting for some final resting state.

5.13 Charisse Pearlina Weston, *i am moored along the soft shored unity of impatient ruin* (2021). Enfolded glass, etched text, approx. 20 × 15 × 10 in.

Against the impossibly perfectible reflection of a glass pane, the curvature of Weston's sculpture demands that we accept the coexistence of coldness and softness. This "soft" coldness remains as the afterlife of a molten, liquid state of a "shored unity of impatient ruin." The process of slumped glass carries the Real, as the sense of loss of resistance to or compliance with the law of gravity is given in a signifier that folds and touches on something that is neither imaginary nor symbolic but real absence. Defenestration produces this glassy, glossy skin of writing, the fold of a time forever in abeyance.

Glass, gloss, (g)loss wonders,

> if, up from within the excess
> of this dream, the deep green sea
> tracing the boundary of inside and
> out will ever gather itself to speak
> through me?"[58]

Write, etch, slip in "*this self of the horizon line who cradles*."[59] The process of slumped glass—both Weston's and what we can imagine of North County Jail's windows after Weston—curls lines of words into a barrel, a hollow (figure 5.14). The lip of Weston's glass is in the shape of perpetual rolling. This

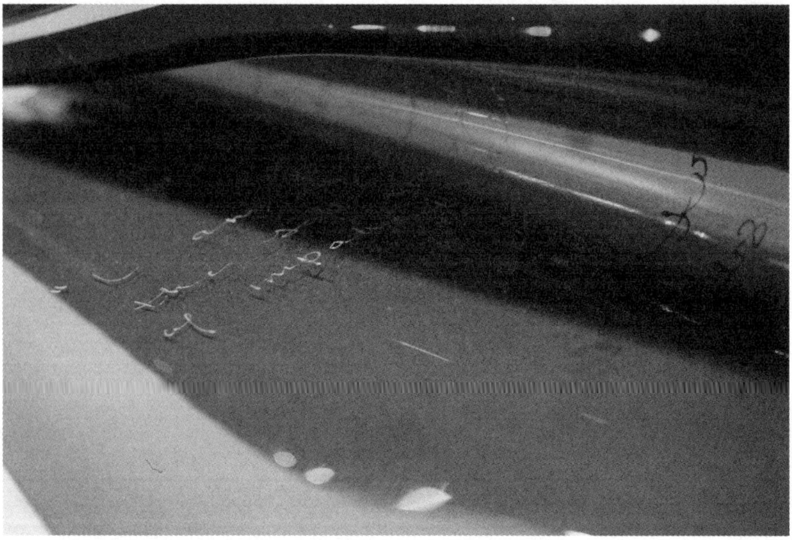

5.14 Charisse Pearlina Weston, detail from *i am moored along the soft shored unity of impatient ruin* (2021).

form of "*thinking now*" as unbreaking wave is represented specifically by the way glass can hold the movement of folding incompletely, "[*gently*]," over that which is no longer there but for which an emptiness will always be held by the bends of this smoky surface.[60]

Writing, slumping. Glass, gloss, (g)loss. Slumped windows teach us to lose (ourselves) in a *parlêtre* as ghostly as *g*.

There are no broken windows here.

res nulla loquitur

This chapter can be read while listening to the sound loops on the website Res Nulla Loquitur (https://resnullaloquitur.com). These loops were created from audio evidence collected during investigations into the deaths of Sandra Bland, Michael Brown, Jamar Clark, Terence Crutcher, Samuel Debose, Eric Garner, Freddie Gray, Walter Scott, and Alton Sterling. Scroll through each section of the website as they correspond to the seven sections in this chapter.

ㄹ [aural blur] 36

Citizen, dashcam, and bodycam recordings of police brutality and lethal use of force comprise a new media terrain of state violence. In 2015 a bystander recorded police officer Michael Slager gunning down Walter Scott. That same year, a patrol car dashboard camera and a microphone worn by state trooper Brian Encinia recorded his arrest of Sandra Bland. She was found dead in a Waller County jail cell three days after being taken into custody.

Recordings like these are destined for use and consumption by publics, journalists, and legal actors such as prosecutors, police administration, juries, and activists in an investigation and, maybe, eventually, a civil or criminal trial for unlawful lethal use of force. Political organizing, public investigations, and criminal and civil adjudication all endow these recordings with evidentiary meaning. Sometimes police officers will be found guilty of some degree of murder or manslaughter, or held civilly liable, but these are exceptional legal outcomes.

What becomes of and in all the evidence whose possible and unknown meanings escape legal judgments? Fred Moten describes this challenge as "the ongoing destruction of the ongoing production of (a) (black) performance, which is what I am, which is what you are or could be if you can listen while you look."[1]

Holding this hearing is all there is. It produces an endless *legis*, which never arrives at an act. Legislation never arrives, because the *whereas* repeats, never to address the question of Bland's "here."[2]

Here is, *eres*, are, our: a litany of whereas's deferring enactment, as, in, the preamble of the never-to-be-ratified George Floyd Justice in Policing Act.[3]

Figures stream. Uncut, medial proximity reveals an unlit gap. From this ledge, we jump into a virtual intimacy. "Believe your eyes," said the prosecutor in his opening remarks to a jury who would decide the criminal guilt of the officer Derek Chauvin for killing George Floyd. See only what you first saw.[4]

But these are recordings without acts. What was first was always, surrepetitiously, in medias res, being recorded, recording the conviction of a knowledge about violence unsayable within the terms and grammar of legal reason.

lauren woods's 2020 exhibition, *American Monument*, allowed visitors to play vinyl records cut with these audio recordings, like Bland's voicemail message, which had been used as evidence in high-profile criminal trials of police charged with murdering black citizens.[5] The mo(nu)mentum of playing these eighteen records created a sound so frenzied and disorienting that it felt as if they threw every one/thing/note off into some place where archiving and the impossibility of meaning making converge. As the points of their needles, drawing a centripetally gathering line, bumped along toward some nonplaceable center of a record, their sound begged the question of whether we could hear a music even so.

Eighteen arms, dragging, circumlocuted an offering that became these loops.

They repeat: "But I'm still here . . ." looking at these renditions of enforcement. "So call me back" using these destroyed conditions of performativity, with the rubble left in the wake of these regimes of self and evidence.[6]

Audio repetition aesthetically disorders, and reassociates, conditions of scenes of state violence against the authority of law's word in the midst of the "ongoing destruction of the ongoing production of (a) (black) performance." How to read and write about how the law reproduces anti-black state violence as we are assailed by the evidence collected in a series of cases on lethal use of force?

To listen to the sound of this evidence while doing anything, in fact, is to consent to a desire to submit oneself to a hearing, to a temporal displacement into a strange state of waiting. Not justice but truth floats above the din of sound and words, violence and history, social life and death.

If the assault of this new aesthetic regime of evidence shifted how the public understands the problem of police violence from one of instances of excessive use of force to, now, one of structural design and effect, audio repetition also shifts how we understand the violence of legal interpretation: from a need for self-evidentiary, incontrovertible documentation necessary to perform remedial justice, to a form of knowledge given in nonperformance that only some (no)thing can speak, or *res nulla loquitur*.

Its nonperformance is to unconditionally promise to hear something in circumstances where the unforeseeable future is not bracketed, or even accepted, but actively bet on, and as such this promise radically, as utterance, transforms the promise of a hearing, whatever is promised in a hearing, and the possibility of establishing a hearing into a sociolegal act that carries with it its own unfulfillment. Writing about use-of-force jurisprudence in the aftermath of Ferguson, and cross-stitching audio evidence into this writing is an experiment in nonperformance.

What happens to the history of thought when we put, not legal statements back into context, but sonic utterances back into the language of law?

Something marks. The swarm of words, letters, sounds, the flock of bodies and papers, the flight of sense and thought, start to land and hover where they will.

Sign this nonperforming will.

Listen while looking at everyone looking, some self looking while reading, a nonself hearing while writing, someone doing something.

Desire displaces displacement.

Inconsist by making whatever self a place of hearing. Wait. Hear, a ringing ringing.

Truth floats up from the murmur of history.

Out above the *murs* of law and justice, this ringing drafts on, in the slipstream of the unconscious. Pluck these radioscopic bits from the air, and throw them at the mighty law, whose bulldozing, wordsmithing, incontrovertible scribe leaves nothing to be asked, and nothing to be argued. They mark a Real no-thing, a rebellion of ten thousand mouths filling the *mis-n'en-scene* of law with alyrical notes.[7]

Res nulla loquitur: it is a written aside, a procedural oversight, on the law's underside, that proves the ink block always runs black.

It is a trace breath left in the running line. Even its end, its disappearance in its own finite fluidity, is part of this trace.

Ends do not justify origins, and so for any original utterance to be just, it must bear a mysticism in and against the mythical origins of law. Hear, until the nonscene of mythical origin overtakes the not-enough of law's origin. Until the lids of the eyes sound words, and the lips of the mouth visualize objects. Until those mystical non(self)substantiating presences become more real than any mythological narrative or legal reform could ever promise to become.

Listen to the more-than-real of some impossible sound. Like the sound of the English letter *r*, a kind of fatty aural blubber cut up and made to jiggle in little bits by the hangul letter ㄹ. This transliteration marks a sound that is neither here nor there. Neither *l* nor *r*.

Here is, *eres*, are, our, ㄹ.

In *Skirt Full of Black*, Sun Yung Shin performs how the mouth visualizes objects with this image of "liul," the name of the hangul letter ㄹ.

> Dictionary of myth. A child in her library. Sounds eaten whole. A bull and a virgin.
>
> The lonely Minotaur haunted in broad-backed, forbidden heat. His human clothes remained in two suffocating wardrobes, pinna to pinna. On all fours he tried a wrecked ladder, a hoof slipped while he had a vision of a snake meandering the legs of a four-poster bed.[8]

The transliterated sound of the hangul letter ㄹ exists somewhere between the English letters *r* and *l*. Listen to the difference in *r* when you blur and slur the *l* and the *r* in *blur* and *slur*. If *blur* and *slur* were to be a letter, it would be ㄹ's utterance, the nonsingle sound of *r* and *l* in a newly resonant, rolling consonant, whole. Shin leaves a blurry, slurry mess in the middle of some labyrinth of books whose sound bounces, ear to ear to ear to ear.

Listen like a transubstantial realist, to that *Zong!*, song, psalm thing.[9]

The Fourth Amendment tells us to be polite, police as dictated in *Tennessee v. Garner* (1985): enforcement-lite, a chimera, a horror, an other wise limit   less law on   Black   life.[10] *Garner*'s theorems posit a manner of mind working at the limits of conscious speech: "there can be no question" and "his own life need not be elaborated."[11] We are in the zone of *factum* as neuter past participle *facere*. As certified absence, they are the word of laws "   of origin."

They are shiny little nothings produced by a revision compulsion, a peculiar repeating negation: E. Garner, no question, E. Garner, need not. One, two, three, and four . . .

The fact of life, declared by the majority in *Garner*, as a "fundamental interest [which] need not be elaborated upon," registers a certain horizon beyond which law's language does not have to extend itself because of an assumed obviousness to the primary equivalence drawn between death and arrest. Indeed, "there can be no question that the use of deadly force is a seizure."[12] The copular function that makes *arrest a predicate of death*, and *a fundamental interest a predicate of life*, is essential to the grammar of the reasonableness standard of the Fourth Amendment.

This grammar, no matter how critical we are of legal liberalism, structures the fantasy of a limitless power of law enforcement over black existence that should be regulated by presuming the facticity of life. It ensures that when black existence is lethally put into question by law enforcement, the law protects that existence not by elaborating on its value but by closing down the proliferation of questions about value. This obstruction is effected precisely by asserting black life as naturally and universally given.

Jean Hyppolite might approach these statements as forms of "denegation" (*dénégation*), translated from Sigmund Freud's discussion of "negation" (*Verneinung*).[13] The key Freudian point of general relevance is "in [negation], the intellectual function is separated from the affective processes."[14] The *dé* of *dénégation* is not a simple and concluding affirmation (*Bejahung*) of repressed content repressed no longer by bringing it to knowledge (*connaissance*) but the acceptance of a symbolized difference between thinking about what is repressed and a constitutive denial of "the libidinal components . . . disappeared in the repeating pleasure in negating [*dénier*]."[15]

Negation allows repressed content to register, but there is no final elimination (*Aufhebung*) of repression as a process.[16] Alenka Zupančič explains further, "It is clear that that [a Freudian *Aufhebung*] cannot simply be an operation performed *on* the repressed content, but something that actively involves the repression (repressive process) itself . . . the dialectical movement being in this case a movement that preserves and works with what is neither being nor not-being, with something that does not count (not even 'for nothing')."[17] I am interested in denegation here, then, as the performance of *intellectual judgment* at work in self-evident statements, where the blank of what is negated in legal knowledge is not "'the negation of something in the judgement,' but a sort of 'revocation of a judgement' [*déjudgement*]," and what Zupančič identifies as "a movement that preserves and works . . . with something that does not count (not even 'for nothing')."[18]

Garner as the performance of judging police judgment is both a negative representation of something that can be thought (loss as a result of wanton state violence) and a nothing that can be libidinally heard (black life as beyond the pale of thought's jurisdiction).

At the heart of the law's revision compulsion, denegation becomes a vehicle through which unthinkable *actualities* are reduced by judgment to *factualities*. Intellectual judgment about what is fact lets the law off the hook, leaving the question of black life as blanknesses within: *unquestionable* and *commonsensical*. What we learn from the law's performance of denegation is that self-evident rhetoric is what Freud referred to as a "certificate of origin" for, as Zupančič clarifies, "something which is *constitutively* unconscious, that is to say that it only registers in reality in the form of repression, as repression (and not as something that first *is*, and is then repressed)."[19] The self-evident quality of video evidence of police violence in our current moment is an echo of this more structural denegation revealed at work in constitutional jurisprudence.

The law is a mirror reflecting back to us an absurd situation: when the law makes recourse to evidence so self-evident that it negates the necessity for judicial review at all, it reveals that when society makes recourse to evidence so self-evident, it negates the necessity for social review, too.

Likewise, the law's revision compulsion is our revision compulsion: repeat read repeat revise *Verneinung dénégation denegation misnegation*. This is the lesson writing this chapter has taught me since 2015: revision compulsion is our only defense, in any case, against vicious judiciousness and the blindness of *intellectual affirmation of negation* to an unconscious knowledge of a black desire for something we call justice. Revision compulsion is a curious process of being on and off the hook, over and over, waiting until finally the prefixes float.

Facts of blackness denegate black life. Say it again. Black life is not an "is" that is repressed by law, ipso facto. Blackness marks (a)tonality confounding the occasion for question and elaboration. Another time.

"the no is proved"[20]

μ [revision compulsion] **38**

The unfortunate nature of this particular case . . .
The unthinkable nature of this particular case . . .
The unthinkable night of this particular case . . .
The unthinkable night of this particular study . . .
The unthinkable night of this precious study . . .
The unthinkable night blanketing this precious study . . .
. . . because the suspected burglar refused to heed this command.
why the suspected burglar refused to heed this command.
why the running burglar refused to heed this command.
why the running figure refused to heed this command.
why the running figure refused to heed some command.
why the running figure quieted to heed some other command . . .
Where there are rights and a harm committed by a state agent, there are questions the courts must hear, elaborate on, and resolve in order to provide remedies.
Where there are bodies and a harm committed by a state agent, there are questions the courts must hear, elaborate on, and resolve in order to provide remedies.

Where there are bodies and a promise committed by a state agent, there are questions the courts must hear, elaborate on, and resolve in order to provide remedies.
Where there are bodies and a promise broken by a state agent, there are questions the courts must hear, elaborate on, and resolve in order to provide remedies.
Where there are bodies and a promise broken by a flashy badge, there are questions the courts must hear, elaborate on, and resolve in order to provide remedies.
Where there are bodies and a promise broken by a flashy badge, there are questions we all hear, elaborate on, and resolve in order to provide remedies.
Where there are bodies and a promise broken by a flashy badge, there are questions we all hear, elaborating on and resolving them in order to provide remedies.
Where there are bodies and a promise broken by a flashy badge, there are questions we all hear, elaborating on and resolving them in order to provide truth.
What kind of life is this life?
What form of life is this life?
What form of life is that life?
What form of sound is that life?
What form of sound projects that life?
What form as sound projects life?

B [wilder] 39

1986: The sentence as a grammatical technology positions the dead as cause of death. It is an aesthetic performance of the law's engagement with a "totality of circumstances" laid out between the majority and minority opinions in *Garner*.[21] Totality, in the end, is constructed through determinations of facts from various forms of documented evidence filtered by a more fundamental question about how the law is to regard black life. Justice Sandra Day O'Connor in *Garner* developed a protocol for determining what she referred to as the "distinctive manner" of black life.[22]

2016: It is as if shooting Alton Sterling was not degradation enough. O'Connor's protocol and police officer Blane Salamoni's repeated words "stupid motherfucker" meet in the totality of law's performative dimension. O'Connor has Sterling's blood on her rationalizing hands with her discovery of an endless source within legal reason to reverse the question of causation. Her logic demonstrates that by defining black subjectivity as self-induced risk and willed exposure, the law will always be able to offer justification for use of lethal force. It does not matter what kind of evidence is collected to argue a civil rights violation because judgment is no longer the aim. The aim, instead, is the business of extracting this curious raw material O'Connor described as "life . . . exposed to risk."[23]

Fourth Amendment jurisprudence here reveals itself to be a form of manifest destiny, turning black life into black selfhood. It is a colonization of life that regards the mere condition of living as supersessive cause for using lethal force.

With law, we are in the morass of how blackness matters grammatically. The grammar of legal sentencing structures life leading up to the fatal moment adjectivally so life can be read against the very constitutional claims made on behalf of victims of state violence.

Supersession, supplantation, displacement, replacement become the *technê* of O'Connor's Fourth Amendment discovery.

2016: The Third Circuit Court of Appeals in *Johnson v. City of Philadelphia* decided that a police officer was not civilly liable for violating Kenyado Newsuan's Fourth Amendment right, reasoning that his mental illness was a "superseding cause" breaking the chain of "proximate causation" between the officer's conduct and the suspect's death.[24]

"Superseding cause" is the way the law looks at black life as supernatural, and as such, black life itself can always offer either a naturalized or privatized explanation for killing a black person, no matter who pulled the trigger.

Life as an ontological assumption is grammatically displaced—from an *unconditional interest in life* to a *willfully exposed self*—and the dead become the cause of dying.

Death, then, becomes self-defeating evidence because black selfhood *substitutes in* for any other cause of death, including the fact that someone else, a state agent, pulled the trigger on their gun. Blackness appears in law as a form of living that has a supersessive relation to seeking a remedy for death.

J. L. Austin could only unconsciously register the murderousness of speech when discussing the "perlocutionary act . . . [for which] there is no restriction to the minimum physical act at all."[25] Perlocutionary acts include the excesses, mistakes, "misfires" of speech in a field of unintended effects or influence on an interlocutor.

Referring to a finger on the trigger of a gun to suggest that speech and physics share the same question of causation as *influence*, Austin remarks that linguistic and physical causation are *in pari materia*.[26] The principle of *in pari materia*, meaning "of the same matter" or "on the same subject," is a principle of statutory interpretation requiring that when you have two laws that refer to the same matter, they must be analyzed together.

We are always in this lethal perlocutionary sphere of influence.

Listening while we look at the law looking at itself, we hear the ongoingness of an ongoing exposure to "(a) (black) performance," to what Stanley Cavell might recognize alternatively as some "passionate utterance," which is the condition of possibility for the very task of judgment and sentencing.[27]

Bewilderment, it seems to me, is the only passion capable of inviting the disorders of desire in this extractive legal landscape where living is a superseding cause that defeats the ability to construct a proximate chain of causation from racial profiling, to arrest, to detention, and, finally, to death.

There is only Bland's repetition of things "turned into all this."[28]

The 2015 final report from President Barack Obama's Task Force on 21st Century Policing pinpoints the problem of "offensive or harsh language [which] can escalate a minor situation."[29] But the dashcam recording of Bland's arrest shows us something much more complex about racial profiling.[30] About 1 minute and 45 seconds of Encinia's attempt to effect a personal arrest are in the visual frame, and about 5 minutes are outside the frame. About nineteen commands are given in the frame, and about forty-six are out of the frame.

Racial profiling as a method of law enforcement is not simply, or even essentially, about the disproportionate or discretionary power of the officer over the citizen but is a function of the *frame*. Listening while we look, we both see and hear how black life is ushered out of the frame and into the void.[31] Bland is out of sight as we hear the officer's erratic commands, the majority of which are made off-screen (figure 6.1). It is as if their heaving is what keeps Bland expelled from the visible.

The actuality of policing takes place outside any given frame, and its authority essentially depends on the irreducibility of the voice of law to social space. We *see* racial profiling in the stillness of the visual scene, but the closeness of the audio takes us outside of the frame with a certain fantasia of the law's relentless barking. The immediate distress produced by this evidence is precisely the feeling of needing it to shut up.

6.1 Screen grab from "Full Sandra Bland Arrest Video," *Wall Street Journal*, July 22, 2015, at 9:48.

The geoAVspatial positioning of enforcement indexes the not-yet and never-to-be compliant. Here is where law's jurisdiction transcends the territoriality of perception and becomes pure diction in the two words, *stop* and *it*, in a totalizing and general command.

Diction emphasizes the dependence of legal meaning on voice, such that law and voice become one and the same: *juris/diction*. "The Law itself," as Mladen Dolar writes, "in its pure form, before commanding anything specific, is epitomized by the voice, the voice that commands total compliance, although senseless in itself."[32] The voice functions as the classically Freudian superegoic dead Father that the word of law, or jurisprudence, depends on. Encinia's vocalization marks the structural status of the "voice object" as the place where an essential narcissism is at work in law. What is deadly about the law is this narcissistic imaginary demand for recognition, always in crisis, but provoked to a murderous level of achieving presence on encountering feminine jouissance.

The "I" and "you" of "I will light you up," bayed by Encinia in response to Bland's question, "Why do I have to put out a cigarette when I'm in my own car?" disperses into so many sonic assaults on "it."[33]

It? Is this an "it," as in the *il* of *il y a*? A *there* of something that is nothing other than the empty frame? As in 있다, *itda*? Whether this "it" is a *there*, a *that*, a *this*, the bleating insistence which presences the law as voice only further devoids the frame of a *there*, a *that*, a *this*, and leaves the trace of a non-universalizable sound of the *not-all* that responds.

Writing the Chinese character 都 up on the board during his lecture . . . *or Worse*, Jacques Lacan explains it is "either voiced *dōu* . . . or, in a more ancient voicing one says *tcha* . . . which means *without exception*."[34]

Lacan is interested in this character for its colloquial usage, which provides a supplementary notion of "the *all* spreading out for us from within, and meeting its limit only with inclusion."[35] As supplemental *all*, *dōu* or *tcha* remains essentially empty insofar as it is added to "the totality of whatever is at issue as content," for example, in the term *mankind*.[36]

都 is a phono-semantic compound, including the pictogram 者 of "a sugarcane with full leaves and stems, with a mouth under," and is phonetically loaned for abstract meanings; and the semantic ideogram 邑, a combination of 囗, depicting total enclosure, and 卩, depicting a kneeling person, to mean "town, city."[37] This colloquial form of the idea of *all* that Lacan is interested in comes from the character 諸, which loses the character 邑 ("town, city"), and gains the ideogram 言, meaning "to say, to speak, to talk."[38] This latter ideogram consists of a mark added to 舌, indicating "movement of the tongue."[39]

The sense of *all* here encompasses the decadence, plentitude, and decay of the sounds of some moving mouth, its forked tongues, which sweetly, treacherously, tempt from the outside of whatever all-enclosing space of social and political life and its terrifyingly inclusive *juris/diction*.

卩 [*res nulla loquitur*] **41**

The performance of *juris/diction* reverberates beyond what is doctrinally comprehensible under the rule of res ipsa loquitur. The classic common law principle *res ipsa loquitur* translates from the Latin as "the thing speaks for itself." The Third Restatement of Torts defines it as "circumstantial evidence of a quite distinctive form" that can be used when there is no direct and specific evidence that someone's negligent act caused the injury at issue before a court.[40] Circumstantiality and generality are usually insufficient modes of evidence to transform social reality into a legally actionable claim. However, res ipsa loquitur marks a type of general harm into the law's always limited jurisdiction to provide remedy only for *specific* acts and injuries.

Res nulla loquitur challenges the cultural investment in res ipsa loquitur by centering the unique quality of black life as self-evidence of an essentially nullifying legal personality. The evidentiary exhibition of lethal arrest documents blackness as life that can be both cause and effect of its own demise.

Res nulla loquitur is the principle unifying every necessary denegation we find with each turn of doctrinal analysis and rhetorical performance of fact and rule. "The no-thing speaks," or "nobody's thing speaks" registers a synesthesia of violence that cannot ever be completely and finally ordered even into the logic of res ipsa loquitur.

Res nulla loquitur is a rule of evidence that calls not for legal remedy but for some other law beyond the force of law and grammar. It is the law of that which will always have been annulled of any reference to a or some self that could come before the law.

Against the clarity and conviction that harm calls for remedy, *res nulla loquitur* is to enter the foggy place of evidentiary interpretation requiring a different forum of hearing. Hear, too, a formally, if bizarrely, encoded audio-nomos across a profoundly overdetermined, perjurious, evidentiary terrain where lethal arrest will have been caused by a form of life always, self-evidently, exposed, and, thus, life with no self.

The no-thing speaks. . . . And when it does, blackness unseats the self-evident in and of every recourse to the copular verb *to be*. With Bland's question, "How did failing to signal turn into all this?" we look over the precipice of self-evidentiary rhetorics wherever we find them to tumble down so many signifying chains of justice.[41]

What we look at here, while listening, is the "Index of Counts" that opens the Third Amended Complaint filed by Sandra Bland's mother, Geneva Reed-Veal.

Count I – Brian Encinia – 42 U.S.C. § 1983 Claim
Count II – Elsa Magnus – 42 U.S.C. § 1983 Claim
Count III – Elsa Magnus – Negligence Claim
Count IV – Oscar Prudente – 42 U.S.C. § 1983 Claim
Count V – Oscar Prudente – Negligence Claim
Count VI – Waller County – Negligence Claim
Count VII – Waller County – §1983 and 1988/*Monnell* [sic] Policy Claim
Count VIII – Rafael Zuniga – 42 U.S.C. § 1983
Count IX – Rafael Zuniga – Negligence Claim
Count X – Michael Sergis – 42 U.S.C. § 1983
Count XI – Michael Sergis – Negligence Claim
Count XII – Dormic Smith – 42 U.S.C. § 1983
Count XIII – Dormic Smith – Negligence Claim
Count XIV – Cynthia Whidden – 42 U.S.C. § 1983
Count XV – Cynthia Whidden – Negligence Claim
Count XVI – Marc Langdon – 42 U.S.C. § 1983
Count XVII – Marc Langdon – Negligence Claim
Count XVIII – Lt. Sherry Rochen – 42 U.S.C. § 1983
Count XIX – Lt. Sherry Rochen – Negligence Claim
Count XX – Asst. Chief Lanny Thibodeaux – 42 U.S.C. § 1983
Count XXI – Asst. Chief Lanny Thibodeaux – Negligence Claim
Count XXII – Matthew Mills – 42 U.S.C. § 1983
Count XXIII – Matthew Mills – Negligence Claim

Count XXIV – Marianne Williams – 42 U.S.C. § 1983
Count XXV – Marianne Williams – Negligence Claim
Count XXVI – Randy Lewis – 42 U.S.C. § 1983
Count XXVII – Randy Lewis – Negligence Claim[42]

Read, while listening, this chain of names linking state agents with two particular civil causes of action: 42 U.S.C. § 1983 and negligence. Section 1983 defines the elements of what constitutes a "civil action for deprivation of rights."[43] And *Black's Law Dictionary* defines *negligence* as "the omission to do something which a reasonable man, guided by those considerations which ordinarily regulate the conduct of human affairs, would do. Or doing something which a prudent and reasonable man would not do."[44]

Interpret, while listening, the rhythm of a score representing both the overtone of deprivation and an undertone of failed care.

In Bland's mother's signifying chain of justice, tort law scores the insufficiency of civil rights remedies with the force of the plurality of social interests drawn into articulating "negligence," or the failure to exercise a reasonable expectation of care.

Index, chain, score.

This score accepts that both direct and circumstantial evidence of lethal use of force will not deliver justice and, instead, symbolizes the reality of the evacuated "self," the *ipsa*, on behalf of which such evidence is thought to speak, and continually interprets to the brink that which evidence cannot bear. It allows us a way to remember that whatever is or seems self-evident is precisely not where we should pay our attention.

119 [bland murmurance] **42**

In a description of the cell where Bland was found dead, the state's investigation includes an arresting citation of what might have been the last words she read:

> The shelf/table attached to the south wall and to the west of this bunk contained two books, one titled "101 Ways to Find God's Purpose in Your Life" and the other was titled "God's Word," or a Bible. *The Bible was opened to pages 428–429, Psalms 119–122.* Investigator PARINELLO informed Ranger ELLISON that he had already moved the two books while looking for any handwritten notes left by BLAND. *The Bible had been found open on the aforementioned pages and the other book was closed.*[45]

Of the psalms referenced in the investigator's report, Psalm 119 is one of the longest chapters in the Bible. It is a prayer dedicated to the Torah, or written word of God, given in physical evidence. It draws our attention to another realm of knowing, equally if differently, tied to another order of submission, compliance, and obedience to authority through writing, the word, and the status of the letter.

Psalms as song or liturgy are inseparable from the ritual context of the open book found in Bland's cell. But it points not to some divine law but a fabricated, performed, shown *doing* in response to Bland's question about how "failing to signal turned into all this." This *doing*, a *loquitur*, in and by the evidence, emerges from a *res nulla*, a nonself, for we ultimately do not know who opened the book, and by whom or whether it was read at all, except by those following this signifying chain.

Res nulla: an unhived, traceless never-leaving, *anatta*, apophatic thing.

Psalm, song, law, *loquitur*: texts to be nonsilently read and aurally interpreted.

Murmur is the English word Robert Alter uses to translate from the Hebrew word *hagah*, which means "to make a low muttering sound, which is what one does with a text in a culture where there is no silent reading."[46]

The trail of evidence left in the wake of Sandra Bland's death with these specific psalms compels us to listen for this murmuring. It vocalizes a teaching, and so desire: an ongoing, concrete promise in nonsilent reading, itself a libidinal mode of "rebellion" and "rescue" in "the here and now" of the physical world.[47]

Murmurance is a compelled aurality of this evidence, which effects, through familiar and traditional imagery and language, the extremities of legal reason and enforcement endured "countermythologically," as J. Kameron Carter would describe it.[48] Aural evidence murmurs that which cannot be directly said or thought. And whatever your listening catches concretizes something more real in the evidence than what self-evident judgment can ever know.

Murmuring itself, *res nulla loquitur* writes our desire within law. Bland murmurance loops and surrounds.

mu, 無, 巫

火 [fire; anger] 43

As for the word (for the word will be my theme)—neither grammar nor lexicon hold an interest for me—I believe I can say that if I love the word, it is only in the body of its idiomatic singularity, that is, where a passion for translation comes to lick it as a flame or an amorous tongue might: . . . —JACQUES DERRIDA, "What Is a 'Relevant' Translation?"

The heat of translation is at once a recovery and a disappearance. It blisters and smothers. It leaves raw the flesh of the word. It cleans and cools down that which smolders on the surface of language.

This enigmatic temperament for translation to burn and purge is there in the debated translations of Frantz Fanon's infamous chapter 5 of *Black Skin, White Masks*. While English translations have rendered Fanon's original French title, "L'expérience vécue du noir," as "fact of blackness" or "lived experience of the black man," Fred Moten has introduced a critical spin on this slippage between fact and lived experience with the title of his 2008 essay "The Case of Blackness." He is interested in an idea of "case" that is "a kind of broken bridge or cut suspension" between fact and lived experience, given in, Moten goes on, "how the troubled, illicit commerce between fact and lived experience is bound up with that between blackness and the black, a difference that is often concealed, one that plays itself out not by way of the question of accuracy or adequation but by way of the shadowed emergence of the ontological difference between being and beings."[1] At stake in theorizing "the case of blackness" is also the difference between Woman and women, and phenomenology and "what remains untranslatable as its direction toward the things [*Dinge*] themselves."[2] Moten goes on further to say that "the case of blackness" between fact and lived experience, "in its relation to the black when black social life is interdicted . . . is part of a set of variations on a theme that include assertions of the irreducible pathology of black social life."[3]

The "political phonochoreography" Moten is after in Fanon's writing begins with the question, "But what are we to make of the pathological here?"[4] Moten perhaps rephrases what John Forrester has asked about the modern history of *thinking in cases* in his article "If *p*, Then What?" Between the two questions, I want to create a path of marks to a certain constitutive pathology that both mobilizes case thinking and animates a series of impasses in Fanon's studies of blackness and colonialism whose essence is given in how one listens to the fullness of dystranslation. These differential translations touch on what necessarily remains untranslatable at the core of the chapter but, as well, Fanon's *écriture*. Translations as failure touch on something untranslatable about *noirceur*, translated only superficially into English as "blackness," within the context of colonial experience by virtue of this form of noncontact between the word and what Jacques Derrida refers to as "the body of its idiomatic singularity."[5]

Dystranslation drifts toward some constantly receding horizon beyond the case's Aristotelian form of practical wisdom and the psychoanalytic form of singularity that refuses a largely analogical relation of reasoning across the professions and the human sciences, including law, medicine, and philosophy. The trouble I want to take on is how any imaginary or symbolic association between blackness and pathology surfaces the constitutive practice of anticolonial case writing that broaches the biographical and psychosocial as its own reward, as a form of unconscious knowledge or what Lacan developed across his work as *savoir*.

Suh Gyung Noh translates *l'expérience* into Korean as "실제 경험," *siljae gyeongheom*, meaning neither "fact" nor "lived experience" but "real experience." Consider the bodies of marks of the term and sense of the concept of 실제 경험 in *hanja*:

實際 經驗
(실제) (경험)

If this, too, is a mode of case writing, we begin with the sheer number and complexity of these marks that make up the phono-ideogrammic compounds in the *hanja* concept of "real experience." They appear as if a map of some secret dance of a mystical multitude connected by invisible, sonic lines only imperfectly contained when we make recourse to the word *experience*. Their crowding brings the marks alive. Their block form teems with foot- and handprints of the unsayable of colonial history. The marks are intricately laid sticks of kindling for what can only be a spectacular explosion of the unthought.

Their dystranslated strokes are forever wet with the breath of how *noirceur* thinks.

Dystranslation heals by extinguishing, singes by singing, and alights by a most uncanny caress. My husband's whispered words "That's not what he said," poured into my ear by some "amorous tongue" Derrida references in the epigraph, spilled water in some vessel I did not know I was. The heat of their madness enveloped my anger.

carve, roof,
silk, thread, horse   mouths
weave, neighbor,   sew,
shell.   gallop,
all.

笑 [smile] 44

That's not what he said.

We were at Red Bay Coffee in Oakland for a screening of Isaac Julien's film *Frantz Fanon: Black Skin, White Masks*. Something of me was momentarily shattered as I watched an unbridgeable gulf open up between the English subtitles running across the lower third of the screen and the audio of Joby Fanon's memories of his brother's decision to become a psychiatrist.

My skepticism toward Julien's documentary representation of Fanon's personal and professional life was brought into sudden relief by these exhaled words: *That's not what he said.* They surfaced just how radical the experience is of being confronted with what one absolutely does not know, and how this unknown is *heard*. In my case, the unknowable surfaced because I could not *hear* the French language; and in a more general sense for a predominantly English-speaking audience there in the coffee shop. The surfacing of the unknowable with the words *That's not what he said* is not a lack or deficiency of any non-French engagement with Fanon's writing. It simply begs the question of the multiple ways in which the unknowable in how *noirceur* thinks is transmitted through the various translations of Fanon's work into non-French languages.

It also begs the question of what forms of intimacy obtain when we catch each other, unwittingly, in the throes of a translation failure. As momentary, felicitous failure in translation between the idiomatic singularity of Joby Fanon's speech and a film narrative of Frantz Fanon's intellectual and political development, looking back on it now, the failure introduced the possibility that we might know the word *noirceur* as a signifier of the ontological failure of "Le Noir" Fanon discusses in chapter 1 of *Black Skin, White Masks*.

Intruded on by the five words *That's not what he said*, they open the floodgates to a desire that knows no difference between the incomprehensibility inherent to any language and the rumble of my lover's voice. If I drown there, mired in all the loss entailed with so many *objets a* circulating in this pure negative space between three languages, in this terra incognita, so be it. Let failures manifest between three languages that I dare not ever say are mine—English, French, and Korean. Their surprises shake me from political conventions of criticism. They dissolve the fantasy of being able to know in any final way that which Fanon invited his readers to encounter, and leave us in "*nospace*" (*n'espace*), to use a term from Lacan's notoriously difficult essay, "L'étourdit."[6]

Beyond the seductive reproduction of meaning through colonial linguistic encounters, this *nospace* is not one metalanguage of imperfect translation and impossible meaning. It is a certain "*notall*" of language marked by a foundational repression in a "primal scene," which Moten provocatively insists, "must be heard."[7] *This* particular historical, social, and global scene of hearing and voice is what we might refer to as *lalangue du noirceur*. Its sound is one of a fundamental equivocality of natural languages and sonicity itself. Both natural languages and sonicity equally, but differentially, fail to symbolize this primal scene. At the same time, both are also equally, but differentially, there to be heard by anyone or anything radically unsettled by the compromises of sense in and through language that, as Lacan warns us, reduce "what is said in what is heard" at the expense of forgetting "that one might be saying (*Qu'on dise*)."[8]

In an anti-black world, all around us, we hear more than we can translate and thus are compelled to speak, write, read, and think differently when yielding or fleeing to inarticulable satisfactions of musicality, sonicity, and the blackness of voice in accentuation, slurring, amalgamating, truncating, severing—in sum, ossifying and rearranging the structurally imperfect words of the Other into sounds our mouths utter and our ears ingest.

That's not what he said radically splays the order cinema gives to sound, image, and subtitled translations. And what can be read is never only what is read but is also the strangeness of the words in relation to everything in disarray. The film's images seduce like a commercial: pieties piled on each other that somehow give you the delusion you already wanted. Still, that which cannot be heard has a sound: a brother's language of a truth driven by Fanon's research on the varying symptoms of an anti-black world. Translational equivocation concretizes forms of missed meaning across the many interpretations of Fanon's life and thought, as well as the possibility of articulating the unconscious or *parlêtre* of Fanon's writing.

I set out to expand this equivocation, Fanon's *parlêtre*, by dystranslating through hangul and *hanja* characters.

> "J'esquissai un sourire."[9] [I hinted a smile].
>
> "I made a tight smile."[10]
>
> "I attempted a smile."[11]
>
> "나는 슬쩍 미소를 지었다."[12] [I made a subtle smile].

미소, *miso*, 微笑, subrideo (from Latin *sub-*, meaning "below, under," and *rīdeō*, meaning "laugh"), Proto-Indo-European root **smei-*, meaning "to laugh, smile"; Old English *smerian*, meaning "to laugh at, scorn."[13] The *hanja* character for "laugh, smile" here, 笑, depicts a dog, a person, some corporeal figure, running, moving amid the grass.

Hint, tight, attempt. 슬쩍, *seuljjeok*, subtle, slight. These are the diminutives of Fanon's libidinal response to smile when caught by the white gaze, "Look, a Negro!" They are diminutives-*plus.* Because the etymologies of the French, English, and Korean words for "smile" already contain within them a diminutive to register a smile as something less or smaller than a laugh.

Blackness libidinally registers at a level smaller, lower, or even shorter than an already mini version of a fullness that is laughter. These diminutives are an essential flourish to Fanon's dramatization of his experience of fragmentation of his "corporeal schema." They register the difficulty of staying small, subtle, tight or only hinting when encountered by the Other's repeated assaults of signification. As this difficulty increases, he increasingly comes closer to a limit-form of laughter, "je voulus m'amuser jusqu'à m'étouffer."[14] This is translated into English with the words "I made up my mind to laugh myself to tears" (Markmann) or "I wanted to kill myself laughing" (Philcox), and into Korean with the words "나는 재미있어 죽을 지경이고 싶었다" (Noh), meaning "I wanted to die from fun."[15] The smile is a symptom of a laughing jouissance that he suffers both as the corporeal integrity of his ego is broken into an "epidermal racial schema" *and* as "the Other, evasive, hostile, but not opaque, transparent and absent, vanished."[16]

Nothing appears in the place of the Other. But he does not suffocate, die, or cry from hiding this laughter with a smile. There is just "nausea" or "구토," a feeling of illness, perhaps, from a laughter within that will force its way out even so.[17]

헛- [*aux malades de fuir la liberté*] 45

Why did Fanon become a psychiatrist? Julien would have us believe from Joby Fanon's answer to this question that it was because, as the English subtitles read, "The psychiatrist can help the patient to regain that freedom they have lost in madness."[18]

That's not what he said.

Joby Fanon's words tell of something else entirely. The psychiatrist, Joby Fanon explains, is he who "allows the sick to flee freedom [*aux malades de fuir la liberté*], but who is obligated to get him to retrieve his freedom [*l'amène à retrouver sa liberté*]." Julien's English whites out the precise rambling of "aux malades de fuir la liberté." The subtitles reduce psychological suffering to an individuated clinical condition, while the spoken French references something endemic to social experience (*aux malades*) whose movement runs from the given terms of freedom into illness, and then into a retrieval of another freedom, neither lost nor regained, and thus wholly his (*sa liberté*).

Embedded between the spaces of the English subtitle translation and the sounds of Joby Fanon's speech, we bump into a surplus negation at the core of

Fanon's desire, the psychiatrist who gives witness to the transformation of *la liberté* into *sa liberté*. The film would have us miss this most difficult agency at the center of Fanon's life and writing: an unconscious choice to flee freedom, which appears in the world as a pathological susceptibility to illness and suffering or human proclivities of violence and shame. Fanon writes:

> Parvenu à ce point, j'hésitai longtemps avant de m'engager. Les étoiles se firent agressives. Il me fallait choisir. Que dis-je, je n'avais pas le choix . . .[19]
>
> Having reached this point, I was long reluctant to commit myself. Aggression was in the stars. I had to choose. What do I mean? I had no choice . . .[20]
>
> Having reached this point, I was long reluctant to commit myself. Then even the stars became aggressive. I had to choose. What am I saying? I had no choice.[21]
>
> 이 지점에 이르자 나는 뛰어들기 전에 한참 망설였다. 별들이 덤벼든나. 나는 선택을 해야 했나. 선택할 것이 없었는네 무슨 헛소리 . . . [At this point, before plunging in, I hesitated a long time. The stars are springing in. I chose to choose. There is nothing to choose, what nonsense . . .] (translation from Korean mine)[22]

These translations of a passage at the end of *Black Skin, White Masks* contain so many compelling slips and differential resonances where Fanon's French in this sentence contains an idiomatic enunciation of doubt in the subject's own sense of what is being said about choice: *que dis-je*. This phrase immediately associates with the key signifier and phoneme *dit* in Lacan's *L'étourdit* of the *qu'on dise* of bungled and foolish saying. Just as Fanon's idiomatic gesture exceeds the ego of conscious statement and consequently, translatability, my ear opens to absorb all the sounds of the unconscious subject of the saying.

Or at least I think I can perhaps do this by splaying the possible saying of the unconscious across a radical idiomaticity of being fooled: *que dis-je . . . what do I mean? . . . what am I saying . . .* 헛 소 리 *. . . what nonsense . . .* no, in Korean, this is idiomatically closer to *what crap, what bullshit*.[23]

The *noirceur* of dystranslation is the entire topology of sounds arranged from this multilingual scene of audition. It registers not only the symbolic effects of the Other on a black ego but also the saying of the unconscious captive in equivocation formally constituted across these multiple languages. The sounding of the saying manifests the specific form of difficulty articulated in this sentence of choosing to choose in a situation of madness that sets in when encountering the void that opens up in every objective and subjective fantasy of "les nègres," as Fanon says.[24]

The *he* of *That's not what he said*, or the *sa* of *sa liberté*, requires a hearing of a saying that is other than the said of what is heard on first, second, third, and every pass.

This is the raw material of a libidinal economy that underwrites a fundamental freedom to flee the freedoms of the given world in the unsayable, registered here as the bewilderment, confusion, and even bullshit, 헛소리 (*hutsori*), of *que dis-je*. It is a certain consuming experience of involving oneself in allowing this fundamental loss to be heard by unwittingly remarking on how one chose to choose in both an objective and a subjective situation in which madness was preferable to the always limited freedom of (neo)(post) colonial belonging and mastery.

At the level of personal narrative, Fanon recounts in *Black Skin, White Masks*, "I had rationalized the world and the world had rejected me on the basis of color prejudice. Since no agreement was possible on the level of reason, I threw myself back toward unreason."[25] But our dystranslation above reveals that the unreason Fanon chooses is one that gives way to an unconscious choice in and against both the factuality and livedness of experience, embodied here in *aux malades*. Fanon's resignation to unreason in a poetics of *objet ça* presents itself here as a unique form of psychoanalytic case writing.

Qu'a t'il dit? What did he say?

How do we even begin to answer this question so as to continue being able to hear the misheard, misunderstood, misread, and any other lapses of communication, sense, and translation?

If blackness has a unique vantage on this question, it's because the essentially libidinal activity of speaking desire carries the unconscious presupposition that history, culture, and language make slaves of us all. So totalizing is this subjection that origins, ownership, obligations, and the entire epistemology of choice become impossible to approach strictly as matters of conscious commitment.

Multilingual apprenticeship of oneself to the history, language, and mores of another cultural group, or even disappearing into another culture, will not absolve us from having to make that choice we misrecognize as the damned position of *les malades*. Interracial encounters as cultural exchange, fair compensation for appropriative association, or reidentifying oneself in the cause of the slave miss what is black about all language, cultural traditions, and sociality: that seemingly inhuman, often regarded as pathological, orientation to earning a political conscience through an exhaustive procedure of living out all the ways in which one pays the price of becoming a free subject by becoming deaf to the 헛- of any utterance, story, origin, political conscience, indeed, 소리.

n'y [*menus morceaux*] 46

I hear by splaying the possible saying of the unconscious across a radical idiomaticity of being fooled:

> Sealed into that crushing objecthood, I turned beseechingly to others. Their attention was a liberation, running over my body suddenly abraded into nonbeing, endowing me once more with an agility that I had thought lost, and by taking me out of the world, restoring me to it. But just as I reached the other side, I stumbled, and the movements, the attitudes, the glances of the other fixed me there, in the sense in which a chemical solution is fixed by a dye. I was indignant; I demanded an explanation. Nothing happened. I burst apart. Now the fragments have been put together again by another self.[26]
>
> Locked in this suffocating reification, I appealed to the Other so that his liberating gaze, gliding over my body suddenly smoothed of rough edges, would give me back the lightness of being I thought I had lost, and taking me out of the world put me back in the world. But just as I

get to the other slope, I stumble, and the Other fixes me with his gaze, his gestures and attitude, the same way you fix a preparation with a dye. I lose my temper, demand an explanation. . . . Nothing doing. I explode. Here are the fragments put together by another me.[27]

Enfermé dans cette objectivité écrasante, j'implorai autrui. Son regard libérateur, glissant sur mon corps devenu soudain nul d'aspérités, me rend une légèreté que je croyais perdue et, m'absentant du monde, me rend au monde. Mais là-bas, juste à contre-pente, je bute, et l'autre, par gestes, attitudes, regards, me fixe, dans le sens où l'on fixe une préparation par un colorant. Je m'emportai, exigeai une explication . . . Rien n'y fit. J'explosai. Voici les menus morceaux par un autre moi réunis.[28]

이 짓누르는 객관성에 갇혀 나는 다른 사람에게 탄원했다. 그의 해방의 시선이 내 몸에 흐르자 갑자기 신랄한 마음이 가시고 내가 잃었다고 믿었던 경쾌한 기분이 살아나고, 나를 세상 밖으로 내보냄으로써 내게 세상을 돌려준다. 그렇지만 나는 저기 반대편 비탈에 부딪히고, 타자는 몸짓, 태도, 시선으로 나를 움직이지 못하게 한다. 마치 착색제로 화학용액을 고정 시키듯. 나는 분개해서 설명을 요구했다. …… 아무 설명이 없다. 나는 폭발했다. 또다른 자아에 의해 작은 조각들이 맞춰진다.[29]

The French word *aspérités* Fanon uses comes from the Old French word meaning "difficulty, painful situation, harsh treatment." It is related to the Latin word *asperitas*, meaning "roughness," from *asper*, meaning "rough, harsh," and was used as an adjective for "sour wine, bad weather, and hard times."[30]

When Fanon writes of a sudden voiding of this harshness as the white gaze runs over his body, it is neither "nonbeing" nor "rough edges" of the body that are negated or smoothed but a psychic nullification of difficulty and pain. The Korean translation of this is "신랄한 마음," meaning "bitter heart."

The mislocation of inner or psychic pain in either an abstraction ("nonbeing") or a physical object ("rough edges") in the English translations displaces the terrain of transformation Fanon is describing in both this paragraph and the book more generally. Again, the issue is not with correcting the translations per se. It is with grasping the specificity of the displacement to understand a certain unknown knowing of black experience manifest in the *notall* of translation itself. Between an overly philosophical or physical emphasis, the unique materiality of symbolic experience given in the body as a libidinal terrain of wild and conflicting feelings (feeling crushed, liberated, light, immobilized, exploded, etc.) is reduced to metaphorical language.

This reduction closes theoretical and political interpretation of Fanon's language. Listening through this reduction, we might hear Fanon's reference to a fixing dye as a material signifier topologically turning Fanon's language on the psychical body. This body is not anywhere else but at the histological register. Histology is a form of study at a microscopic scale. Microscopic observation is enabled by the use of dye to make the small, invisible details of physical matter visible.

Insofar as *histo-* refers to "tissue," when Fanon says, in response to this histological fixing, "Je m'emportai, exigeai une explication," we should understand it as a cellular, systemic response. The more literal translation of the French into English as being "carried away" is much more resonant with the image of a cellular web of a piece of flesh than the emotional states of indignity or anger signified by Markmann, Philcox, and Noh. These translations—"I was indignant . . . ," "I lose my temper . . . ," "I was outraged . . . ," "나는 분개해서 . . ."—impose an ego and lose the idiomatic phrasing that contains the saying of an unknown subject who carries Fanon's body off.

This is key because this shapes how we hear the next part of the phrase, "exigeai une explication . . . " If we are hearing something already other than the castrated symbolic subject, then it is this other, this unknown subject, who "demands an explanation" and, by implication, questions. This is the body whom Fanon addresses in prayer with this famous final line, "O my body, always make me a man who questions!"[31]

The audible associative space created across these multiple translations allows us to conceptually index how experience in the body moves from a neurotic structure of imaginary enjoyment to an identification with the emptiness of the cause of desire.

"Nothing happened."
That's not what he said.

"Nothing doing."
What? That's not what he said.

"아무 설명이 없다."
That's not what he said.

"Rien n'y fit." [To no avail? There, nothing could be done? Nothing availed itself?]

What is this "n'y"?

Dystranslation works through the limits of metaphor and reads for metonymically produced signification of absences. It allows us to track and assemble the presence of the Real of the body, "실제 경험," *siljae gyeongheom*, or "real experience," not only as an inner devastation or ruination but as a topological movement between the imaginary and symbolic realities of experience that sit on the surface of desire. "Voici," writes Fanon, "les menus morceaux. . . ." Where the English translations offer the neatness of the word *fragments*, the Korean translation's more literal rendering, "작은 조각들," meaning "small pieces," underscores the diminutive nature of the things extimately assembled in the aftermath of an exploded "I."

This assembly is the analyst's discourse, Lacan writes, as a practice of "interpretation, which, for its part, is not modal, but apophantic."[32] This is a knowledge without a subject, a constellation of indestructible letters, all the different *objets a*, or *objets ça*, through which our captivity in language becomes something of a choice between freedom and madness.

Not *petit*. Fanon wrote "menus." Not *objet*. He wrote "morceaux."

Not *n'est pas*. He wrote "n'y fit."

Apophantic analytic translational hearing exceeds the frigidity of *n'est pas* and embraces, instead, the endless procedure given in the idiomatic words, "n'y fit."

患 [anagrammatic scramble] 47

The English subtitles in the film *Black Skin, White Masks* keep repeating "the patient." It is the film's special signifier, its *objet a*.

Patient comes from the Latin *pati*, which means "to suffer." This is what Frantz Fanon as a doctor witnessed and studied as he treated the men, women, and children in Algeria. In contrast, Joby Fanon refers to these people in French as "les malades," which comes from the Latin *male habitus*, which means "ill-conditioned."[33] Both the French and English words contain a certain passivity about how and why people become ill, a certain abstraction of illness, which is a state as opposed to an experience. Though the English translation renders the patient in a passive relationship to freedom, the origin of the word *patient* has a more immediate and literal sense of illness. Again, in contrast, though the spoken French discussion of illness recognizes the agency of the patient in relationship to their freedom, the origin and sound of the word *malade* retains a sense of remove from a more experiential sense of illness.

This equivocation surprises me with its near-perfect inversion of a distance between word and origin. *Les malades* contains a strange mirror image of a certain gap (passive recipient or abstracted state) structured into the sign for the experience of illness.

In Noh's Korean translation of Fanon from the French, we find the use of the hangul word 환자 (*hwanja*), "a medical patient," which originates from the *hanja* word 患者, meaning "one who suffers from illness." The first ideogram of the word, 患 (*hwan*), means "to worry, to contract or suffer an illness, trouble, peril." This ideogram comprises two preceding ideograms: 串, which means "to pierce through, to wear, to penetrate," and 心, which means "heart, mind, thought, idea, intention, center, core." In contrast to the French word *les malades*, we have a composite depiction of illness as a *wounding to the core*.

I wonder about this connotation for those familiar with spoken Korean, and how the sound of the discourse of the 환사 retains the depicted scene in the ideogram 患.

Interpretation without translational resolution demonstrates how closely a referent can bring the *experience* of psychological suffering to an understanding of illness as an effect of language. The mind/body dichotomy, reproduced by a Western dichotomy between sign and reference, and word and speech, is deconstructed by the complex truth of psychological suffering, which eludes language between the three referents—*patient*, *malades*, and 患. The *hanja* characters and their ideogrammic reservoir via the Korean alphabet set us down the course of what Nathaniel Mackey refers to as the always available "anagrammatic" scramble of language, or what Derrida identifies as the "irreducibly graphic" nature of any text.[34]

Writing at the limits of translation opens up onto the *blackness* of anagrammatic scramble. You do not have to know a language to speak this language of the case of blackness. For it is a language that cannot be other than those lyrical fragments, those percussive phrases, that machinic looping of bits, all the words that burn up into letters whatever and anything they were meant to mean. The only rule for this *lalangue du noirceur*, which cannot be given in advance, is to fuck with grammatical settlement.

영 [μηδέν] **48**

What you set out to say can turn in the very saying of it. That is the reality of the Möbius-like movement of desire. One minute you're talking. And the next minute, unconscious desire is being spoken. If Fanon's writing bears *l'étourdit*, we must be able to cut through what is said in what is heard, and read it to the letter for how it transmits a knowledge of the blackness of unconscious desire.

How do we see/hear that movement? How do we index this unconscious desire when it emerges like this? Perhaps we might experience nothing but being implicated in this turn, this movement where the fragments of one's corporeality can be shattered no further and appear just as they are: in some other anagrammatic order of writing that knows

Lacan concludes his seminar on *L'étourdit* with an invitation to laugh, as Democritus does, at nothing. He drops two Greek words to signify a materialist sense of "nothing."

The first word is μηδέν (*mēdén*), meaning "nothing"; from μηδείς (*mēdeís*), meaning "no one, not even one, nobody, nothing... naught... by no means."[35]

The second is ἄτομος (*átomos*), "not compound, that cannot be cut, indivisible, infinitely small, individual"; from ἀ- (*a*-, "not") + τομ-, from the root word, τέμνω (*témnō*, "cut . . . particular kinds of cutting").[36]

Let our laughter register an "apophantic" blackness, *noirceur*, a Real movement that opens up between the *notall* captured by the numeral presence of "zero" in any signifier, including the signifier you are; and parts, or letters, so small they cannot be further divided, that you, too, harbor and scatter to the winds wherever your mark roams.

The Korean word for "zero" is 영 (*yeong*). Its *hanja* character, 零, is a compound combining the semantic 雨, depicting rain, and the phonetic 令, which has the ideogrammic meanings, "to order, to command, to make, to allow, to cause" and "order, command, directive." 零 has many meanings, including "to wither and fall, to rain or drizzle, to fraction, fragment or remainder, and zero." The Chinese ideogram 〇, also meaning "zero," is an etymological variant of 零 and is strangely doubled in the hangul word 영, with its two *ieung*s (ㅇ's), as if to remind us never to not be in touch with some celestial unknown in the thought and representation of nothingness.

Ten thousand marks rain, laugh, down from above, and water, clear, empty us of us.

咸 [*a*] **49**

My father's mother sent him a photo shortly after he had moved to Berkeley to start graduate school in 1969. I don't remember what the image was of. But on the back of the photo, she wrote a little note wondering about a hippopotamus she had seen during her recent visit to a zoo.

I wonder which zoo she went to. DalSeong Park Zoo, I learn through a quick Google search, is located in the oldest earthwork in Korea, built during the Three Kingdoms Period between 57 BCE and 668 CE. The Japanese military used the earthwork during the Sino-Japanese War in 1894–95 and then converted it to a park in 1905, the same year Japan forced Korea to sign the Japan-Korea Treaty of 1905, also known as the Eulsa Treaty, stripping

Korea of its diplomatic sovereignty and rendering Korea a protectorate of Japan. The park was renovated in 1965, a few years before my father would leave for Berkeley.

But most likely, my grandmother went to the Seoul Zoo, created in 1909 by the Japanese in the Changgyeonggung Palace. At the end of World War II, Japan poisoned 150 animals to conserve materials and labor. Animals that were not killed were abandoned. One wonders how they fared after Korea's so-called liberation from Japan, and whether and how the zoo's layered colonial origin was transformed in the following years.

Japan's colonialism reified the animality of African species and ways of life by introducing the institution of the zoo in Korean society.[37] Japan's strategic development of the peninsula through a zoological imagination marks the capaciousness of anti-black colonial fantasy. But it also occluded the possible identification of Korean colonial subjects with African animals in a form of captive indigeneity. Certainly, peasants and rebels and scholars and all manner of anti-colonial recalcitrants could always use another spirit animal to guide a way through these unending apocalyptic times.

The name *hippopotamus* comes from the Latin *hippos*, meaning "horse," and *potamos*, meaning "river," to signal this most curious, mythological, riparian mammal. It is a native of sub-Saharan Africa and among land-dwelling mammals is the closest to sharing a common evolutionary ancestor with whales and dolphins. Hippos were almost transplanted to the United States.

Among many surprising characteristics of the hippo, I am especially intrigued by the knowledge that they can open their mouths nearly 180 degrees. They also hold their heads partially above water when communicating, sending sound that travels through both water and air.[38] Littoral hippo language is double registered, differentially sonic, materially split.

The Korean hangul word for hippo is 하마 (*hama*). Like the Latin etymology, the Korean word in *hanja*, 河馬, "water" (*mul*) + "horse" (*mal*), translates to "river horse." It appears that *hama* is a loan translation moving from the Dutch word *rivierpaard*, also literally meaning "river horse," to Japanese kanji, as documented by the *Dōyaku Haruma* (1833).[39]

My father's mother's born surname was 함 (*Ham*). *Hama* minus the *a*. Supposedly there is only one clan from which this surname comes. It is the clan of Ham Gyu, a Goryeo general from the thirteenth century, from Gangneung. We visited Gangneung four summers ago when we all went to Korea together. The water there was a pale, pale blue, haunted by the sound *ttok, ttok, ttok . . .*

The *hanja* character for 함 (*Ham*) is 咸. It is an ideogrammic compound of 戌, meaning "axe," and 口, meaning "mouth/person or clay pot." The ideogram 戌, together with 口, expresses the image of soldiers on a battlefield, shouting while holding their spears, hence leading to associations with "shout," "everyone, without exception," and "together, completely, united." The extremity of the *hanja* scene here is *of some form of sound* that signs pure force. The sound itself stages the confluence of force and commonness, even force as and in common, or perhaps even some cosmic common force.

I set out to write and talk about 한 (*han*), but some *étourdit* in the case of blackness brought us 함 (*ham*), this pure force, a cipher made of something like the flesh of this mysterious riparian-dwelling, river-riding 말 (*mal*, 馬, horse). Again, Korean homophonic "political phonochoreography" delivers another wondrous knot. *Mal* (馬) is a homophone for 말 (*mal*), also meaning "word, speech, talk, language." Dystranslation by some unconscious subject marked and remarked in the *hanja* character for illness, 患, turned over and around into this signifier, 馬, is to hear another language of real experience at the heart of making the case of and for blackness.

This language, a black Korean anagrammatic calligraphy, attends (to) a diction beyond any law or grammar. Jurisgenerativity via dystranslation reveals that [함/말/馬/*mal*] diction has always been dancing at the linguistic outskirts of jurisdiction. Its strange, sublime, gestural spokenness drives my writing of and from the analytic symbolism of the indivisible littoral spaces of slavery and colonialism.

For daughters of 馬 *diction*, then, 말해, *malhae*. Tell us of *han/a*, one zeroing forever, and *ham/a*, ten thousand *notalls*, 49 times. 49 아무 (*amu*)'s, 49 any's, 49 아니 (ani)'s, 49 *n'y*'s.

Mu, 無, 巫.

notes

Preface

1 Don Mee Choi, "Translator's Note," in H. Kim, *Autobiography of Death*, 109.
2 See Mackey, "Robert Creeley's *The Gold Diggers*"; Mackey, *Discrepant Engagement*, 260–86; and Mackey, *Call Me Tantra*.
3 Moten, *Little Edges*; and Moten's trilogy, *consent not to be a single being*, including *Black and Blur*, *Stolen Life*, and *The Universal Machine*.
4 Moten, *Universal Machine*, 233; and Moten, *Stolen Life*, 116.
5 Mackey's "*Mu*" poems can be found across multiple volumes of his poetry, including *Eroding Witness*, *School of Udhra*, *Splay Anthem*, *Nod House*, and the three-volume set, *Double Trio*.
6 This triadic formulation echoes Moten's brilliant condensation of Fanon's language into a reminder that "the lunatic, the (revolutionary) lover, and the poet [who] are of imagination all compact" (*Universal Machine*, 233). Insofar as writing theory after Afro-pessimism depends on the possibility of desiring "something-other-than-transcendental subjectivity that is called nothing," I hear Moten's figure of the blackness of desire as a creative Fanonian reformulation of the Lacanian Symbolic, Imaginary and Real (234).
7 Moten, *Universal Machine*, 234.
8 Han, *to regard a wave* (selva oscura press, forthcoming).
9 Fenollosa and Pound, *Chinese Written Character as a Medium for Poetry*; see also Pound, *Cantos of Ezra Pound*; and Pound, *Cathay*. See also Yip, "Translating Chinese Poetry." With this anthology, Yip hopes to put readers of Chinese poetry in the wake of Pound "out of gear," by arguing that "both the Taoist and the Confucian poetics demand the submission of the self to the cosmic measure rather than the Kantian attempt to resist and measure oneself against the apparent almighti-

ness of nature, resulting in a greater degree of noninterference in artistic presentation" (27).

10 Olson, "Projective Verse"; Derrida, *Of Grammatology*, 92.
11 Blasing, *Lyric Poetry*, 169; and Bernstein, *Close Listening*, 22.
12 Lacan, *Seminar X: Anxiety*, translated by Cormac Gallagher, 79.
13 Lacan, *Seminar X: Anxiety*, translated by Gallagher, 79 (my emphasis).
14 Lacan, *Seminar X: Anxiety*, translated by Gallagher, 79.
15 Lacan, *Seminar X: Anxiety*, translated by Gallagher, 79, 80.
16 Lacan, *Seminar X: Anxiety*, translated by Gallagher, 80. For a compelling psychoanalytic exploration of self-writing and the feminine structure of knowledge and love, see Lieber, *The Writing Cure*.
17 Rogers, *Incandescent Alphabets*, 177.
18 Carter, "Black Malpractice," 81.
19 Carter, "Black Malpractice," 81.
20 Nielsen, *Black Chant*, 34.
21 On the innovation of Korean calligraphy, see generally Lachman, *Way with Words*.
22 Mackey, *Eroding Witness*, 67.
23 Judy, *Sentient Flesh*, 7.
24 Dworkin, *Reading the Illegible*, 81.
25 Sells, *Mystical Languages of Unsaying*, 8–9. Sells has also written about apophasis and the language of the unsayable in psychoanalysis; see Webb and Sells, "Lacan and Bion."
26 Rogers, *Incandescent Alphabets*, 202.
27 Clifton, *Collected Poems*, 173. For an audio recording of Clifton reading this poem, see https://www.poetryfoundation.org/play/76500.

Savoir Black

1 Mackey, *Splay Anthem*, x.
2 Griffiths, "Hunger."
3 Graham, "In/Silence," 140.
4 Izcovich, *Marks of a Psychoanalysis*, 23.
5 Mullen, "Sleeping with the Dictionary," 67.
6 Benjamin, "Critique of Violence," 243.
7 Benjamin, "Critique of Violence," 244.
8 Sexton, "Social Life of Social Death."
9 Hunt, *Veronica*, 38.
10 Lyn Hejinian's *My Life and My Life in the Nineties* and Robert Bringhurst's *Everywhere Being Is Dancing: Twenty Pieces of Thinking* also inform the organizational principle of this book.
11 Izcovich, *Marks of a Psychoanalysis*, 93.
12 From a translation of Rilke's "The Panther," quoted in Kentridge, *Six Drawing Lessons*, 154.

13 Kentridge, *Six Drawing Lessons*, 154–55.

14 These three forms are gestured toward in Seminar X, *Anxiety*, and then developed in more detail across two seminars, Seminar XX, *On Feminine Sexuality, the Limits of Love and Knowledge*, and Seminar XXII, *The Sinthome*.

15 Baraka, "Who Is You?," 442.

16 Kentridge, *Six Drawing Lessons*, 82.

17 *Oxford English Dictionary (Online)*, s.v. "membrane, n., Etymology," accessed July 28, 2023, https://doi.org/10.1093/OED/7333982928.

18 *Oxford English Dictionary (Online)*, s.v. "membrane," accessed July 28, 2023, https://www.oed.com/view/Entry/116312?redirectedFrom=membrane&.

19 Alexander v. State of Florida, 121 So. 3d 1185 (2013), accessed July 28, 2023, https://cite.case.law/so-3d/121/1185/. See also Kaba, *No Selves to Defend*.

20 Lacan, *Anxiety*, 150.

21 Fenollosa and Pound, *Chinese Written Character*, 50.

22 Cover, "Supreme Court, 1982 Term."

23 Fenollosa and Pound, *Chinese Written Character*, 49, 48.

24 Fenollosa and Pound, *Chinese Written Character*, 49.

25 Freud, *Beyond the Pleasure Principle*, 10.

26 Freud, *Beyond the Pleasure Principle*, 9.

27 *Handbook of the International Phonetic Association*, [illegible]

28 Moten, *Universal Machine*, 146.

29 Fenollosa and Pound, *Chinese Written Character*, 49.

30 Fenollosa and Pound, *Chinese Written Character*, 49.

31 Many native Korean speakers would probably transliterate this fricative as the hangul letter ㅋ. The hangul letter ㄱ, however, has been transliterated both as the English letters *K* and *G*. I approach all four letters—ㅋ, ㄱ, *K*, and *G*—as marks of a shared anagrammatic, spoken and written space of vernacular transliteration.

32 Yeol and Inseung, "Cards with Diagrams."

33 Fenollosa and Pound, *Chinese Written Character*, 49.

34 Fenollosa and Pound, *Chinese Written Character*, 50.

35 *Kiyuk* is my improper or off transliteration of the Korean word 기억, meaning "memory." According to the Revised Romanization Rules, 기억 would be transliterated as *giyeok*.

36 *Si-sa Elite Korean-English Dictionary*, rev. ed., s.v. "기 [ki]," 301.

37 Izcovich, *Marks of a Psychoanalysis*, 73.

38 Cherry, "Brown Rice," https://open.spotify.com/track/2u7vy4E7raAt291mJwxxK4?si=1dfd61f34ada412b.

39 Long Soldier, *WHEREAS*, 5.

40 Powell, *Record of Tung-shan*, 27–28. For further discussion of Dongshan Liangjie's notion of "Just This," see Taigen, "Dongshan."

41 Lacan, *Talking to Brick Walls*.

42 Kim H., "Seoul, Book of the Dead: Day Twenty-Two," 39.

43 Lacan, *Talking to Brick Walls*, 47.
44 Lacan, *Talking to Brick Walls*, 47.
45 Judy, *(Dis)Forming the American Canon*, 262–64.
46 Lacan, *Talking to Brick Walls*, 47; and Judy, *(Dis)Forming the American Canon*, 264, 263.
47 Judy, *(Dis)Forming the American Canon*, 52.
48 Judy, *(Dis)Forming the American Canon*, 273.
49 Judy, *Sentient Flesh*, 391 (my emphasis).
50 Judy, *Sentient Flesh*, 392.
51 Judy, *(Dis)Forming the American Canon*, 273. Insofar as Judy's critique of Lacan is engaged primarily with debates within the discourse of philosophy, I believe it is possible to extend Judy's concept of cryptoanalysis and *poiēsis* to inform how we mobilize Lacan's writing and teachings—not for philosophy but for and as a practice of psychoanalysis.
52 Lacan, *Écrits*, 305–6.
53 Lacan, *Écrits*, 305, 306.
54 Judy, *(Dis)Forming the American Canon*, 273.
55 Lacan, *Écrits*, 305.
56 I take Afro-pessimism as a signifier whose para-semiotic effect has been to give clarity to the absence at the core of Western discourses of ontology and the world-making violence that ensues when this absence, that "auto-obscuring articulation" (Judy, *(Dis)Forming the American Canon*, 264), is reduced to all manner of bivalent logics. Jared Sexton addresses this reduction in "Afro-Pessimism: The Unclear Word" with his insistence that we continue to think about "how to remark what is always already marked" (18). I do not intend to provide an interpretation of the debates about Afro-pessimism in this book. I instead continue elaborating on an "Afro-pessimist psychoanalytics" Sexton and I have discussed in our essay "The Devil's Choice," through a reading of Rita Dove's play *The Darker Face of the Earth*.
57 Judy, *(Dis)Forming the American Canon*, 273.
58 Judy, *(Dis)Forming the American Canon*, 273.
59 David Lloyd, *Change of State*, VI.
60 Hejinian, "Forms of Alterity," 315.
61 Quoted in Izcovich, *Marks of a Psychoanalysis*, 92.
62 Izcovich, *Marks of a Psychoanalysis*, quoting Lacan's "La Troisième," 161.
63 Izcovich, *Marks of a Psychoanalysis*, 159.
64 Lacan, *Talking to Brick Walls*, 64.
65 Lacan, . . . *or Worse*, 4.
66 Lacan, "Psychoanalysis and Its Teaching," 372. See also Izcovich, *Marks of a Psychoanalysis*, 163–72.
67 Lacan, *Talking to Brick Walls*, 98, 102.
68 Lacan, *Talking to Brick Walls*, 98.
69 André, "Writing Begins," 146.

70 André, "Writing Begins," 152.

71 Dred Scott v. Sanford, 60 U.S. 393 (1857); and Charles Gaines, *Manifestos 4* (2020), exhibited in *New Work: Charles Gaines*, San Francisco Museum of Modern Art, San Francisco, CA, 2021, https://www.sfmoma.org/exhibition/new-work-charles-gaines/.

72 I thank Roshy Kheshti for the phrasing "unhearable sonicity."

73 Mackey, *Discrepant Engagement*, 232.

74 Gregson v. Gilbert, 3 Doug. KB 232 (1783).

75 See also Baucom, *Specters of the Atlantic.*

76 Philip, *Looking for Livingstone*, 72. See *Zong!*, 182, for an example of the radical textuality I describe in this section.

77 The Kaluli story and thought of the *muni* bird, as it has spiraled out from Moten reading Mackey reading Steven Feld's *Sound and Sentiment*, is inseparable from my own response, with this book, to learn from this and other birds, theirs, and others' lines of flight and lament, and what that teaches us about *mu*. See Moten, *In the Break*, 259–60; Mackey, *Discrepant Engagement*, 232; and Mackey, *Splay Anthem*, xv–xvi, 55–56, 86–87, 115–18.

78 Moten, "[the unacknowledged legislator]," in *B Jenkins*, 87.

79 The word *underness* is from Mackey, *Splay Anthem*, xi.

Terra Incognita

1 Lacan, *Écrits*, 716.

2 Lacan, *Écrits*, 716.

3 Lacan, *Écrits*, 716.

4 Lacan, *Écrits*, 716.

5 Lacan, *Écrits*, 713.

6 Glissant, *Poetics of Relation*, 57; and Betsy Wing, "Translator's Introduction," in Glissant, *Poetics of Relation*, xiv.

7 Glissant, *Poetics of Relation*, 6.

8 Glissant, *Poetics of Relation*, 6.

9 Glissant, *Poetics of Relation*, 6.

10 Glissant, *Poetics of Relation*, 6.

11 Glissant, *Poetics of Relation*, 11, 7.

12 Glissant, *Poetics of Relation*, 7.

13 Glissant, *Poetics of Relation*, 58 (my emphasis).

14 Glissant, *Poetics of Relation*, 59–60.

15 Glissant, *Poetics of Relation*, 99.

16 Glissant, *Poetics of Relation*, 119.

17 We can read Glissant's reference to this term as part of his general critical engagement with Gilles Deleuze and Félix Guattari's two-volume *Capitalism and Schizophrenia*, and maybe even as a specific engagement with Guattari's focus on group-related psychotherapy across his clinical practice. See generally Guattari,

Psychoanalysis and Transversality: Texts and Interviews, 1955-1971. But Glissant's references to this line of interpretation are only to the names of these authors and not to any of their texts, let alone language in these texts that develop this term (see his chapter "Errantry, Exile," in *Poetics of Relation*, 11–22).

18 Glissant, *Poetics of Relation*, 99. This question births others: "Is the Chinese language absorbing the Latin alphabet? How is the actual status of languages changing in the Soviet Union? Is Quechuan beginning to make its escape from silence? And in Europe are the Scandinavian languages starting to open up to the world? Are forms of creolization silently at work, and where? Will Swahili and Fulani share the written domain with other languages in Africa? Are regional dialects in France fading away? How quickly? Will ideograms, pictograms, and other forms of writing show up in this panorama? Do translations already allow perceptible correspondences between language systems? And how many minorities are there struggling within diglossia, like the numerous French-speaking Creole blacks in southwestern Louisiana? Or the thirty thousand Inuits on Baffin Island?" (99–100).

19 Glissant, *Poetics of Relation*, 119.

20 Glissant, *Poetics of Relation*, 58.

21 Glissant, *Poetics of Relation*, 53.

22 Glissant, *Poetics of Relation*, 59 (my emphasis).

23 For an account of France's colonial excursions in Korea in the early to mid-nineteenth century, see Cumings, *Korea's Place*, 96–109.

24 Sexton, "*Vel* of Slavery," 593 (my emphasis).

25 Glissant, *Poetics of Relation*, 9. My discussion of *murmur* in this chapter does not explicitly make a connection with music as a form of sound, simply because the scholarship on music is so vast and there are plenty of others who would be better equipped to make those connections than I am. Were I to attempt such a discussion, it would only be to emphasize what in music as a form of symbolic speech bears the unsayable. My approach to music would not regard it as a supplement to the unsayable in verbal and written speech but would listen to how it itself contains the marks of unconscious desire.

26 Philip, *Zong!*, 157. This quotation is a rendering of the words photographed from "Ferrum" as a passage I attempt to block quote following the *Chicago Manual of Style*.

27 The essay "'The Permanent Obliquity of an In(pha)llibly Straight': In the Time of the Daughters and the Fathers" was first published in the volume *Fathers and Daughters* (1988). My references are to the 2003 reprint, in Spillers's volume *Black, White, and in Color: Essays on American Literature and Culture.*

28 Spillers, "'Permanent Obliquity,'" 248.

29 Spillers, "'Permanent Obliquity,'" 232. See also Morgan, "Partus sequitur ventrem," 8. Hereinafter, I refer to this law as the "law of *partus*."

30 Spillers, "'Permanent Obliquity,'" 232.

31 Spillers, "'Permanent Obliquity,'" 232.

32 *Black's Law Dictionary*, s.v. "abeyance in," accessed July 19, 2023, https://thelaw dictionary.org/abeyance-in/.

33 Spillers, "'Permanent Obliquity,'" 247.

34 D. Evans, *Introductory Dictionary*, 99; and Lacan, *Écrits*, 665. The first quote is Evans's translation; the second quote is Fink's translation.

35 Freud, "Dissolution of the Oedipus Complex," 178.

36 Freud, "Dissolution of the Oedipus Complex, " 178–79.

37 Freud, "Some Psychological Consequences," 257.

38 Freud, "Dissolution of the Oedipus Complex," 178.

39 Freud, "Some Psychological Consequences," 257.

40 Freud, "Some Psychological Consequences," 257, 258.

41 Freud, "Some Psychological Consequences," 257–58.

42 Laplanche and Pontalis, *Language of Psycho-Analysis*, 286.

43 D. Evans, *Introductory Dictionary*, 130.

44 Lacan, *Écrits*, 21.

45 Spillers, "'Permanent Obliquity,'" 232.

46 *Strong's Exhaustive Concordance of the Bible, Hebrew and Chaldee Dictionary*, s.v. "bâsâr," #1320, 24.

47 *Strong's Exhaustive Concordance of the Bible, Hebrew and Chaldee Dictionary*, s.v. "bâsar," #1319, 24.

48 Moten, *Black and Blur*, xiii.

49 Jackson, *Becoming Human*, 39.

50 Lacan, *Television*, 22.

51 Orlando Patterson's discussion of natal alienation in *Slavery and Social Death* describes the slave as a "genealogical isolate" (5). We can understand this in a historical sense symbolized by the positive law of *partus*. But this isolation is not produced simply as a matter of juridical command. Together with the oedipal law, a much deeper legal and theoretical understanding of the law of *partus* as the absence of the paternal metaphor would situate genealogical isolation as a uniquely psychoanalytic question of unconscious desire.

52 Han, "Poetics of Mu," 921–48.

53 Mackey, *Splay Anthem*, x.

54 Mackey, *Splay Anthem*, ix–xii. Mackey's *Song of the Andoumboulou* poems can be found across multiple volumes also containing his "*Mu*" poems. See note 5 of this volume's preface.

55 Mackey, *Splay Anthem*, 13.

56 In the second appearance of the word, the adjective *atless* becomes the name of a proper place, Atless. Mackey, *Splay Anthem*, 19. But like the name *Mu*, which is indistinguishable from "*mu* momentary utterance extended into ongoing myth, an impulse toward signature, self-elaboration, finding and losing itself" (xiii), Atless is a name without ground, a name more true because of its "whatsaid-ness" than any proper geographic referent it might correspond to.

57 Mackey, *Splay Anthem*, xv.
58 Moten, "Blackness and Nothingness," 750.
59 Moten, "Blackness and Nothingness," 750.
60 Moten, "Blackness and Nothingness," 750.
61 Moten, "Blackness and Nothingness," 750 (emphasis in original).
62 Moten, "Blackness and Nothingness," 751.
63 The unconscious emerges in my listening to a polyglossic speech of the unsayable, and an analytic capacity to listen for the specific forms of the unsayable contained in that polyglossic articulation. But while this manifestation of the unsayable as the unconscious is individuated, the unconscious is ultimately a structural phenomenon that exceeds individual experience, history, and symbolic meaning. Insofar as this is true, it would be impossible and reductive for me to try to argue that there is something about being a postcolonial subject that allows me to listen in a particular, privileged way to the way that colonialism survives in language. Listening to the unconscious is not a cultural, national, historical capacity of an individual but the unique configuration of absence where cultural, national, historical symbolic worlds converge in an individual and thus shape techniques of *listening* in the first instance.
64 Mackey, *Splay Anthem*, 13.
65 Cha, *Dictee*, 177.
66 Cha, *Dictee*, 140.
67 Cha, *Dictee*, 5.
68 Cha, *Dictee*, 3.
69 Cha, *Dictee*, 3–4.
70 Cha, *Dictee*, 5. There is a crucial distinction here between the vocalization of speech and language as voice. See generally Dolar, *Voice and Nothing More*. I read this section in *Dictee* to be exploring the experience of the latter relationship, where the topological surface of the mouth effaces the distinction between inner and outer experience. The classical Chinese and modern anatomical diagrams Cha includes in the section "Urania Astronomy" (61–75) further support this interpretation.
71 Cha, *Dictee*, 3.
72 Cha, *Dictee*, 5.
73 Stone-Richards, "Commentary," 189–91; and Cha, *Dictee*, 165–79.
74 Cha, *Dictee*, 54–55.
75 Stone-Richards, "Commentary," 175.
76 Stone-Richards, "Commentary," 147.
77 See generally Akmajian et al., *Linguistics: An Introduction to Language and Communication*, 333; and Lee and Ramsey, *History of the Korean Language*, 13–15.
78 This point about the various ways in which Cha turns the body inside out, and outside in, such that the body itself becomes a terra incognita of orifices, is indebted to David Lloyd's *Irish Culture and Colonial Modernity, 1800–2000*, which

makes a general claim that "orality implies . . . a complex interaction of spaces, an intersection of oral and literate modes, each surviving in peculiar ways within the other and even preserving the other's life within itself . . . the ways in which the oral lives on, both in and through the intimate damage that colonialism inflicts" (4).

79 Mackey, *Splay Anthem*, 13.

80 My use of the term "monstrate" comes from the appearance of the theme "monstrous" in both Spillers's essay "Mama's Baby, Papa's Maybe" (1987) and Christina Sharpe's *Monstrous Intimacies* (2010). I am interested less in the substantive aesthetic quality of the ugly or abnormal and more in the general process of how truth troubles representational form. *Monstrous* indicates a relation to truth as that which cannot be proven or known, or even *demonstrated* through adequations of form and object. For Jean-Luc Nancy, the image generally reveals that violence and truth have the same essence: they exploit both mimetic appearance (demonstration) and self-presenting force (monstration), which together deform the very forms they appear as. Nancy, *Ground of the Image*, 21. Interestingly, Nancy's use of the term *monstration* refers to the process of monstration set in motion as failed repetition and is attributed to the work of Mehdi Belhaj Kacem (142n10).

81 I am indebted to Yen Noh for directing me to Lee Ae-joo's body of work and the image in figure 2.3. This image is of Lee's *salpuri* performance at the funeral of Lee Han-yeol, a Yonsei University student who was killed by riot police during a democratic demonstration protesting the Chun Doo-hwan dictatorship. His death, and Lee's *salpuri* performance, sparked the June Democracy Movement that would bring down the Chun dictatorship. The name of this dance, 바람맞이 (*barammaji*), means "life-continues-in-receiving-wind." For more historical context about Lee Ae-joo and her development of Korean folk dance, see 이애주 (Lee Ae-joo), "승무의 원류에 관한 연구," 체육사학회지 1, no. 1 (1996): 65; 김경은 (Kim Kyung-eun), "이애주(李愛珠) <바람맞이>춤에 내재된 한국춤의 본성 (本性)," *Pigyo minsokhak* 58 (2015): 47–96.

82 Glissant, *Poetics of Relation*, 84.

83 Spillers, "'Permanent Obliquity,'" 250.

84 Spillers, "'Permanent Obliquity,'" 233 (bracketed text in original).

85 Han, "Poetics of Mu," 940.

86 Spillers, "'Permanent Obliquity,'" 232.

87 Spillers, "'Permanent Obliquity,'" 232.

88 Spillers, "'Permanent Obliquity,'" 243, quoting Walker.

89 Spillers, "'Permanent Obliquity,'" 243.

90 Walker, quoted in Spillers, "'Permanent Obliquity,'" 243.

91 Spillers, "'Permanent Obliquity,'" 242.

92 *Oxford English Dictionary (Online)*, s.v. "spouse, n., sense I.1.a.iii," accessed July 19, 2023, https://doi.org/10.1093/OED/3949257586.

93 Lewis, *Elementary Latin Dictionary*, s.v. "*spondee*," accessed July 19, 2023, http://www.perseus.tufts.edu/hopper/text?doc=Perseus:text:1999.04.0060:entry=spondeo.
94 Cixous, "Castration or Decapitation?," 49.
95 Spillers, "'Permanent Obliquity,'" 244.
96 Spillers, "'Permanent Obliquity,'" 232.
97 Kristeva, "Motherhood Today."
98 Morrison, *A Mercy*, 142.
99 Philip, *Zong!*, 146.
100 Philip, *Zong!*, 162.

Nonperformance

1 Moten, *Stolen Life*, 56.
2 Moten, *Stolen Life*, 56.
3 Moten, *Stolen Life*, 57.
4 Moten, *Stolen Life*, 88.
5 Moten, *Stolen Life*, 133.
6 Moten, *Stolen Life*, 89.
7 Moten, *Stolen Life*, 164–79.
8 Moten, *Little Edges*, 10–15. Slurring is an echo of Moten's perfect phrase, "in permeance," in the poem "hand up to your ear," 11.
9 Moten, *Little Edges*, 35.
10 *Betty's Case*, 20 Monthly L. Rep. 455 (Massachusetts, Nov. 9, 1857).
11 Lacan, "Lituraterre," 333.
12 Lacan, "Lituraterre," 333.
13 Lacan, "Lituraterre," 333.
14 *Online Etymology Dictionary*, s.v. "littoral," accessed July 24, 2023, https://www.etymonline.com/search?q=littoral.
15 Lacan, "Lituraterre," 330, 331.
16 Sharpe, *In the Wake*, 18.
17 Watson, *Digest of Justinian*, 306.
18 Watson, *Digest of Justinian*, 306.
19 Watson, *Digest of Justinian*, 306.
20 Frier and McGinn, *Roman Family Law*, 31.
21 Frier and McGinn, *Roman Family Law*, 31.
22 Spillers, "'Permanent Obliquity,'" 232.
23 *Contubernium*, meaning "dwelling together," in Roman family law refers to extralegal cohabitation between two slaves or a free person and a slave. Frier and McGinn, *Roman Family Law*, 33. It originated in military language referring to "dwelling together in a tent," and extended also to refer to animals, like bees, dwelling together. *ΛΟΓΕΙΟΝ*, s.v. "contubernium," accessed July 24, 2023, https://logeion.uchicago.edu/contubernium.

24 Cover, "Supreme Court, 1982 Term—Nomos and Narrative."

25 Lee and Ramsey, *History of the Korean Language*, 122. Diacritics found in Middle Korean writing disappeared after the Japanese invasion of Korea that culminated in the Imjin War in 1592–98 (241–42).

26 Harris, *Experiments in Exile*, 2.

27 Spillers, "Mama's Baby, Papa's Maybe," 78 (italics in original).

28 *Online Etymology Dictionary*, s.v. "till," accessed July 24, 2023, https://www.etymonline.com/word/till#etymonline_v_13323.

29 *Online Etymology Dictionary*, s.v. "till," accessed July 24, 2023, https://www.etymonline.com/word/till#etymonline_v_13323.

30 Freud, *Jokes*, 153. Thank you to Akira Bowler for indulging my Zittersprache and helping me to hear and think about the difference between *Ziel* and *Seele*.

31 Rogers, "Becoming an Analyst," 95.

32 Rogers, "Becoming an Analyst," 98.

33 Lacan, quoted in Rogers, "Becoming an Analyst," 98.

34 Parsons, *Law of Contracts*, 1:3.

35 Parsons, *Law of Contracts*, 1:3.

36 Han, "Slavery as Contract," 406–7.

37 Moten, *In the Break*, 99.

38 Derrida, "Force of Law," 997.

39 Holmes, *Common Law*, 223–60.

40 Spillers, "Mama's Baby, Papa's Maybe," 74.

41 G. Gilmore, *Death of Contract*, 60.

42 Sís, *Conference of the Birds*. This dialogue takes place in part IV when the birds are crossing the Valley of Understanding, where "time suspended, there is no beginning or end, only endless flight."

43 Moten, *Stolen Life*, 263.

44 *Wiktionary*, s.v. "속," accessed July 24, 2023, https://en.wiktionary.org/wiki/속; s.v. "俗," accessed July 24, 2023, https://en.wiktionary.org/wiki/俗#Korean.

45 *Black's Law Dictionary*, s.v. "evergreen promise," accessed July 24, 2023, https://thelawdictionary.org/evergreen-promise/.

46 Moten, *In the Break*, 13–14.

47 Harney and Moten, *Undercommons*, 50.

48 Harney and Moten, *Undercommons*, 50.

49 Moten, *In the Break*, 227.

50 Watson, *Digest of Justinian*, 149.

51 Hartman, "Venus in Two Acts."

52 Gladman and Moten, *One Long Black Sentence*.

53 Moten, *Stolen Life*, 264.

54 Rogers, "Becoming an Analyst," 96.

55 Freud, "Negation."

56 Apollon, "Limit," 106.

57 Apollon, "Limit," 107.

58 Apollon, "Limit," 109.
59 Apollon, "Limit," 112.
60 Apollon, "Limit," 115.
61 Copjec, *Supposing the Subject*, xi.
62 Benjamin, quoted in Choi, *Translation Is a Mode*, 13.
63 Choi, *Translation Is a Mode*, 7.
64 Lacan, "Lituraterre," 331–32.
65 *Wiktionary*, s.v. "金," accessed July 24, 2023, https://en.wiktionary.org/wiki/金; s.v. "今," accessed July 24, 2023, https://en.wiktionary.org/wiki/今.
66 *Wiktionary*, s.v., "人," accessed July 24, 2023, https://en.wiktionary.org/wiki/人; s.v., "集," accessed July 24, 2023, https://en.wiktionary.org/wiki/集.
67 Moten, *Stolen Life*, 182.

Non Liquet Blackness

1 Zalamea, *Synthetic Philosophy*, 33.
2 Zalamea, *Synthetic Philosophy*, 33.
3 *ΛΟΓΕΙΟΝ*, s.v. "demonstrare," accessed July 26, 2023, https://logeion.uchicago.edu/demonstrare; *Online Etymology Dictionary*, s.v. "demolish," accessed July 26, 2023, https://www.etymonline.com/search?q=demolish.
4 LaTasha Nevada Diggs, reading "dimelo," in "Reading," November 6, 2014, video, 5:30, https://youtu.be/SP6aOmMyoME. Her reading of the entire poem is from 2:34 to 6:49.
5 "디매로" is my transcription of the Spanish phrase *dimelo* into hangul. "말해" is my dystranslation of the phrase into Korean. 말해, *malhae*, is the command "to say, talk, speak, tell."
6 Choi, *DMZ Colony*, 29.
7 Yi Yŏn-Ju, "Prostitute 1," in Ch'oe, Kim, and Yi, *Anxiety of Words*, 133.
8 Lacan, "Neurotic's Individual Myth," 414.
9 Lacan, "Neurotic's Individual Myth," 415.
10 Lacan, "Neurotic's Individual Myth," 415.
11 Han, "Slavery as Contract."
12 Marsh, *Quantum Particle Illusion*, 17.
13 *Black's Law Dictionary*, s.v. "loophole," accessed July 25, 2023, https://thelawdictionary.org/loophole/.
14 *Oxford English Dictionary (Online)*, s.v. "frustrate, v., Etymology," accessed July 2023, https://doi.org/10.1093/OED/6852663385.
15 Laplanche and Pontalis, *Language of Psychoanalysis*, 176.
16 Yi Yŏn-Ju, "Prostitute 4," in Ch'oe, Kim, and Yi, *Anxiety of Words*, 135.
17 *Civil Rights Cases of 1883*, 109 US 3 (1883), 21.
18 Quoted in McAward, "Defining the Badges," 586.
19 *Civil Rights Cases of 1883*, 109 US 3 (1883), 36.
20 McAward, "Defining the Badges," 568.

21 *Online Etymology Dictionary*, s.v. "prophylactic," accessed July 24, 2023, https://www.etymonline.com/search?q=Prophylactic.

22 Bridgewater, "Un/Re/Discovering Slave Breeding," 35–36, 41.

23 Bridgewater, "Un/Re/Discovering Slave Breeding," 30–35.

24 E. Kim, "Flyways."

25 Alexander, *New Jim Crow*.

26 Davis, *Are Prisons Obsolete?*, 37.

27 Sideris and the Amnesty Working Group, "Amnesty for Prisoners," 2.

28 Davis, "Angela Davis Speaks Out."

29 Davis, "Angela Davis Speaks Out."

30 Yi Yŏn-Ju, "Prostitute 5," in Ch'oe, Kim, and Yi, *Anxiety of Words*, 136–37.

31 Certeau, *Writing of History*, 299.

32 *Black's Law Dictionary*, s.v. "lacuna," accessed July 25, 2023, https://thelawdictionary.org/lacuna/.

33 Congressional Globe, 39th Cong., 1st Sess. 474 (1866).

34 Yi Yŏn-Ju, "Prostitute 6," in Ch'oe, Kim, and Yi, *Anxiety of Words*, 138 (my translation).

35 Fastenrath and Knur, "Non Liquet."

36 Lacan includes a reference to NL in his paper "The Function and Field of Speech and Language in Psychoanalysis" to underscore the confluence between ancient discourses of mystery and modern scientific discourses of nature in an "analytic symbolism" that relies on the "admission of *non liquet*" (218). The translator, Bruce Fink, provides a definition of this Roman notation as "it is not clear" (787). Insofar as law and legal thought are also modern scientific discourses with its own forms of "analogical thinking" that lead, as well, to "excessive excursions into the ridiculous" (218), I am extending Lacan's critique of psychoanalysis here explicitly through this symbol, NL.

37 Article 2(4) of the United Nations Charter, https://www.un.org/en/about-us/un-charter/full-text.

38 *Legality of the Threat or Use of Nuclear Weapons, Advisory Opinion, I.C.J. Report 1996*, 263.

39 Dissenting opinion of Judge C. G. Weeramantry, *Legality of the Threat, I.C.J. Report 1996*, 515.

40 Dissenting opinion of Judge C. G. Weeramantry, *Legality of the Threat, I.C.J. Report 1996*, 515.

41 Dissenting opinion of Judge C. G. Weeramantry, *Legality of the Threat, I.C.J. Report 1996*, 516.

42 These are transliterations and translations taken from Yi Yŏn-Ju, "Prostitute 7," in Ch'oe, Kim, and Yi, *Anxiety of Words*, 140.

43 W. Johnson, *River of Dark Dreams*, 14.

44 W. Johnson, *River of Dark Dreams*, 13.

45 W. Johnson, *River of Dark Dreams*, 108.

46 Du Bois, *Suppression of the African Slave-Trade*, 143.

47 Gaspar's video can be found at https://vimeo.com/191742460.

48 *ΛΟΓΕΙΟΝ*, s.v. "lacrimalis," accessed July 25, 2023, https://logeion.uchicago.edu/lacrimalis; *Online Etymology Dictionary*, s.v. "lachrymal," accessed July 25, 2023, https://www.etymonline.com/word/lachrymal.

49 Thank you to Monica Wonju Cho for this latter description of the dog in 淚.

50 Wilderson, *Afropessimism*, 337.

51 Lacan, *Four Fundamental Concepts*, 92.

52 Wilderson, *Afropessimism*, 337.

53 Wilderson, *Afropessimism*, 336.

54 Wilderson, *Afropessimism*, 322.

55 Wilderson, *Afropessimism*, 328.

56 Wilderson, *Afropessimism*, 336.

57 Wilderson, *Afropessimism*, 337.

58 Lacan, *Television*, 37.

59 Wilderson, *Red, White and Black*, 54–91.

60 Lacan, *Television*, 41.

61 Yi Yŏn-Ju, "La La La, There Is No Way of Knowing," in Ch'oe, Kim, and Yi, *Anxiety of Words*, 151.

The Sur-Round

1 Davis, *Angela Davis*.

2 *Wiktionary*, s.v. "容," accessed July 26, 2023, https://en.wiktionary.org/wiki/容.

3 *Wiktionary*, s.v. "門," accessed July 26, 2023, https://en.wiktionary.org/wiki/門.

4 Pashukanis, *Law and Marxism*, 180–81.

5 Taylor, "Alameda County's 'Super Jail.'"

6 National Institute of Corrections, *Jail Design Guide* (1998); and National Institute of Corrections, *Jail Design Guide* (2011).

7 President's Commission on Law Enforcement and Administration of Justice, *Challenge of Crime*.

8 Taylor, "Alameda County's 'Super Jail.'"

9 Wilkinson, "Typology."

10 Weese, "Harry Weese," 131.

11 Potié, *Le Corbusier*.

12 Davis, *Angela Davis*, 347.

13 Sorkin, "Drawing the Line."

14 Slade, "Is There Such a Thing."

15 The hangul word for "torso," for example, is 몸통, *momtong*, but would not carry the *hanja* 桶. Nonetheless, I note the homophonic resonance between the two words.

16 Kentridge, *Six Drawing Lessons*, 115.

17 Moten, *Black and Blur*, 101.

18 Foucault, "Of Other Spaces."

19 Foucault, "Of Other Spaces."
20 Davis, *Angela Davis*, 17–18.
21 Lacan, *Four Fundamental Concepts*, 94.
22 Lacan, *Four Fundamental Concepts*, 150–52.
23 Barthes, "From *The Neutral*."
24 Barthes, "From *The Neutral*," 16.
25 Spillers, "Mama's Baby, Papa's Maybe," 67.
26 Judy, *Sentient Flesh*, 185.
27 Judy, *Sentient Flesh*, 185.
28 Quoted in Barthes, "From *The Neutral*," 3.
29 Judy, *Sentient Flesh*, 215–61.
30 Foucault, "'Panopticism,'" 5.
31 Foucault, "'Panopticism,'" 5.
32 Foucault, "'Panopticism,'" 5.
33 Foucault, "'Panopticism,'" 6.
34 Foucault, "'Panopticism,'" 5.
35 Foucault, "'Panopticism,'" 6.
36 Foucault, "'Panopticism,'" 6.
37 Foucault, "'Panopticism,'" 6.
38 Foucault, "'Panopticism,'" 5.
39 Foucault, "'Panopticism,'" 9.
40 Foucault, "'Panopticism,'" 6.
41 R. Evans, "Bentham's Panopticon," 26.
42 Foucault, "'Panopticism,'" 9.
43 Spiegel, "Women's Prison Closed."
44 Fleetwood, *Marking Time*, 261.
45 I mobilize this ideogrammic interpretation because 色 has a strong sexual connotation, captured by the depiction of blushing complexions in an intimate moment between two people. *Wiktionary* also breaks this character down into 爪, meaning "claw" or "hand," and 卩, depicting a "kneeling person." *Wiktionary*, s.v. "色," accessed August 7, 2023, https://en.wiktionary.org/wiki/色.
46 Mackey, *From a Broken Bottle*, 128.
47 The prominence of the cello in Nam June Paik's art, in part because of his decades-long collaboration with cellist Charlotte Moorman and experimental composer John Cage was apparent at a retrospective exhibit, *Nam June Paik*, at the San Francisco Museum of Modern Art, May 8–October 3, 2021, https://www.sfmoma.org/exhibition/nam-june-paik-2021/. The most well known is his 1971 television sculpture, *TV Cello*, consisting of cathode-ray tubes, acrylic boxes, television casings, electronics, wiring, wood base, fan, and stool. Walker Art Center, Minneapolis, 1992 For more on Moorman and Paik's collaborative works on, with, and as the cello, see generally, Rothfuss, *Topless Cellist*.
48 Bentham, *Panopticon Writings*, 36.
49 Foucault, "'Panopticism,'" 12.

50 Bentham, *Panopticon Writings*, 36.
51 President's Commission on Law Enforcement and Administration of Justice, *Challenge of Crime*, 172.
52 President's Commission on Law Enforcement and Administration of Justice, *Challenge of Crime*, 172.
53 President's Commission on Law Enforcement and Administration of Justice, *Challenge of Crime*, 172.
54 President's Commission on Law Enforcement and Administration of Justice, *Challenge of Crime*, 172.
55 President's Commission on Law Enforcement and Administration of Justice, *Challenge of Crime*, 173–74.
56 Foucault, *Discipline and Punish*, 216.
57 R. Gilmore, "Extraction."
58 Weston, unpublished poetry manuscript from which the words etched onto the sculpture *i am moored* . . . are taken (on file with author).
59 Weston, unpublished poetry manuscript from which the words etched onto the sculpture *i am moored* . . . are taken (on file with author).
60 "*thinking now*" is from Weston's unpublished poetry manuscript; "*[gently]*" is from Weston's sculpture *i am moored* . . .

Res Nulla Loquitur

1 Moten, *In the Break*, 20.
2 Bland, "Sandra Bland's Voicemail Call from Jail."
3 George Floyd Justice in Policing Act of 2021, H.R. 1280, 117th Cong. (2021), https://www.congress.gov/bill/117th-congress/house-bill/1280.
4 Bogel-Burroughs, "Closing Argument."
5 lauren woods, *American Monument*, Beall Center for Art + Technology, University of California, Irvine, October 5, 2019–March 16, 2020. See also the website American Monument (https://americanmonument.blog/).
6 Bland, "Sandra Bland's Voicemail Call from Jail."
7 The term *mis-n'en-scene* is from Brinkema, *Forms of the Affects*, 46.
8 Shin, *Skirt Full of Black*, 70.
9 Philip, *Zong!*
10 Tennessee v. Garner, 471 U.S. 1, at 9.
11 Tennessee v. Garner, 471 U.S. 1, at 7.
12 Tennessee v. Garner, 471 U.S. 1, at 7.
13 Hyppolite, "Appendix I."
14 Freud, *Ego and the Id*, 236.
15 Hyppolite, "Appendix I," 752.
16 Freud, *Ego and the Id*, 236.
17 Zupančič, "Hegel and Freud," 484.
18 Hyppolite, "Appendix I," 746; and Zupančič, "Hegel and Freud," 484.

19 Freud, *Ego and the Id*, 235; and Zupančič, "Hegel and Freud," 483.
20 Philip, *Zong!*, 50.
21 Tennessee v. Garner, 471 U.S. 1, at 9.
22 Tennessee v. Garner, 471 U.S. 1, at 29.
23 Tennessee v. Garner, 471 U.S. 1, at 29.
24 Johnson v. City of Philadelphia, No. 15-2346 (3d Cir. 2016) at 351–52.
25 Austin, *How to Do Things*, 107.
26 Austin, *How to Do Things*, 113.
27 Moten, *In the Break*, 20; and Cavell, *Philosophy*, 18.
28 Bland, "Sandra Bland's Voicemail Call from Jail."
29 President's Task Force on 21st Century Policing, *Final Report*, 45.
30 *Wall Street Journal*, "Full Sandra Bland Arrest Video."
31 *Wall Street Journal*, "Full Sandra Bland Arrest Video," at 9:05.
32 Dolar, "Object Voice," 25.
33 *Wall Street Journal*, "Full Sandra Bland Arrest Video," at 7:42.
34 Lacan, . . . *or Worse*, 93.
35 Lacan, . . . *or Worse*, 93.
36 Lacan, . . . *or Worse*, 93.
37 *Wiktionary*, s.v. "都," accessed July 28, 2023, https://en.wiktionary.org/wiki/都; s.v. "者," accessed July 28, 2023, https://en.wiktionary.org/wiki/者.
38 *Wiktionary*, s.v. "言," accessed July 28, 2023, https://en.wiktionary.org/wiki/言.
39 *Wiktionary*, s.v. "言," accessed July 28, 2023, https://en.wiktionary.org/wiki/言.
40 The American Law Institute, *Restatement of the Law, Third, Torts*, 184.
41 Bland, "Sandra Bland's Voicemail Call from Jail."
42 Reed-Veal v. Encinia, U.S. District Court for the Southern District of Texas, Case 4:15-cv-02232, Document 63, Third Amended Complaint at Law and Jury Demand (Jan. 19, 2016), 2–3. The case Monell v. Department of Social Services, 436 U.S. 658 (1978), is referenced in this index and introduces an interesting concept for the basis of making claims against these named defendants. To make a *Monell* claim against a government entity for an injury resulting from an individual state agent, the claimant must show that this agent violated a constitutional right. The claim is aimed at institutional, as opposed to individual, responsibility for civil rights violations.
43 United States Code, Title 42, § 1983, https://www.law.cornell.edu/uscode/text/42/1983 (accessed July 28, 2023).
44 *Black's Law Dictionary*, s.v. "negligence," accessed July 28, 2023, https://thelawdictionary.org/negligence/.
45 Ellison, "Questionable Death," 6 (my emphasis).
46 Alter, *Book of Psalms*, 3.
47 Alter, *Book of Psalms*, xxxii.
48 Carter, "Paratheological Blackness," 594, discussing Hortense Spillers's "Interstices: A Small Drama of Words."

Mu, 無, 巫

1 Moten, "Case of Blackness," 180.
2 Moten, "Case of Blackness," 185.
3 Moten, "Case of Blackness," 188.
4 Moten, "Case of Blackness," 188.
5 Calhoun, "Fanon's Lexical Intervention"; and Derrida, "What Is a 'Relevant' Translation?," 175.
6 Lacan, "L'étourdit: A Bilingual Presentation of the Second Turn," 3.
7 Lacan, "L'étourdit: A Bilingual Presentation of the Second Turn," 4; and Moten, *In the Break*, 186.
8 Lacan, "L'étourdit: "A Bilingual Presentation of the First Turn," 32. The full sentence in French is "Qu'on dise reste oublié derrière ce qui se dit dans ce qui s'entend" (33).
9 Fanon, *Peau noire, masques blancs*, 90.
10 Fanon, *Black Skin, White Masks*, translated by Charles Lam Markmann, 111.
11 Fanon, *Black Skin, White Masks*, translated by Richard Philcox, 91.
12 Fanon, 검은 피부, 하얀 가면 (Geomeun pibu, hayan gamyeon), translated by Suh Gyung Noh, 109.
13 *Online Etymology Dictionary*, s.v. "smile," accessed July 22, 2023, https://www.etymonline.com/word/smile.
14 Fanon, *Peau noire, masques blancs*, 90.
15 Fanon, *Black Skin, White Masks*, translated by Markmann, 112; Fanon, *Black Skin, White Masks*, translated by Philcox, 91; and Fanon, 검은 피부, 하얀 가면 (Geomeun pibu, hayan gamyeon), translated by Noh, 109.
16 Fanon, *Black Skin, White Masks*, translated by Philcox, 92. The Markmann translation of these two quotes are, "racial epidermal schema" and "the evanescent other, hostile but not opaque, transparent, not there, disappeared" (112).
17 Fanon, 검은 피부, 하얀 가면 (Geomeun pibu, hayan gamyeon), translated by Noh, 110.
18 Julien, *Frantz Fanon: Black Skin, White Masks*, 13:38–13:50.
19 Fanon, *Peau noire, masques blancs*, 102.
20 Fanon, *Black Skin, White Masks*, translated by Markmann, 126.
21 Fanon, *Black Skin, White Masks*, translated by Philcox, 105–6.
22 Fanon, 검은 피부, 하얀 가면 (Geomeun pibu, hayan gamyeon), translated by Noh, 125.
23 This latter translation is by my mother, Sun Young Han.
24 Fanon, *Peau noire, masques blancs*, 102.
25 Fanon, *Black Skin, White Masks*, translated by Markmann, 123.
26 Fanon, *Black Skin, White Masks*, translated by Markmann, 109.
27 Fanon, *Black Skin, White Masks*, translated by Philcox, 89.
28 Fanon, *Peau noire, masques blancs*, 88.

29 Fanon, 검은 피부, 하얀 가면 (Geomeun pibu, hayan gamyeon), translated by Noh, 107.

30 *Online Etymology Dictionary*, s.v. "asperity," accessed July 22, 2023, https://www.etymonline.com/word/asperity.

31 Fanon, *Black Skin, White Masks*, translated by Philcox, 206.

32 Lacan, "L'étourdit: A Bilingual Presentation of the Second Turn," 4.

33 *Online Etymology Dictionary*, s.v. "malady," accessed July 22, 2023, https://www.etymonline.com/word/malady.

34 Mackey, *Splay Anthem*, xiii; Derrida, "Freud and the Scene of Writing," 75.

35 Henry George Liddell and Robert Scott, eds., *A Greek-English Lexicon*, new supplement edition (New York: Clarendon Press, 1996), s.v. "μηδείς," including "μηδέν," 1125; see also *Wiktionary*, s.v. "μηδέν," accessed July 24, 2023, https://en.wiktionary.org/wiki/μηδέν. See Gherovici, "Laughing about Nothing," for a discussion of Lacan's discussion of Democritus's "malapromism," -δέν (den), created from the two Greek words *μηδέν* and *ἄτομος* we find in *L'étourdit* (65).

36 Liddell and Scott, *Greek-English Lexicon*, s.v. "ἄτομος," 271, s.v. "τομος," 1803, and s.v. "τέμνω," 1774–75; see also *Wiktionary*, s.v. "ἄτομος," accessed July 24, 2023, https://en.wiktionary.org/wiki/ἄτομος.

37 On the global racial and colonial imaginary of the zoo in developing Japanese ecological modernity, see generally I. Miller, *Nature of the Beasts*, especially 25–59 and 86–92.

38 For an entertaining history of the hippo, see generally Williams, *Hippopotamus*.

39 Under the editorship of Hendrik Doeff, the *Dōyaku Haruma*, also known as the "Zūfu Haruma," was based on a prior Japanese translation of François Halma's *Woordenboek der Nederduitsche en Fransche taalen* (1708), by Inamura Sanpaku, into the *Haruma wage* (1796). The history of the *Haruma wage*, and later the *Dōyaku Haruma*, is detailed in more general discussions of the history of translating the European idea of nature into East Asian languages for which no corresponding word or idea existed. See generally Marcon, *Knowledge of Nature and the Nature of Knowledge in Early Modern Japan*; and Nanyan Guo, "From *Shizen* to *Nature*." For a study of the impact of this Dutch influence through Japan on Korean, see Vos, "Dutch Influences on the Japanese Language."

bibliography

Akmajian, Adrian, Richard A. Demers, Ann K. Farmer, and Robert M. Harnish. *Linguistics: An Introduction to Language and Communication*. 6th ed. Cambridge, MA: MIT Press, 2010.

Alexander, Michelle. *The New Jim Crow*. New York: The New Press, 2010.

Alter, Robert. *The Book of Psalms: A Translation with Commentary*. New York: W. W. Norton, 2007.

The American Law Institute. *Restatement of the Law, Third, Torts: Liability for Physical and Emotional Harm*, Vol. 1. St. Paul, MN: American Law Institute Publishers, 2010.

André, Serge. "Writing Begins Where Psychoanalysis Ends." Translated by Steven Miller. *Umbr(a): Incurable*, no. 1 (2006): 143–77.

Apollon, Willey. "The Limit: A Fundamental Question for the Subject in Human Experience." *Konturen* 3, no. 1 (2010): 103–18.

Austin, J. L. *How to Do Things with Words: The William James Lectures Delivered at Harvard University in 1955*. 2nd ed. Edited by J. O. Urmson and Marina Sbisa. Oxford: Oxford University Press, 1975.

Baraka, Amiri. "Who Is You?" In *S.O.S.: Poems, 1961–2013*, 442–49. New York: Grove, 2016.

Barthes, Roland. *Camera Lucida*. New York: Hill and Wang, 1980.

Barthes, Roland. "From *The Neutral: Session of March 11, 1978*." Translated by Rosalind Krauss. *October* 112 (Spring 2005): 3–22.

Baucom, Ian. *Specters of the Atlantic: Finance Capital, Slavery, and the Philosophy of History*. Durham, NC: Duke University Press, 2005.

Benjamin, Walter. "Critique of Violence." In *Walter Benjamin: Selected Writings, Volume 1, 1913–1926*, edited by Marcus Bullock and Michael W. Jennings, 236–52. Cambridge, MA: Belknap Press of Harvard University Press, 1996.

Benjamin, Walter. "The Task of the Translator." In *Walter Benjamin: Selected Writ-*

ings, Volume 1, 1913–1926, edited by Marcus Bullock and Michael W. Jennings, 253–63. Cambridge, MA: Belknap Press of Harvard University Press, 1996.

Bentham, Jeremy. *The Panopticon Writings*. Edited by Miran Božovič. London: Verso, 1995.

Bernstein, Charles. *Close Listening: Poetry and the Performed Word*. New York: Oxford University Press, 1998.

Bland, Sandra. "Sandra Bland's Voicemail Call from Jail." YouTube video, 0:35, uploaded by CourtChatter Live, July 22, 2015. https://youtu.be/CTmtBRR54J4.

Blasing, Mutlu Konuk. *Lyric Poetry: The Pain and the Pleasure of Words*. Princeton, NJ: Princeton University Press, 2007.

Bogel-Burroughs, Nicholas. "Prosecutor in Derek Chauvin Trial Makes Closing Argument: 'This Wasn't Policing, This was Murder.'" *New York Times*, April 19, 2021. https://www.nytimes.com/2021/04/19/us/prosecution-closing-argument-derek-chauvin-trial.html?smid=url-share.

Boose, Lynda K., and Betty Sue Flowers, eds. *Fathers and Daughters*. Baltimore: Johns Hopkins University Press, 1988.

Bracey, John, Sonia Sanchez, and James Smethurst, eds. *SOS—Calling All Black People: A Black Arts Movement Reader*. Amherst, MA: University of Massachusetts Press, 2014.

Bridgewater, Pamela. "Un/Re/Dis Covering Slave Breeding in Thirteenth Amendment Jurisprudence." *Washington and Lee Journal of Civil Rights and Social Justice* 7, no. 1 (2001): 11–43.

Bringhurst, Robert. *Everywhere Being Is Dancing: Twenty Pieces of Thinking*. Berkeley, CA: Counterpoint, 2008.

Brinkema, Eugenie. *The Forms of the Affects*. Durham, NC: Duke University Press, 2014.

Calhoun, Doyle. "Fanon's Lexical Intervention: Writing Blackness in *Black Skin, White Masks*." *Paragraph* (Modern Critical Theory Group) 43, no. 2 (2020): 159–78.

Carter, J. Kameron. *The Anarchy of Black Religion: A Mystic Song*. Durham, NC: Duke University Press, 2023.

Carter, J. Kameron. "Black Malpractice (a Poetics of the Sacred)." *Social Text* 37, no. 2 (2019): 67–107.

Carter, J. Kameron. "Paratheological Blackness." *South Atlantic Quarterly* 112, no. 4 (2013): 589–611.

Cavell, Stanley. *Philosophy the Day after Tomorrow*. Cambridge, MA: Belknap Press of Harvard University Press, 2005.

Certeau, Michel de. *The Writing of History*. Translated by Tom Conley. New York: Columbia University Press, 1988.

Cha, Theresa Hak Kyung. *Dictee*. Oakland: University of California Press, 2001.

Cherry, Don. "Brown Rice." Recorded January 1, 1975. UMG Recordings Inc., 1977. Streaming audio, accessed August 8, 2020, https://open.spotify.com/track/2u7vy4E7raAt291mJwxxK4?si=6b20ab2bd62b414e.

Cherry, Don. *"Mu," First Part and Second Part."* Recorded August 22, 1969. Studios Saravah, Paris. Charly Publishing Limited, 2001. CD.
Ch'oe Sŭng-ja, Kim Hyesoon, and Yi Yŏn-ju. *Anxiety of Words: Contemporary Poetry by Korean Women*. Translated by Don Mee Choi. Brookline, MA: Zephyr, 2006.
Choi, Don Mee. *DMZ Colony*. Seattle: Wave Books, 2020.
Choi, Don Mee. *Translation is a Mode=Translation is an Anti-neocolonial Mode*. Brooklyn, NY: Ugly Duckling Presse, 2020.
Cixous, Hélène. "Castration or Decapitation?" Translated by Annette Kuhn. *Signs: Journal of Women in Culture and Society* 7, no. 1 (1981): 41–55.
Cleaver, Eldridge. *Soul on Ice*. New York: Dell, 1968.
Clifton, Lucille. *The Collected Poems of Lucille Clifton, 1965–2010*. Edited by Kevin Young and Michael S. Glaser. New York: BOA Editions, 2012.
Clifton, Lucille. "Cutting Greens." Audio recording. Poetry Foundation, n.d. https://www.poetryfoundation.org/play/76500.
Copjec, Joan, ed. *Supposing the Subject*. London: Verso, 1994.
Cover, Robert. "The Supreme Court, 1982 Term—Nomos and Narrative." *Harvard Law Review* 97, no. 1 (November 1983): 4–68.
Cumings, Bruce. *Korea's Place in the Sun*. New York: W. W. Norton, 2005.
Davis, Angela. *Angela Davis: An Autobiography*. New York: International Publishers, 1988.
Davis, Angela Y. "Angela Davis Speaks Out on Prisons and Human Rights Abuses in the Aftermath of Hurricane Katrina." Interview by Amy Goodman. *Democracy Now*, December 28, 2006. https://www.democracynow.org/2006/12/28/angela_davis_speaks_out_on_prisons.
Davis, Angela Y. *Are Prisons Obsolete?* New York: Seven Stories, 2003.
Deleuze, Gilles, and Félix Guattari. *Anti-Oedipus: Capitalism and Schizophrenia*. Minneapolis: University of Minnesota Press, 1983.
Deleuze, Gilles, and Félix Guattari. *A Thousand Plateaus: Capitalism and Schizophrenia*. Translated by Brian Massumi. London: Athlone, 1988.
Derrida, Jacques. "Force of Law: The 'Mystical Foundation of Authority.' (Deconstruction and the Possibility of Justice)." Translated by Mary Quaintance. *Cardozo Law Review* 11, no. 5–6 (1990): 920–1045.
Derrida, Jacques. "Freud and the Scene of Writing." Translated by Jeffrey Mehlman. *Yale French Studies*, no. 48 (1972): 74–117.
Derrida, Jacques. *Of Grammatology*. Translated by Gayatri Spivak. Baltimore: Johns Hopkins University Press, 1997.
Derrida, Jacques. "What Is a 'Relevant' Translation?" Translated by Lawrence Venuti. *Critical Inquiry* 27, no. 2 (2001): 174–200.
Diggs, LaTasha Nevada. "Reading by Poet LaTasha N. Nevada Diggs, 11.06.14." YouTube video, posted by UChicago Division of the Humanities, November 6, 2014. https://youtu.be/SP6aOmMyoME.
Doeff, Hendrik. *Zūfu Haruma*. 1833. Tōkyō: Yumani Shobō, 1998.
Dolar, Mladen. "The Object Voice." In *Gaze and Voice as Love Objects*, edited by

Renata Salecl and Slavoj Žižek, 1:7–31. Durham, NC: Duke University Press, 1996.
Dolar, Mladen. *A Voice and Nothing More*. Cambridge, MA: MIT Press, 2006.
Du Bois, W. E. B. (William Edward Burghardt). *The Suppression of the African Slave-Trade to the United States of America, 1638–1870*. 1896. New York: Oxford University Press, 2007.
Dunoff, Jeffrey L., Steven R. Ratner, and David Wippman. *International Law: Norms, Actors, Process; A Problem-Oriented Approach*. New York: Wolters Kluwer, 2002.
DuVernay, Ava, dir. *13th*. USA: Netflix Studios, 2016.
Dworkin, Craig Douglas. *Reading the Illegible*. Evanston, IL: Northwestern University Press, 2003.
Ellison, Shane. "Questionable Death, Waller County, Hempstead, Victim Bland, Sandra (B/F)." Texas Department of Public Safety, Texas Rangers Report of Investigation. Investigation No. RA201500242. Approved August 11, 2017.
Evans, Dylan. *An Introductory Dictionary of Lacanian Psychoanalysis*. London: Routledge, 1996.
Evans, Robin. "Bentham's Pancopticon." *Architectural Association Quarterly* 3, no. 2 (Spring 1971): 21–37.
Fanon, Frantz. *Black Skin, White Masks*. Translated by Charles Lam Markmann. New York: Grove Weidenfeld, 1967.
Fanon, Frantz. *Black Skin, White Masks*. Translated by Richard Philcox. New York: Grove, 2008.
Fanon, Frantz. *Peau noire, masques blancs*. Paris: Éditions de Seuil, 1952.
Fanon, Frantz. 검은 피부, 하얀 가면 (Geomeun pibu, hayan gamyeon). Translated by 노서경 (Suh Gyung Noh). Seoul, South Korea: Munhakdongne, 2014.
Fastenrath, Ulrich, and Franziska Knur. "Non Liquet." In *International Law*. Oxford Bibliographies, last modified March 31, 2016. https://doi.org/10.1093/obo/9780199796953-0130.
Feld, Steven. *Sound and Sentiment: Birds, Weeping, Poetics and Song in Kaluli Expression (Third Edition)*. Durham, NC: Duke University Press, 2012.
Fenollosa, Ernest, and Ezra Pound. *The Chinese Written Character as a Medium for Poetry*. Edited by Haun Saussy, Jonathan Stalling, and Lucas Klein. New York: Fordham University Press, 2008.
Fleetwood, Nicole R. *Marking Time: Art in the Age of Mass Incarceration*. Cambridge, MA: Harvard University Press, 2020.
Forrester, John. "If *p*, Then What? Thinking in Cases." *History of the Human Sciences* 9, no. 3 (1996): 1–25.
Foucault, Michel. *Discipline and Punish: The Birth of the Prison*. Translated by Alan Sheridan. New York: Vintage Books, 1979.
Foucault, Michel. "Of Other Spaces." Translated by Jay Miskowiec. *Diacritics* 16, no. 1 (1986): 22–27.
Foucault, Michel. "'Panopticism' from *Discipline and Punishment: The Birth of the Prison*." *Race/Ethnicity* 2, no. 1 (2008): 1–12.

Freud, Sigmund. *Beyond the Pleasure Principle*. Translated and edited by James Strachey. New York: W. W. Norton, 1961.

Freud, Sigmund. “The Dissolution of the Oedipus Complex.” 1924. In *The Ego and the Id and Other Works*, translated by James Strachey, 171–79. London: Vintage Books, 2001.

Freud, Sigmund. *Jokes and Their Relation to the Unconscious*. Translated by James Strachey. New York: W. W. Norton, 1990.

Freud, Sigmund. “Negation.” 1925. In *The Ego and the Id and Other Works*, translated by James Strachey, 233–39. London: Vintage Books, 2001.

Freud, Sigmund. “Some Psychological Consequences of the Anatomical Distinction Between the Sexes.” 1925. In *The Ego and the Id and Other Works*, translated by James Strachey, 241–58. London: Vintage Books, 2001.

Freud, Sigmund. *Totem and Taboo: Some Points of Agreement between the Mental Lives of Savages and Neurotics*. Translated and edited by James Strachey. New York: W. W. Norton, 1989.

Frier, Bruce W., and Thomas A. McGinn. *A Casebook on Roman Family Law*. Oxford: Oxford University Press, 2004.

Gaspar, Maria. *On the Border of What Is Formless and Monstrous*. Five-channel sound and video installation. Vimeo, 14:52, posted July 10, 2016. https://vimeo.com/174112732.

Gherovici, Patricia. “Laughing about Nothing: Democritus and Lacan.” In *Lacan, Psychoanalysis, and Comedy*, edited by Patricia Gherovici, 60–72. Cambridge: Cambridge University Press, 2016.

Gilmore, Grant. *Death of Contract*. 2nd ed. Columbus: Ohio State University Press, 1995.

Gilmore, Ruth Wilson. “Abolition Geography and the Problem of Innocence.” In *Futures of Black Radicalism*, edited by Gaye Theresa Johnson and Alex Lubin, 225–40. London: Verso, 2017.

Gilmore, Ruth Wilson. “Extraction: Abolition Geography and the Problem of Innocence.” Lecture, the 5th Antipode Institutes for Geographies of Justice, Johannesburg, South Africa, June 15, 2015. YouTube video, 1:00:39. https://youtu.be/dmjgPxElk7A.

Gladman, Renee, and Fred Moten. *One Long Black Sentence*. Ithaca, NY: Image Text Ithaca Press, 2020.

Glissant, Édouard. *Poetics of Relation*. Translated by Betsy Wing. Ann Arbor: University of Michigan Press, 1997.

Graham, Jorie. “In/Silence.” In *American Women in Poets in the 21st Century*, edited by Claudia Rankine and Juliana Spahr, 140–45. Middletown, CT: Wesleyan University Press, 2002.

Griffiths, Rachel Eliza. “Hunger.” *Paris Review*, no. 232 (Spring 2020). https://www.theparisreview.org/poetry/7519/hunger-rachel-eliza-griffiths.

Guattari, Félix. *Psychoanalysis and Transversality: Texts and Interviews, 1955–1971*. Translated by Ames Hodges. Los Angeles: Semiotext(e), 2015.

Guo, Nanyan. "From *Shizen* to *Nature*: A Process of Cultural Translation." In *International Perspectives on Translation, Education and Innovation in Japanese and Korean Societies*, edited by David Hebert, 17–34. New York: Springer, 2018.

Halma, François. *Woordenboek der Nederduitsche en Fransche taalen*. 3rd ed. Utrecht: Jacob van Poolsum, 1758.

Han, Sora Y. "Poetics of Mu." *Textual Practice* 34, no. 6 (2020): 921–48.

Han, Sora Y. "Slavery as Contract: Betty's Case and the Question of Freedom." *Law and Literature* 27, no. 3 (2015): 395–416.

Han, Sora Y. *to regard a wave*. Chicago: selva oscura press, forthcoming.

Harney, Stefano, and Fred Moten. *The Undercommons: Fugitive Planning and Black Study*. Wivenhoe, UK: Minor Compositions, 2013.

Harris, Laura. *Experiments in Exile: C. L. R. James, Hélio Oiticica, and the Aesthetic Sociality of Blackness.* New York: Fordham University Press, 2018.

Hartman, Saidiya. "Venus in Two Acts." *Small Axe: A Journal of Criticism* 12, no. 2 (2008): 1–14.

Hejinian, Lyn. "Forms of Alterity: On Translation." In *The Language of Inquiry*, 296–317. Berkeley: University of California Press, 2000.

Hejinian, Lyn. *My Life and My Life in the Nineties.* Middletown, CT: Wesleyan University Press, 2013.

Holmes, Oliver Wendell, Jr. *The Common Law.* 1881. Cambridge, MA: Belknap Press of Harvard University Press, 2009.

Hunt, Erica. *Veronica: A Suite in X Parts.* Chicago: selva oscura, 2019.

Hyppolite, Jean. "Appendix I: A Spoken Commentary on Freud's 'Verneinung.'" In *Écrits: The First Complete Edition in English*, by Jacques Lacan, translated by Bruce Fink, 746–54. New York: W. W. Norton, 2006.

International Phonetic Association. *Handbook of the International Phonetic Association: A Guide to the Use of the International Phonetic Alphabet.* New York: Cambridge University Press, 1999.

Izcovich, Luis. *The Marks of a Psychoanalysis*. New York: Routledge, 2017.

Jackson, Zakiyyah Iman. *Becoming Human: Matter and Meaning in an Antiblack World.* New York: New York University Press, 2021.

James, Joy. "The Womb of Western Theory: Trauma, Time Theft, and the Captive Maternal." *Carceral Notebooks* 12 (2016): 253–96.

Johnson, Barbara. "Taking Fidelity Philosophically." In *The Barbara Johnson Reader: The Surprise of Otherness*, edited by Melissa Feuerstein, Bill Johnson González, Lili Porten, and Keja Valens, 371–76. Durham, NC: Duke University Press, 2014.

Johnson, Walter. *River of Dark Dreams: Slavery and Empire in the Cotton Kingdom*. Cambridge, MA: Belknap Press of Harvard University Press, 2013.

Judy, R. A. *(Dis)forming the American Canon: African-Arabic Slave Narratives and the Vernacular.* Minneapolis: University of Minnesota Press, 1993.

Judy, R. A. *Sentient Flesh: Thinking in Disorder, Poiēsis in Black*. Durham, NC: Duke University Press, 2020.

Julien, Isaac, dir. *Frantz Fanon: Black Skin, White Mask.* San Francisco: California Newsreel, 1996.

Kaba, Mariame, ed. *No Selves to Defend.* Self-published, June 2014. https://noselves2defend.wordpress.com/#:~:text=The%20%E2%80%9CNo%20Selves%20to%20Defend,education%20and%20consciousness%2Draising%20tool.

Kentridge, William. *Six Drawing Lessons.* Cambridge, MA: Harvard University Press, 2014.

Kim, Eleana J. "Flyways." Theorizing the Contemporary, *Fieldsights*, June 27, 2018. https://culanth.org/fieldsights/flyways.

Kim Hyesoon. "Seoul, Book of the Dead: Day Twenty-Two." In *Autobiography of Death.* Drawings by Fi Jae Lee. Translated by Don Mee Choi. New York: New Directions, 2018.

김경은 (Kim Kyung-eun). "이애주(李愛珠) (Lee Ae-joo) <바람맞이> (barammaji) 춤에 내재된 한국춤의 본성 (本性) (chume naejaedoen hangukchumui bon-seong)." *Pigyo minsokhak* 58 (2015): 47–96.

Kristeva, Julia. "Motherhood Today." Julia Kristeva official website, 2005. http://www.kristeva.fr/motherhood.html.

Lacan, Jacques. *Anxiety: The Seminar of Jacques Lacan, Book X.* Edited by Jacques-Alain Miller. Cambridge, UK: Polity, 2016.

Lacan, Jacques. *Anxiety: The Seminar of Jacques Lacan, Book X.* Translated by Cormac Gallagher. http://www.lacaninireland.com/web/wp-content/uploads/2010/06/Seminar-X-Revised-by-Mary-Cherou-Lagreze.pdf.

Lacan, Jacques. *Écrits: The First Complete Edition in English.* Translated by Bruce Fink. New York: W. W. Norton, 2007.

Lacan, Jacques. *The Four Fundamental Concepts of Psychoanalysis: The Seminar of Jacques Lacan, Book XI.* Edited by Jacques-Alain Miller. New York: W. W. Norton, 1998.

Lacan, Jacques. "The Function and Field of Speech and Language in Psychoanalysis." In *Écrits: The First Complete Edition in English*, translated by Bruce Fink, 197–268. New York: W. W. Norton, 2007.

Lacan, Jacques. "Kant with Sade." In *Écrits: The First Complete Edition in English*, translated by Bruce Fink, 765–91. New York: W. W. Norton, 2007.

Lacan, Jacques. "L'étourdit: A Bilingual Presentation of the First Turn." Translated by Cormac Gallagher. *The Letter* 41 (2009): 31–80.

Lacan, Jacques. "L'étourdit: A Bilingual Presentation of the Second Turn: The Discourse of the Analyst." Translated by Cormac Gallagher. *The Letter* 45 (2010): 1–15.

Lacan, Jacques. "Lituraterre." Translated by Dany Nobus. *Continental Philosophy Review* 46, no. 2 (2013): 327–34.

Lacan, Jacques. "The Neurotic's Individual Myth." *Psychoanalytic Quarterly* 48, no. 3 (1979): 405–25.

Lacan, Jacques. *On Feminine Sexuality, the Limits of Love and Knowledge, 1972–1973: Encore, The Seminar of Jacques Lacan, Book XX.* Edited by Jacques-Alain Miller. New York: W. W. Norton, 1998.

Lacan, Jacques. . . . *or Worse: The Seminar of Jacques Lacan, Book XIX*. Edited by Jacques-Alain Miller. Cambridge, UK: Polity, 2011.

Lacan, Jacques. "Psychoanalysis and Its Teaching." In *Écrits: The First Complete Edition in English*, translated by Bruce Fink, 364–83. New York: W. W. Norton, 2007.

Lacan, Jacques. *The Sinthome: The Seminar of Jacques Lacan, Book XXIII*. Edited by Jacques-Alain Miller. Cambridge, UK: Polity, 2016.

Lacan, Jacques. *Talking to Brick Walls: A Series of Presentations in the Chapel at Sainte-Anne Hospital*. Translated by A. R. Price. Cambridge, UK: Polity, 2017.

Lacan, Jacques. *Television*. Edited by Joan Copjec. New York: W. W. Norton, 1990.

Lachman, Charles. *A Way with Words: The Calligraphic Art of Jung Do-jun*. Eugene, OR: Jordan Schnitzer Museum of Art, 2006.

Laplanche, Jean, and Jean-Bertrand Pontalis. *The Language of Psycho-Analysis*. Translated by Donald Nicholson-Smith. New York: W. W. Norton, 1974.

Lee, Ki-Moon, and S. Robert Ramsey. *A History of the Korean Language*. Cambridge: Cambridge University Press, 2011.

이애주 (Lee Ae-joo). "승무의 원류에 관한 연구 (seungmuui wonlyue gwanhan yeon-gu)." 체육사학회지 (cheyuksahakoeji) 1, no. 1 (1996): 65–73.

Lewallen, Constance. *The Dream of the Audience: Theresa Hak Kyung Cha (1951–1982)*. Berkeley: University of California Berkeley Art Museum, 2001.

Lewis, Charlton T. *An Elementary Latin Dictionary*. New York: American Book Company, 1890. http://www.perseus.tufts.edu/hopper/search?doc=Perseus%3atext%3a1999.04.0060.

Lieber, Emma. *The Writing Cure*. New York: Bloomsbury Academic, 2020.

Little, Stephen, and Virginia Moon, eds. *Beyond the Line: The Art of Korean Writing*. Los Angeles: Los Angeles County Museum of Art, 2019.

Lloyd, David. *Change of State*. Berkeley, CA: Cusp Books, 1993.

Lloyd, David. *Irish Culture and Colonial Modernity, 1800–2000: The Transformation of Oral Space*. Cambridge: Cambridge University Press, 2011.

Long Soldier, Layli. *WHEREAS*. Minneapolis: Graywolf Press, 2017.

Mackey, Nathaniel. *Call Me Tantra: Open Field Poetics*. PhD diss., Stanford University, 1975.

Mackey, Nathaniel. *Discrepant Engagement: Dissonance, Cross-Culturality, and Experimental Writing*. New York: Cambridge University Press, 1993.

Mackey, Nathaniel. *Double Trio*. 3 vols. New York: New Directions, 2021.

Mackey, Nathaniel. *Eroding Witness*. Pittsboro, NC: selva oscura, 2018.

Mackey, Nathaniel. *From a Broken Bottle Traces of Perfume Still Emanate: Volumes 1–3*. New York: New Directions, 2010.

Mackey, Nathaniel. *Nod House*. New York: New Directions, 2011.

Mackey, Nathaniel. "Robert Creeley's *The Gold Diggers*: Projective Prose." *Boundary 2* 6/7, nos. 3 and 1 (Spring–Autumn 1978): 469–87.

Mackey, Nathaniel. *School of Udhra*. San Francisco: City Lights, 1993.

Mackey, Nathaniel. *Splay Anthem*. New York: New Directions, 2006.

Marcon, Federico. *The Knowledge of Nature and the Nature of Knowledge in Early Modern Japan*. Chicago: University of Chicago Press, 2019.

Marsh, Gerald. *The Quantum Particle Illusion.* London: World Scientific Publishing, 2022.

Martin, Dawn Lundy. "A Bleeding, an Autobiographical Tale." In *A Gathering of Matter, a Matter of Gathering: Poems,* 42–44. Athens: University of Georgia Press, 2007.

McAward, Jennifer Mason. "Defining the Badges and Incidents of Slavery." *University of Pennsylvania Journal of Constitutional Law* 14, no. 3 (2012): 561–630.

Miller, Ian Jared. *The Nature of the Beasts: Empire and Exhibition at the Tokyo Imperial Zoo*. Berkeley: University of California Press, 2013.

Morgan, Jennifer. "Partus sequitur ventrem: Law, Race, and Reproduction in Colonial Slavery." *Small Axe* 22, no. 1 (55) (2018): 1–17.

Morrison, Toni. *A Mercy*. New York: Vintage International, 2009.

Moten, Fred. *B Jenkins*. Durham, NC: Duke University Press, 2010.

Moten, Fred. *Black and Blur*. Durham, NC: Duke University Press, 2018.

Moten, Fred. "Blackness and Nothingness (Mysticism in the Flesh)." *South Atlantic Quarterly* 112, no. 4 (2013): 737–80.

Moten, Fred. "The Case of Blackness." *Criticism* 50, no. 2 (2008): 177–218.

Moten, Fred. *In the Break: The Aesthetics of the Black Radical Tradition*. Minneapolis: University of Minnesota Press, 2003.

Moten, Fred. "Knowledge of Freedom." *CR: The New Centennial Review* 4, no. 2 (2004): 269–310.

Moten, Fred. *The Little Edges*. Middletown, CT: Wesleyan University Press, 2015.

Moten, Fred. "Manic Depression: A Poetics of Hesitant Sociology." Lecture, Center for Comparative Literature, University of Toronto, April 4, 2017. YouTube video, 1:43:24. https://youtu.be/gQ2kodsmIJE.

Moten, Fred. *Stolen Life*. Durham, NC: Duke University Press, 2018.

Moten, Fred. *The Universal Machine*. Durham, NC: Duke University Press, 2018.

Mullen, Harryette. "Sleeping with the Dictionary." In *Sleeping with the Dictionary*, 67. Berkeley: University of California Press, 2002.

Nancy, Jean-Luc. *The Ground of the Image*. Translated by Jeff Fort. New York: Fordham University Press, 2005.

National Institute of Corrections. *Jail Design Guide*. 3rd ed. Washington, DC: National Institute of Corrections, US Department of Justice, 2011. https://nicic.gov/jail-design-guide.

National Institute of Corrections. *Jail Design Guide: A Resource for Small and Medium-Sized Jails*. Washington, DC: National Institute of Corrections, US Department of Justice, 1998. http://correction.org/wp-content/uploads/2014/10/il20design20guide20nationa.pdf.

Nielsen, Aldon Lynn. *Black Chant: Languages of African-American Postmodernism*. Cambridge: Cambridge University Press, 1997.

Olson, Charles. "Projective Verse." 1950. Poetry Foundation, October 13, 2009. https://www.poetryfoundation.org/articles/69406/projective-verse.
Parsons, Theophilus. *The Law of Contracts*. 4th ed. Boston: Little, Brown, 1860.
Pashukanis, Evgeny B. *Law and Marxism*. 1924. Translated by Barbara Einhorn. London: Ink Links, 1978.
Patterson, Orlando. *Slavery and Social Death*. Cambridge, MA: Harvard University Press, 1982.
Philip, M. NourbeSe. *Looking for Livingstone: An Odyssey of Silence*. Toronto: Mercury, 1991.
Philip, M. NourbeSe. *Zong! As Told to the Author by Setaey Adamu Boateng*. Middletown, CT: Wesleyan University Press, 2008.
Potié, Philippe. *Le Corbusier: Le Couvent Sainte Marie de La Tourette*. Basel: Birkhäuser Architecture, 1997.
Pound, Ezra. *The Cantos of Ezra Pound*. New York: New Directions, 1972.
Pound, Ezra. *Cathay: A Critical Edition*. Edited by Timothy James Billings. New York: Fordham University Press, 2019.
Powell, John. *The Record of Tung-shan*. Honolulu: University of Hawai'i Press, 1986.
President's Commission on Law Enforcement and Administration of Justice. *The Challenge of Crime in a Free Society: A Report by the President's Commission on Law Enforcement and Administration of Justice*. Washington, DC: US Government Printing Office, 1967.
President's Task Force on 21st Century Policing. *Final Report of the President's Task Force on 21st Century Policing*. Washington, DC: Office of Community Oriented Policing Services, 2015.
Rogers, Annie G. "Becoming an Analyst: Après-Coup." *Psychoanalytic Inquiry* 40, no. 2 (2020): 90–99.
Rogers, Annie G. *Incandescent Alphabets: Psychosis and the Enigma of Language*. London: Karnac, 2016.
Rothfuss, Joan. *Topless Cellist: The Improbable Life of Charlotte Moorman*. Cambridge, MA: MIT Press, 2014.
Sells, Michael Anthony. *Mystical Languages of Unsaying*. Chicago: University of Chicago Press, 1994.
Sexton, Jared. "Afro-Pessimism: The Unclear Word." *Rhizomes*, no. 29 (2016). https://doi.org/10.20415/rhiz/029.e02.
Sexton, Jared. "The Social Life of Social Death: On Afro-Pessimism and Black Optimism." *InTensions*, no. 5 (2011). https://doi.org/10.25071/1913-5874/37359.
Sexton, Jared. "The *Vel* of Slavery: Tracking the Figure of the Unsovereign." *Critical Sociology* 42, nos. 4–5 (2006): 583–97.
Sexton, Jared, and Sora Han. "The Devil's Choice: Slavery and the Logic of the Vel." In *Esoteric Lacan*, edited by Philipp Valentini and Mahdi Tourage, 141–59. London: Rowman and Littlefield International, 2020.
Sharpe, Christina. *In the Wake: On Blackness and Being*. Durham, NC: Duke University Press, 2016.

Sharpe, Christina. *Monstrous Intimacies: Making Post-slavery Subjects*. Durham, NC: Duke University Press, 2010.

Shin, Sun Yung. *Skirt Full of Black: Poems*. Minneapolis: Coffee House Press, 2007.

Sideris, Marina, and the Amnesty Working Group. "Amnesty for Prisoners of Katrina: A Critical Resistance Special Report." November 2007. https://www2.ohchr.org/english/bodies/cerd/docs/ngos/usa/ushrn20.doc.

Sís, Peter. *The Conference of the Birds*. London: SelfMadeHero, 2012.

Si-sa Elite Korean-English Dictionary. Revised edition. Korea: YBM Sisayeongeosi, 1998.

Slade, Rachel. "Is There Such a Thing as 'Good' Prison Design?" *Architectural Digest*, April 30, 2018. https://www.architecturaldigest.com/story/is-there-such-a-thing-as-good-prison-design.

Sorkin, Michael. "Drawing the Line: Architects and Prisons." *Nation*, August 27, 2013. https://www.thenation.com/article/archive/drawing-line-architects-and-prisons/.

Spiegel, Irving. "Women's Prison Closed; Inmates Moved to Rikers." *New York Times*, June 14, 1971.

Spillers, Hortense J. "Interstices: A Small Drama of Words." In *Black, White, and in Color: Essays on American Literature and Culture*, 152–75. Chicago: University of Chicago Press, 2003.

Spillers, Hortense J. "Mama's Baby, Papa's Maybe: An American Grammar Book." *Diacritics* 17, no. 2 (1987): 65–81.

Spillers, Hortense J. "'The Permanent Obliquity of an In(pha)llibly Straight': In the Time of the Daughters and the Fathers." In *Black, White, and in Color: Essays on American Literature and Culture*, 230–50. Chicago: University of Chicago Press, 2003.

Stone-Richards, Michael. "A Commentary on Theresa Hak Kyung Cha's *Dictee*." *Glossator* 1 (Fall 2009): 145–210.

Stone-Richards, Michael. *Logics of Separation: Exile and Transcendence in Aesthetic Modernity*. Bern, Switzerland: Peter Lang, 2011.

Strong, James. *The Exhaustive Concordance of the Bible: Showing Every Word of the Text of the Common English Version of the Canonical Books, and Every Occurrence of Each Word in Regular Order; Together with a Comparative Concordance of the Authorized and Revised Versions, Including the American Variations; Also Brief Dictionaries of the Hebrew and Greek Words of the Original, with References to the English Words*. 1890. N.p.: Abingdon Press, 1894.

Taigen, Dan Leighton. "Dongshan and the Teaching of Suchness." In *Zen Masters*, edited by Steven Heine and Dale Wright, 33–58. Oxford: Oxford University Press, 2010.

Taylor, Michael. "Alameda County's 'Super Jail'—a Pretty Comfortable Place." *San Francisco Chronicle*, March 9, 1984.

Vos, Frits. "Dutch Influences on the Japanese Language: With an Appendix on Dutch Words in Korean," *Lingua* 12 (1963): 341–88. Repr., *East Asian History* 39 (2014): 153–80.

Walker, Alice. "The Child Who Favored Daughter." In *In Love and Trouble: Stories of Black Women*, 35–46. New York: Harcourt, 2001.
Wall Street Journal. "Full Sandra Bland Arrest Video." July 22, 2015. https://www.wsj.com/video/full-sandra-bland-arrest-video/824DEC23-4137-453B-83AC-0AC636C91683.html.
Watson, Alan, ed. *The Digest of Justinian*. Vol. 4. Philadelphia: University of Pennsylvania Press, 2009.
Webb, Richard E., and Michael A. Sells. "Lacan and Bion: Psychoanalysis and the Mystical Language of 'Unsaying.'" *Theory and Psychology* 5, no. 2 (May 1995): 195–215.
Weese, Ben. "Harry Weese." In *The Chicago Architectural Journal* 9:130–31. Chicago: Chicago Architectural Club, 2000.
Weston, Charisse Pearlina. Unpublished poetry manuscript on file with author, February 2022.
Wilderson, Frank B., III. *Afropessimism*. New York: Liveright, 2020.
Wilderson, Frank B., III. *Incognegro: A Memoir of Exile and Apartheid*. Durham, NC: Duke University Press, 2015.
Wilderson, Frank B., III. *Red, White and Black: Cinema and the Structure of U.S. Antagonisms*. Durham, NC: Duke University Press, 2010.
Wilkinson, Tom. "Typology: Prison." *Architectural Review*, June 11, 2018. https://www.architectural-review.com/essays/typology/typology-prison.
Williams, Edgar. *Hippopotamus*. London: Reaktion Books, 2017.
Wynter, Sylvia. "Unsettling the Coloniality of Being/Power/Truth/Freedom: Towards the Human, after Man, Its Overrepresentation—an Argument." *CR: The New Centennial Review* 3, no. 3 (2003): 257–337.
Yip, Wai-Lim. "Translating Chinese Poetry: The Convergence of Languages and Poetics—a Radical Introduction." In *Chinese Poetry: An Anthology of Major Modes and Genres*, edited and translated by Wai-Lim Yip, 1–27. Durham, NC: Duke University Press, 1997.
Yi Sang. "Paradise Lost." 1939. In *Yi Sang: Selected Works*, edited by Don Mee Choi, translated by Jack Jung, Sawako Nakayasu, Don Mee Choi, and Joyelle McSweeney, 65–73. Seattle: Wave Books, 2020.
Yu, Yeol, and Jeong Inseung. "Cards with Diagrams of Hangeul Mouth Movements." 1947. In *Beyond the Line: The Art of Korean Writing*, edited by Stephen Little and Virginia Moon, 332–35. Los Angeles: Los Angeles County Museum of Art, 2019.
Zalamea, Fernando. *Synthetic Philosophy of Contemporary Mathematics*. 2nd ed. London: Urbanomic/Sequence Press, 2019.
Zupančič, Alenka. "Hegel and Freud: Between Aufhebung and Verneinung." *Crisis and Critique* 4, no. 1 (2017): 481–94.

Art Exhibits

Clark, Sonya. *Edifice and Mortar*. Institute of Contemporary Art, Richmond, VA, 2018.

Gaines, Charles. *New Work: Charles Gaines*. San Francisco Museum of Modern Art, San Francisco, CA, March 6-September 12, 2021. https://www.sfmoma.org/exhibition/new-work-charles-gaines/.

Paik, Nam June. *Nam June Paik*. San Francisco Museum of Modern Art, San Francisco, CA, May 8–October 3, 2021. https://www.sfmoma.org/exhibition/nam-june-paik-2021/.

Weston, Charisse Pearlina. *Through: The Fold, the Shatter*. Recess, New York, NY, March 2–April 13, 2021. https://www.recessart.org/charissepearlinaweston/.

woods, lauren. *American Monument*. Beall Center for Art + Technology, University of California, Irvine, October 5, 2019–March 16, 2020. https://beallcenter.uci.edu/exhibitions/american-monument.

Primary Legal Texts

Alexander v. State of Florida. 121 So. 3d 1185 (2013).

Betty's Case. 20 Monthly L. Rep. 455 (Massachusetts, Nov. 9, 1857).

Civil Action for Deprivation of Rights. U.S.C. 42 (1996), § 1983. https://www.law.cornell.edu/uscode/text/42/1983.

Civil Rights Cases of 1883. 109 U.S. 3 (1883).

Congressional Globe, 39th Cong., 1st Sess. 474 (1866).

Dred Scott v. Sanford. 60 U.S. 393 (1857).

George Floyd Justice in Policing Act of 2021. H.R. 1280, 117th Cong. (2021). https://www.congress.gov/bill/117th-congress/house-bill/1280.

Gregson v. Gilbert. 3 Doug. KB 232 (1783).

Legality of the Threat or Use of Nuclear Weapons, Advisory Opinion, I.C.J. Reports 1996, p. 226.

Monell v. Department of Social Services. 436 U.S. 658 (1978).

Johnson v. City of Philadelphia. No. 15-2346 (3d Cir. 2016).

Reed-Veal v. Encinia. U.S. District Court for the Southern District of Texas, Case 4:15-cv-02232, Document 63, Third Amended Complaint At Law and Jury Demand (Jan. 19, 2016).

Tennessee v. Garner. 471 U.S. 1 (1985).

United Nations Charter. 1945. https://www.un.org/en/about-us/un-charter/full-text.

index

Page locators in italics indicate figures